The Simple
MEDITERRANEAN
DIET COOKBOOK for Beginners

2000 Days Tasty, Quick & Easy-to-Make Recipes Book for Everyday Meals | Includes a 30-Day Meal Plan

Clatihzra Danmilielsen

Copyright© 2025 By Clatihzra Danmilielsen

All rights reserved worldwide.

No part of this book may be reproduced or transmitted in any form or by any means, electronic or mechanical, including photo- copying, recording or by any information storage and retrieval system, without written permission from the publisher, except for the inclusion of brief quotations in a review.

Warning-Disclaimer

The purpose of this book is to educate and entertain. The author or publisher does not guarantee that anyone following the techniques, suggestions, tips, ideas, or strategies will become successful. The author and publisher shall have neither liability or responsibility to anyone with respect to any loss or damage caused, or alleged to be caused, directly or indirectly by the information contained in this book.

TABLE OF CONTENTS

Introduction
Chapter 1   The Mediterranean Diet: A Healthier and Longer Life / 4
Chapter 2   Breakfasts / 10
Chapter 3   Beans and Grains / 18
Chapter 4   Poultry / 26
Chapter 5   Beef, Pork, and Lamb / 33
Chapter 6   Fish and Seafood / 40
Chapter 7   Vegetables and Sides / 49
Chapter 8   Vegetarian Mains / 58
Chapter 9   Salads / 64
Chapter 10   Snacks and Appetizers / 72
Chapter 11   Pizzas, Wraps, and Sandwiches / 78
Chapter 12   Desserts / 83
Chapter 13   Pasta / 89
Chapter 14   Staples, Sauces, Dips, and Dressings / 93
Appendix 1:   Measurement Conversion Chart / 97
Appendix 2:   The Dirty Dozen and Clean Fifteen / 98
Appendix 3:   Recipes Index / 99

INTRODUCTION

In a world where time is often limited and health is a priority, cooking healthy, delicious meals at home can be a challenge. But with The Simple Mediterranean Diet Cookbook for Beginners, that challenge becomes an opportunity. This cookbook is a comprehensive guide to preparing nutritious, flavorful meals with ease. Whether you are just starting your journey into the Mediterranean diet or are an experienced home cook looking for fresh ideas, this book will help you create meals that nourish your body and delight your taste buds.

A Path to Health and Wellness

The Mediterranean diet is well known for its heart-healthy benefits, focusing on fresh fruits, vegetables, whole grains, lean proteins, healthy fats, and legumes. It's a way of eating that emphasizes balance, fresh ingredients, and a sustainable lifestyle. The Mediterranean diet has been linked to lower rates of chronic diseases, such as heart disease, stroke, and diabetes, and is often celebrated for promoting weight loss and overall well-being. This diet is not just about what you eat but how you eat, encouraging mindful eating, social connection, and enjoying meals with loved ones.

Quick and Easy Mediterranean Recipes for Busy Lives

This cookbook focuses on making the Mediterranean diet accessible, practical, and enjoyable. Designed for beginners, it includes a wide variety of easy-to-follow recipes that can be prepared with minimal time and effort. Each recipe is carefully crafted to ensure a balance of taste and nutrition. With over 2000 days of tasty, quick, and easy-to-make recipes, you'll never run out of delicious meal ideas. From vibrant salads to flavorful fish and seafood dishes, hearty soups, roasted vegetables, and even healthy desserts, every recipe is designed to fit into your daily routine, making cooking a fun and rewarding experience.

Air Frying Made Easy: Healthier, Faster Cooking

One of the key features of this cookbook is the use of the air fryer, which makes preparing Mediterranean meals faster, healthier, and more convenient. Air frying reduces the amount of oil needed for cooking while still achieving that crispy, golden texture we all love. This is especially beneficial for those looking to reduce their calorie intake without sacrificing taste. You'll find air fryer-friendly recipes for everything from crispy falafel to roasted vegetables, chicken, and even healthy snacks like kale chips and cheesy dates. The air fryer will become your best friend in the kitchen, making meal prep quicker and more efficient.

A Convenient and Flexible Meal Planning Guide

In addition to a wealth of recipes, this cookbook provides a comprehensive meal planning guide to simplify your Mediterranean diet journey. Designed to take the guesswork out of what to eat, the plan offers a balanced approach that incorporates a wide variety of nutrient-dense meals. The meal plan focuses on using fresh, seasonal ingredients, making it easy to enjoy flavorful, wholesome dishes every day. Whether you're cooking for yourself or feeding a group, the plan is adaptable, allowing you to adjust portion sizes and swap ingredients based on your personal tastes and dietary requirements. With this guide, healthy eating becomes a stress-free and enjoyable part of your daily routine.

Embrace a Holistic Approach to Health and Cooking

In addition to the recipes and meal plan, The Simple Mediterranean Diet Cookbook for Beginners provides tips and tricks for easy, everyday cooking. You'll learn how to stock your pantry with the essential ingredients needed to create Mediterranean dishes, how to prepare your meals efficiently, and how to customize recipes to suit your personal taste preferences. With simple ingredients, minimal prep time, and straightforward techniques, cooking Mediterranean meals will feel like second nature.

The cookbook emphasizes the importance of a balanced approach to health and lifestyle. Alongside the recipes, you'll find insights into how the Mediterranean diet promotes a holistic, healthy lifestyle. The book encourages you to take your time while eating, to savor your meals, and to focus on the joy of food. This is a lifestyle that goes beyond the kitchen—it's about building healthy habits that can improve your long-term health and well-being.

Introduction

A Simple, Enjoyable Way to Eat Healthier

Whether you are new to the Mediterranean diet or looking for ways to streamline your cooking routine, The Simple Mediterranean Diet Cookbook for Beginners is the perfect resource. With clear instructions, detailed nutrition information, and a variety of recipes to suit all tastes, this cookbook will empower you to create healthy, vibrant meals that nourish both your body and soul. Whether you're making a quick dinner after a long day or preparing a special meal for friends and family, this book makes cooking fun and effortless. Get ready to enjoy the flavors, benefits, and lifestyle of the Mediterranean—one meal at a time!

Chapter 1
The Mediterranean Diet: A Healthier and Longer Life

Chapter 1 The Mediterranean Diet: A Healthier and Longer Life

The Mediterranean Diet is not just about food; it's a lifestyle that focuses on balance, fresh ingredients, and mindful eating. Renowned for its heart-healthy benefits, the Mediterranean Diet emphasizes not only what you eat but how you approach food, health, and life. In this chapter, we will explore the key principles of the Mediterranean Diet, its impact on overall wellness, and how adopting this way of eating can improve your health and enrich your life. From heart disease prevention to weight management, the Mediterranean Diet provides a holistic approach to living, benefiting both body and mind.

The Mediterranean Diet Pyramid: A Visual Guide to Healthy Eating

The Mediterranean Diet Pyramid serves as a simple yet effective guide to the foods that should make up the majority of your diet. As you can see from the image below, the pyramid is divided into different sections, each representing a category of foods that should be incorporated into your daily meals. At the base of the pyramid, you'll find fruits, vegetables, whole grains, legumes, and olive oil. These foods form the foundation of every meal, providing essential vitamins, minerals, fiber, and healthy fats that contribute to overall health.

As you move up the pyramid, you'll see that fish and seafood should be consumed frequently—at least twice a week. These nutrient-dense foods are excellent sources of protein, omega-3 fatty acids, and antioxidants, which contribute to heart health. Further up, you find poultry, eggs, cheese, and yogurt. These foods should be eaten in moderate portions, and they provide essential nutrients like protein, calcium, and probiotics. The tip of the pyramid suggests that meats and sweets should be consumed sparingly, reinforcing the idea that moderation is key to maintaining a healthy diet.

The Mediterranean Diet Pyramid not only simplifies the decision-making process when planning meals but also helps you focus on the foods that will provide you with the most health benefits. It encourages eating fresh, whole foods while minimizing processed items, which is a fundamental principle of the Mediterranean way of eating.

The Role of Fresh, Seasonal Ingredients

The Mediterranean Diet places great emphasis on using fresh, seasonal ingredients. Fruits, vegetables, and herbs should be consumed in abundance, as they provide a rich source of essential vitamins, minerals, fiber, and antioxidants. The diet encourages variety, so you can enjoy a diverse range of produce, ensuring you're getting a wide array of nutrients. By eating seasonally, you're also supporting local, sustainable farming practices, which is good for both your health and the environment.

In addition to providing essential nutrients, fresh, seasonal ingredients enhance the flavor of meals. The Mediterranean Diet encourages cooking with ingredients that are flavorful on their own, meaning less reliance on added sugars, salts, or preservatives. Fresh, locally grown produce is not only more nutritious but also more vibrant, which makes every meal a sensory experience.

Olive Oil: The Heart of the Mediterranean Diet

Olive oil is one of the defining components of the Mediterranean Diet. It's used in cooking, drizzled over salads, and even served as a dip for bread. Olive oil is a source of monounsaturated fats, which have been shown to lower bad cholesterol levels and improve heart health. Additionally, it's rich in antioxidants, such as polyphenols, which can help reduce inflammation and protect against chronic diseases.

Research consistently shows that olive oil can help prevent cardiovascular disease and support overall well-being. The Mediterranean Diet recommends using extra virgin olive oil as the primary fat in cooking, which further boosts its health benefits. Not only does olive oil improve the taste and texture of dishes, but it also enhances the nutritional profile of the foods you prepare, making it a crucial ingredient in every Mediterranean meal.

Be Physically Active and Enjoy Meals with Others

While the Mediterranean Diet emphasizes what to eat, it also encourages a lifestyle that integrates physical activity and social connection. Regular physical activity is a vital part of maintaining a healthy weight and promoting cardiovascular health. The Mediterranean lifestyle encourages walking, cycling, and engaging in physical activities that are part of daily life. In many Mediterranean cultures, exercise is a natural part of the day, whether it's walking to the market, gardening, or taking part in a recreational sport.

In addition to being physically active, the Mediterranean Diet encourages enjoying meals in the company of others. Meals are seen as a time to connect with family and friends, fostering social interaction and a sense of community. Eating together promotes mindful eating, where you can slow down, enjoy the flavors, and appreciate the experience of sharing food. This social aspect of the Mediterranean Diet has been linked to improved mental health, as it reduces stress and promotes positive social relationships.

Summary

The Mediterranean Diet isn't just about food; it's about creating a balanced lifestyle that enhances your physical, mental, and emotional well-being. By incorporating fresh, nutrient-dense foods into your daily routine, using healthy fats like olive oil, and enjoying meals with others, you can cultivate a sustainable and rewarding approach to living.

The lifestyle promoted by the Mediterranean Diet also emphasizes the importance of reducing stress, getting enough sleep, and staying connected with nature. It's about embracing a holistic approach to health that encompasses not only what you eat but how you live. This balanced lifestyle is a key reason why the Mediterranean Diet has become one of the most widely recommended eating patterns for long-term health and longevity.

Let's get cooking!

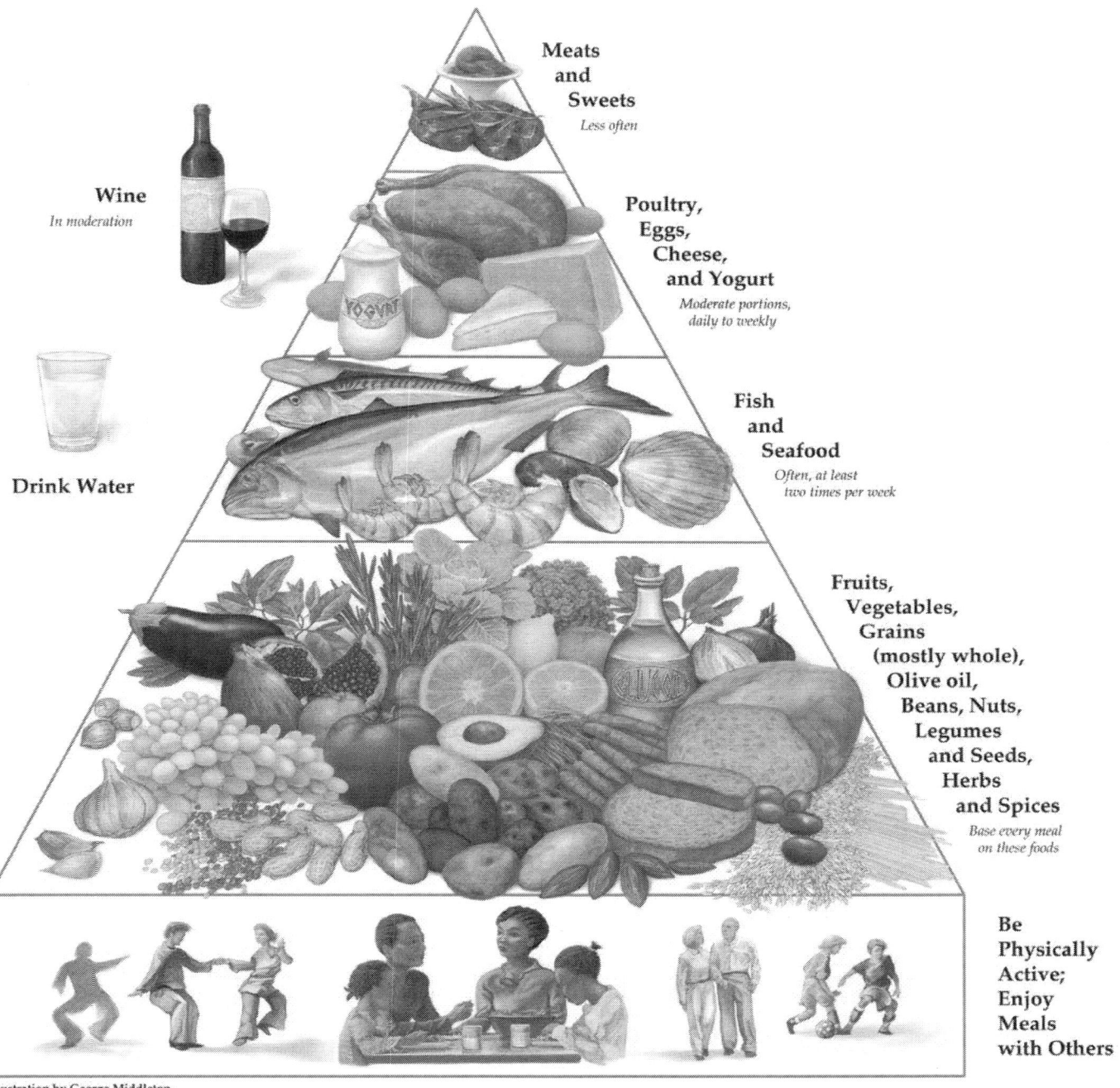

30-Day Meal Plan

DAYS	BREAKFAST	LUNCH	DINNER	SNACK/DESSERT
1	Veggie Breakfast Hash with Eggs 11	Flavorful Venetian Pasta with Beans 21	Tangy Chicken Jalfrezi 31	Delicious Nut and Apple Salad 73
2	Greek Yogurt Parfait 11	Wild Rice and Orange Salmon Bowl 43	Greek-Style Roast Turkey Breast 29	Black-Eyed Pea "Caviar" 73
3	Mini Shrimp Frittata Bites 11	Kale and Chickpea Delight 19	Zesty Spanish Lemon and Garlic Chicken 29	Pea and Arugula Crostini 77
4	Greek Breakfast Power Bowl 12	Amaranth Salad 20	Skillet Greek Turkey and Rice 29	Taste of the Mediterranean Fat Bombs 74
5	Nutty Fruit Oatmeal 12	Sautéed Lentil Spinach Curry 19	Feta and Spinach Stuffed Chicken Breasts 29	Cheese-Stuffed Dates 74
6	Mediterranean Breakfast Pita Sandwiches 12	Classic Margherita Pizza 79	Lemon Chicken 27	Roasted Chickpeas 74
7	Golden Apple Tahini Toast 15	Artichoke Quinoa Delight 22	Coconut Chicken Bites 27	Savory Mackerel Goat Cheese Bites 74
8	Egg Baked in Avocado 11	Giant Beans with Tomato and Parsley 24	Garlic-Lemon Chicken and Potatoes 27	Stuffed Cucumber Cups 74
9	Apple-Spiced Oatmeal 15	Lentil and Spinach Medley 22	Lemon-Infused Chicken with Asparagus 31	Black Bean Corn Spread 73
10	Olive Oil Breakfast Cakes with Berry Syrup and Lemon 15	Sautéed Tomato Rice 20	Grape Chicken Panzanella 32	Savory Mediterranean Popcorn 73
11	Steel-Cut Oats with Flax, Dates, and Walnuts 17	Zesty Spanish Rice Bowl 20	Savory Chicken and Mushroom Medley 30	Pita Pizza with Olives and Feta 77
12	Gluten-Free Granola Cereal 12	Fava Beans with Ground Meat 20	Pork Rind Fried Chicken 28	Baby Artichokes with Lemon-Garlic Aioli 76
13	Herb and Cheese Fritters 13	Nutty Brown Rice with Cherries and Apricots 20	Sweet and Tangy Mango Chutney Chicken 28	Spicy White Bean Harissa Dip 76
14	Egg and Pepper Pita 13	Wild Mushroom Farrotto 21	Spinach and Feta Stuffed Chicken Breasts 28	Shrimp Pirogues 75
15	Sun-Dried Tomato and Spinach Egg Wrap 13	Zesty Farro Bowl with Avocado 21	Duck with Fennel Root 27	Manchego Cheese Crackers 75
16	Spiced Potatoes with Chickpeas 13	Wild Rice and Mushroom Soup 24	Tex-Mex Chicken Roll-Ups 28	Classic Hummus with Tahini 75

DAYS	BREAKFAST	LUNCH	DINNER	SNACK/DESSERT
17	Savory Farro with Nuts and Dried Fruit 17	Date and Pistachio Rice Pilaf 24	Lemon Mushroom Chicken Piccata 32	Smoky Eggplant Dip 77
18	Baked Ricotta with Pears 17	Brown Rice Salad with Zucchini and Tomatoes 25	One-Pan Parsley Chicken and Potatoes 30	Mexican Potato Skins 76
19	Mini Spinach Mushroom Quiche Cups 15	Velvety Thyme-Infused Polenta 25	Flavorful Herb-Marinated Chicken 30	Stuffed Mushrooms 76
20	Hearty Almond Date Oatmeal 14	Creamy Lima Bean Soup 24	Sumac Chicken with Cauliflower and Carrots 30	Steamed Artichokes with Herbs and Olive Oil 75
21	Spinach and Feta Breakfast Bake 14	Endive Boats with Quinoa Salad 22	Savory Pork Chops with Peppers and Onions 34	Crispy Kale Chips 77
22	Mediterranean Omelet 14	Herbed Polenta 23	Stuffed Flank Steak 34	Asian Five-Spice Wings 77
23	Delicious Polenta with Chard and Eggs 14	Mediterranean Bulgur Mix 23	Stuffed Cube Steak Rolls 35	Light Baklava Rolls 87
24	Turkish Egg Bowl 16	Quinoa Salad with Chicken, Chickpeas, and Spinach 22	Greek Stuffed Tenderloin 34	Grilled Stone Fruit 84
25	Warm Fava Bean Dip with Pita Wedges 16	Savory Herbed Lima Beans 23	Savory Herb Lamb Loin Chops 35	Espresso Chocolate Honey Ricotta 84
26	Ricotta and Fruit Bruschetta 17	White Beans with Kale 23	Flank Steak and Blue Cheese Wraps 35	Toasted Almonds with Honey 84
27	Red Pepper, Spinach, and Feta Muffins 16	Moist Greek Yogurt Corn Bread 19	Lamb Chops with Fresh Zucchini Slaw 35	Refreshing Red Grapefruit Granita 86
28	Sunshine Overnight Oats 15	Garbanzo and Pita No-Bake Casserole 23	Greek Meatball Soup 36	Ricotta Cheesecake 87
29	Tuna Tortilla with Roasted Peppers 17	Black Chickpea Snack 25	Zesty Mustard-Glazed Lamb Chops 36	Dark Chocolate Fruit and Nut Bark 84
30	Kagianas 16	Spicy Black Beans with Root Veggies 25	Pepper Steak 36	Roasted Honey-Cinnamon Apples 86

Chapter 2

Breakfasts

Chapter 2 Breakfasts

Veggie Breakfast Hash with Eggs

Prep time: 20 minutes | Cook time: 6¼ hours | Serves 2

- Nonstick cooking spray
- 1 onion, chopped
- 2 garlic cloves, minced
- 1 red bell pepper, chopped
- 1 yellow summer squash, chopped
- 2 carrots, chopped
- 2 Yukon Gold potatoes, peeled and chopped
- 2 large tomatoes, seeded and chopped
- ¼ cup vegetable broth
- ½ teaspoon salt
- ⅛ teaspoon freshly ground black pepper
- ½ teaspoon dried thyme leaves
- 3 or 4 eggs
- ½ teaspoon ground sweet paprika

1. Coat the inside of the slow cooker with nonstick cooking spray. 2. Add all the ingredients to the slow cooker, except for the eggs and paprika, then give everything a good stir. 3. Place the lid on the slow cooker and let it cook on low for 6 hours. 4. Remove the lid and create indentations in the vegetable mixture, one for each egg. Crack an egg into a small cup, then carefully pour it into one of the indentations. Continue this process with the remaining eggs, then sprinkle paprika over the top. 5. Cover again and cook on low for 10 to 15 minutes, or until the eggs have set. Serve immediately.

Per Serving:
calories: 381 | fat: 8g | protein: 17g | carbs: 64g | fiber: 12g | sodium: 747mg

Greek Yogurt Parfait

Prep time: 5 minutes | Cook time: 0 minutes | Serves 1

- ½ cup plain whole-milk Greek yogurt
- 2 tablespoons heavy whipping cream
- ¼ cup frozen berries, thawed with juices
- ½ teaspoon vanilla or almond extract (optional)
- ¼ teaspoon ground cinnamon (optional)
- 1 tablespoon ground flaxseed
- 2 tablespoons chopped nuts (walnuts or pecans)

1. In a small bowl or glass, combine the yogurt, heavy whipping cream, thawed berries in their juice, vanilla or almond extract (if using), cinnamon (if using), and flaxseed and stir well until smooth. Top with chopped nuts and enjoy.

Per Serving:
calories: 333 | fat: 27g | protein: 10g | carbs: 15g | fiber: 4g | sodium: 71mg

Egg Baked in Avocado

Prep time: 5 minutes | Cook time: 15 minutes | Serves 2

- 1 ripe large avocado
- 2 large eggs
- Salt
- Freshly ground black pepper
- 4 tablespoons jarred pesto, for serving
- 2 tablespoons chopped tomato, for serving
- 2 tablespoons crumbled feta, for serving (optional)

1. Preheat the oven to 425°F(220°C). 2. Slice the avocado in half and remove the pit. Scoop out about 1 to 2 tablespoons from each half to create a hole large enough to fit an egg. Place the avocado halves on a baking sheet, cut-side up. 3. Crack 1 egg in each avocado half and season with salt and pepper. 4. Bake until the eggs are set and cooked to desired level of doneness, 10 to 15 minutes. 5. Remove from oven and top each avocado with 2 tablespoons pesto, 1 tablespoon chopped tomato, and 1 tablespoon crumbled feta (if using).

Per Serving:
calories: 248 | fat: 23g | protein: 10g | carbs: 2g | fiber: 1g | sodium: 377mg

Mini Shrimp Frittata Bites

Prep time: 15 minutes | Cook time: 20 minutes | Serves 4

- 1 teaspoon olive oil, plus more for spraying
- ½ small red bell pepper, finely diced
- 1 teaspoon minced garlic
- 1 (4-ounce / 113-g) can of tiny shrimp, drained
- Salt and freshly ground black pepper, to taste
- 4 eggs, beaten
- 4 teaspoons ricotta cheese

1. Lightly spray four ramekins with olive oil. 2. Heat 1 teaspoon of olive oil in a medium skillet over medium-low heat. Add the bell pepper and garlic, and sauté for about 5 minutes until the bell pepper becomes tender. 3. Add the shrimp, season with salt and pepper, and cook for 1 to 2 minutes until just warmed through. Remove from heat. 4. Pour in the eggs and stir until everything is well combined. 5. Evenly distribute the mixture into the four ramekins. 6. Place two ramekins in the air fryer basket and bake at 350°F (177°C) for 6 minutes. 7. Take the air fryer basket out, stir the contents of each ramekin, and add 1 teaspoon of ricotta cheese to each. Put the basket back in and continue baking for another 4 to 5 minutes, until the eggs are set and the tops are golden brown.8. Repeat the process with the remaining two ramekins.

Per Serving:
calories: 114 | fat: 6g | protein: 12g | carbs: 1g | fiber: 0g | sodium: 314mg

Greek Breakfast Power Bowl

Prep time: 15 minutes | Cook time: 20 minutes | Serves 2

- 3 tablespoons extra-virgin avocado oil or ghee, divided
- 1 clove garlic, minced
- 2 teaspoons chopped fresh rosemary
- 1 small eggplant, roughly chopped
- 1 medium zucchini, roughly chopped
- 1 tablespoon fresh lemon juice
- 2 tablespoons chopped mint
- 1 tablespoon chopped fresh oregano
- Salt and black pepper, to taste
- 6 ounces (170 g) Halloumi cheese, cubed or sliced
- ¼ cup pitted Kalamata olives
- 4 large eggs, soft-boiled (or hard-boiled or poached)
- 1 tablespoon extra-virgin olive oil, to drizzle

1. Heat a skillet (with a lid) greased with 2 tablespoons (30 ml) of the avocado oil over medium heat. Add the garlic and rosemary and cook for 1 minute. Add the eggplant, zucchini, and lemon juice. Stir and cover with a lid, then reduce the heat to medium-low. Cook for 10 to 15 minutes, stirring once or twice, until tender. 2. Stir in the mint and oregano. Optionally, reserve some herbs for topping. Season with salt and pepper to taste. Remove from the heat and transfer to a plate. Cover with the skillet lid to keep the veggies warm. 3. Grease the same pan with the remaining 1 tablespoon (15 ml) avocado oil and cook the Halloumi over medium-high heat for 2 to 3 minutes per side until lightly browned. Place the slices of cooked Halloumi on top of the cooked veggies. Top with the olives and cooked eggs and drizzle with the olive oil. 4. Always serve warm, as Halloumi hardens once it cools. Reheat before serving if necessary.

Per Serving:
calories: 748 | fat: 56g | protein: 40g | carbs: 25g | fiber: 10g | sodium: 275mg

Nutty Fruit Oatmeal

Prep time: 10 minutes | Cook time: 7 minutes | Serves 2

- 1 cup rolled oats
- 1¼ cups water
- ¼ cup orange juice
- 1 medium pear, peeled, cored, and cubed
- ¼ cup dried cherries
- ¼ cup chopped walnuts
- 1 tablespoon honey
- ¼ teaspoon ground ginger
- ¼ teaspoon ground cinnamon
- ⅛ teaspoon salt

1. Add the oats, water, orange juice, pear, cherries, walnuts, honey, ginger, cinnamon, and salt to the Instant Pot®. Stir everything together until well mixed. 2. Secure the lid, set the steam release to Sealing, press the Manual button, and set the cooking time to 7 minutes. When the cooking cycle is complete, allow the pressure to release naturally for about 20 minutes. 3. Press the Cancel button, carefully open the lid, and give the mixture a thorough stir. Serve warm and enjoy.

Per Serving:
calories: 362 | fat: 8g | protein: 7g | carbs: 69g | fiber: 8g | sodium: 164mg

Gluten-Free Granola Cereal

Prep time: 7 minutes | Cook time: 30 minutes | Makes 3½ cups

- Oil, for spraying
- 1½ cups gluten-free rolled oats
- ½ cup chopped walnuts
- ½ cup chopped almonds
- ½ cup pumpkin seeds
- ¼ cup maple syrup or honey
- 1 tablespoon toasted sesame oil or vegetable oil
- 1 teaspoon ground cinnamon
- ½ teaspoon salt
- ½ cup dried cranberries

1. Preheat the air fryer to 250ºF (121ºC). Line the air fryer basket with parchment and spray lightly with oil. (Do not skip the step of lining the basket; the parchment will keep the granola from falling through the holes.) 2. In a large bowl, mix together the oats, walnuts, almonds, pumpkin seeds, maple syrup, sesame oil, cinnamon, and salt. 3. Spread the mixture in an even layer in the prepared basket. 4. Cook for 30 minutes, stirring every 10 minutes. 5. Transfer the granola to a bowl, add the dried cranberries, and toss to combine. 6. Let cool to room temperature before storing in an airtight container.

Per Serving:
calories: 322 | fat: 17g | protein: 11g | carbs: 35g | fiber: 6g | sodium: 170mg

Mediterranean Breakfast Pita Sandwiches

Prep time: 5 minutes | Cook time: 7 minutes | Serves 2

- 2 eggs
- 1 small avocado, peeled, halved, and pitted
- ¼ teaspoon fresh lemon juice
- Pinch of salt
- ¼ teaspoon freshly ground black pepper
- 1 (8-inch) whole-wheat pocket pita bread, halved
- 12 (¼-inch) thick cucumber slices
- 6 oil-packed sun-dried tomatoes, rinsed, patted dry, and cut in half
- 2 tablespoons crumbled feta
- ½ teaspoon extra virgin olive oil

1. Fill a small saucepan with water and place it over medium heat. When the water is boiling, use a slotted spoon to carefully lower the eggs into the water. Gently boil for 7 minutes, then remove the pan from the heat and transfer the eggs to a bowl of cold water. Set aside. 2. In a small bowl, mash the avocado with a fork and then add the lemon juice and salt. Mash to combine. 3. Peel and slice the eggs, then sprinkle the black pepper over the egg slices. 4. Spread half of the avocado mixture over one side of the pita half. Top the pita half with 1 sliced egg, 6 cucumber slices, and 6 sun-dried tomato pieces. 5. Sprinkle 1 tablespoon crumbled feta over the top and drizzle ¼ teaspoon olive oil over the feta. Repeat with the other pita half. Serve promptly.

Per Serving:
calories: 427 | fat: 28g | protein: 14g | carbs: 36g | fiber: 12g | sodium: 398mg

Chapter 2 Breakfasts

Egg and Pepper Pita

Prep time: 10 minutes | Cook time: 10 minutes | Serves 4

- 2 pita breads
- 2 tablespoons olive oil
- 1 red or yellow bell pepper, diced
- 2 zucchini, quartered lengthwise and sliced
- 4 large eggs, beaten
- Sea salt
- Freshly ground black pepper
- Pinch dried oregano
- 2 avocados, sliced
- ½ to ¾ cup crumbled feta cheese
- 2 tablespoons chopped scallion, green part only, for garnish
- Hot sauce, for serving

1. In a large skillet, heat the pitas over medium heat until warmed through and lightly toasted, about 2 minutes. Remove the pitas from the skillet and set aside. 2. In the same skillet, heat the olive oil over medium heat. Add the bell pepper and zucchini and sauté for 4 to 5 minutes. Add the eggs and season with salt, black pepper, and the oregano. Cook, stirring, for 2 to 3 minutes, until the eggs are cooked through. Remove from the heat. 3. Slice the pitas in half crosswise and fill each half with the egg mixture. Divide the avocado and feta among the pita halves. Garnish with the scallion and serve with hot sauce.

Per Serving:
calories: 476 | fat: 31g | protein: 17g | carbs: 36g | fiber: 11g | sodium: 455mg

Herb and Cheese Fritters

Prep time: 10 minutes | Cook time: 15 minutes | Serves 5

- 3 medium zucchini
- 8 ounces (227 g) frozen spinach, thawed and squeezed dry (weight excludes water squeezed out)
- 4 large eggs
- ½ teaspoon salt
- ¼ teaspoon black pepper
- 3 tablespoons flax meal or coconut flour
- ¼ cup grated Pecorino Romano
- 2 cloves garlic, minced
- ¼ cup chopped fresh herbs, such as parsley, basil, oregano, mint, chives, and/or thyme
- ¼ cup extra-virgin avocado oil or ghee

1. Grate the zucchini and transfer it to a bowl lined with cheesecloth. Let it sit for 5 minutes, then gather the cheesecloth around the zucchini and squeeze firmly to remove as much moisture as possible. You should have about 13 ounces (370 g) of drained zucchini. 2. In a mixing bowl, combine the zucchini, spinach, eggs, salt, and pepper. Add the flax meal and Pecorino cheese, stirring well. Mix in the garlic and herbs until fully incorporated. 3. Heat a large pan over medium heat and grease it with 1 tablespoon of ghee. Once the pan is hot, scoop the mixture with a ¼-cup measuring cup (about 57 g/2 ounces per fritter) and place it in the pan. Flatten and shape the fritters with a spatula. Cook for 3 to 4 minutes on each side until golden and crispy. Cook in batches, adding more ghee to the pan as needed, until all the mixture is used up. 4. Serve the fritters warm or cold as a breakfast, side dish, or snack. Store them in the fridge for up to 4 days or freeze for up to 3 months.

Per Serving:
calories: 239 | fat: 20g | protein: 10g | carbs: 8g | fiber: 3g | sodium: 426mg

Sun-Dried Tomato and Spinach Egg Wrap

Prep time: 10 minutes | Cook time: 7 minutes | Serves 2

- 1 tablespoon olive oil
- ¼ cup minced onion
- 3 to 4 tablespoons minced sun-dried tomatoes in olive oil and herbs
- 3 large eggs, beaten
- 1½ cups packed baby spinach
- 1 ounce (28 g) crumbled feta cheese
- Salt
- 2 (8-inch) whole-wheat tortillas

1. Heat the olive oil in a large skillet over medium-high heat. Add the onion and tomatoes, and sauté for about 3 minutes until softened. 2. Reduce the heat to medium, pour in the beaten eggs, and stir continuously to scramble them. 3. Add the spinach and stir until it wilts. Sprinkle feta cheese over the eggs and season with salt to taste. 4. Microwave the tortillas for about 20 seconds each until warm and pliable. 5. Spoon half of the egg mixture into each tortilla. Fold the tortillas in half or roll them up, then serve immediately.

Per Serving:
calories: 435 | fat: 28g | protein: 17g | carbs: 31g | fiber: 6g | sodium: 552mg

Spiced Potatoes with Chickpeas

Prep time: 10 minutes | Cook time: 10 minutes | Serves 4

- ¼ cup olive oil
- 3 medium potatoes, peeled and shredded
- 2 cups finely chopped baby spinach
- 1 medium onion, finely diced
- 1 tablespoon minced fresh ginger
- 1 teaspoon ground cumin
- 1 teaspoon ground coriander
- ½ teaspoon ground turmeric
- ½ teaspoon salt
- 1 (15-ounce / 425-g) can chickpeas, drained and rinsed
- 1 medium zucchini, diced
- ¼ cup chopped cilantro
- 1 cup plain yogurt

1. Heat the olive oil in a large skillet over medium heat. Add the potatoes, spinach, onions, ginger, cumin, coriander, turmeric, and salt and stir to mix well. Spread the mixture out into an even layer and let cook, without stirring, for about 5 minutes until the potatoes are crisp and browned on the bottom. 2. Add the chickpeas and zucchini and mix to combine, breaking up the layer of potatoes. Spread the mixture out again into an even layer and continue to cook, without stirring, for another 5 minutes or so, until the potatoes are crisp on the bottom. 3. To serve, garnish with cilantro and yogurt.

Per Serving:
calories: 679 | fat: 20g | protein: 28g | carbs: 100g | fiber: 24g | sodium: 388mg

Mediterranean Omelet

Prep time: 10 minutes | Cook time: 12 minutes | Serves 2

- 2 teaspoons extra-virgin olive oil, divided
- 1 garlic clove, minced
- ½ red bell pepper, thinly sliced
- ½ yellow bell pepper, thinly sliced
- ¼ cup thinly sliced red onion
- 2 tablespoons chopped fresh basil
- 2 tablespoons chopped fresh parsley, plus extra for garnish
- ½ teaspoon salt
- ½ teaspoon freshly ground black pepper
- 4 large eggs, beaten

1. In a large, heavy skillet, heat 1 teaspoon of the olive oil over medium heat. Add the garlic, peppers, and onion to the pan and sauté, stirring frequently, for 5 minutes. 2. Add the basil, parsley, salt, and pepper, increase the heat to medium-high, and sauté for 2 minutes. Slide the vegetable mixture onto a plate and return the pan to the heat. 3. Heat the remaining 1 teaspoon olive oil in the same pan and pour in the beaten eggs, tilting the pan to coat evenly. Cook the eggs just until the edges are bubbly and all but the center is dry, 3 to 5 minutes. 4. Either flip the omelet or use a spatula to turn it over. 5. Spoon the vegetable mixture onto one-half of the omelet and use a spatula to fold the empty side over the top. Slide the omelet onto a platter or cutting board. 6. To serve, cut the omelet in half and garnish with fresh parsley.

Per Serving:
calories: 218 | fat: 14g | protein: 14g | carbs: 9g | fiber: 1g | sodium: 728mg

Delicious Polenta with Chard and Eggs

Prep time: 5 minutes | Cook time: 20 minutes | Serves 4

For the Polenta:
- 2½ cups water
- ½ teaspoon kosher salt
- ¾ cups whole-grain cornmeal

For the Chard:
- 1 tablespoon extra-virgin olive oil
- 1 bunch (about 6 ounces / 170 g) Swiss chard, leaves and stems chopped and separated

For the Eggs:
- 1 tablespoon extra-virgin olive oil

- ¼ teaspoon freshly ground black pepper
- 2 tablespoons grated Parmesan cheese
- 2 garlic cloves, sliced
- ¼ teaspoon kosher salt
- ⅛ teaspoon freshly ground black pepper
- Lemon juice (optional)
- 4 large eggs

Make the Polenta: 1. In a medium saucepan, bring the water and salt to a boil over high heat. Gradually pour in the cornmeal, whisking continuously to prevent clumps. 2. Lower the heat to low, cover, and cook for 10 to 15 minutes, stirring frequently to keep it smooth. Mix in the pepper and Parmesan, then portion the polenta into 4 bowls.
Make the Chard: 3. In a large skillet, heat the oil over medium heat. Add the chard stems, garlic, salt, and pepper, and sauté for 2 minutes. Stir in the chard leaves and cook for 3 to 5 minutes until they wilt. 4. Add a squeeze of lemon juice if you like, toss everything together, and evenly distribute the chard over the polenta in each bowl.
Make the Eggs: 5. In the same skillet, heat the oil over medium-high heat. Crack the eggs into the skillet, spacing them apart to avoid overcrowding. Cook for 2 to 3 minutes until the whites are set and the edges are golden. 6. Serve the eggs sunny-side up or carefully flip them and cook for 1 minute longer for over-easy eggs. Top each bowl of polenta and chard with one egg.

Per Serving:
calories: 310 | fat: 18g | protein: 17g | carbs: 21g | fiber: 1g | sodium: 500mg

Hearty Almond Date Oatmeal

Prep time: 5 minutes | Cook time: 12 minutes | Serves 4

- 1 cup sliced almonds
- 4 cups water
- 2 cups rolled oats
- 1 tablespoon extra-virgin olive oil
- ¼ teaspoon salt
- ½ cup chopped pitted dates

1. Press the Sauté button on the Instant Pot® and add almonds. Toast, stirring constantly, until almonds are golden brown, about 8 minutes. Press the Cancel button and add water, oats, oil, salt, and dates to the pot. Stir well. Close lid and set steam release to Sealing. Press the Manual button and set time to 4 minutes. 2. When the timer beeps, quick-release the pressure until the float valve drops, open lid, and stir well. Serve hot.

Per Serving:
calories: 451 | fat: 25g | protein: 14g | carbs: 52g | fiber: 9g | sodium: 320mg

Spinach and Feta Breakfast Bake

Prep time: 7 minutes | Cook time: 23 to 25 minutes | Serves 2

- Avocado oil spray
- ⅓ cup diced red onion
- 1 cup frozen chopped spinach, thawed and drained
- 4 large eggs
- ¼ cup heavy (whipping) cream
- Sea salt and freshly ground black pepper, to taste
- ¼ teaspoon cayenne pepper
- ½ cup crumbled feta cheese
- ¼ cup shredded Parmesan cheese

1. Lightly spray a deep pan with oil. Add the onion to the pan and place it in the air fryer basket. Set the air fryer to 350ºF (177ºC) and cook for 7 minutes. 2. Evenly sprinkle the spinach over the cooked onion. 3. In a medium bowl, whisk together the eggs, heavy cream, salt, black pepper, and cayenne. Pour the egg mixture over the vegetables in the pan. 4. Sprinkle feta and Parmesan cheese on top. Return the pan to the air fryer and bake for 16 to 18 minutes, until the eggs are fully set and the top is lightly browned.

Per Serving:
calories: 366 | fat: 26g | protein: 25g | carbs: 8g | fiber: 3g | sodium: 520mg

Chapter 2 Breakfasts

Golden Apple Tahini Toast

Prep time: 10 minutes | Cook time: 0 minutes | Serves 1

- 2 tablespoons tahini
- 2 slices whole-wheat bread, toasted
- 1 small apple of your choice, cored and thinly sliced
- 1 teaspoon honey

1. Evenly spread the tahini over the toasted bread. 2. Arrange the apple slices on top and drizzle with honey. Serve right away.

Per Serving:
calories: 439 | fat: 19g | protein: 13g | carbs: 60g | fiber: 10g | sodium: 327mg

Apple-Spiced Oatmeal

Prep time: 10 minutes | Cook time: 7 minutes | Serves 4

- 1 tablespoon light olive oil
- 1 large Granny Smith, Honeycrisp, or Pink Lady apple, peeled, cored, and diced
- ½ teaspoon ground cardamom
- 1 cup steel-cut oats
- 3 cups water
- ¼ cup maple syrup
- ½ teaspoon salt

1. Press the Sauté button on the Instant Pot® and warm the oil. Add the apple and cardamom, cooking for about 2 minutes until the apple is just tender. Press the Cancel button. 2. Add the oats, water, maple syrup, and salt to the pot, stirring until well combined. Secure the lid, set the steam release to Sealing, press the Manual button, and set the timer for 5 minutes. 3. Once the timer goes off, let the pressure release naturally for 10 minutes, then perform a quick release until the float valve lowers. Press the Cancel button, open the lid, and stir thoroughly. Serve hot.

Per Serving:
calories: 249 | fat: 6g | protein: 6g | carbs: 48g | fiber: 5g | sodium: 298mg

Olive Oil Breakfast Cakes with Berry Syrup and Lemon

Prep time: 5 minutes | Cook time: 10 minutes | Serves 4

For the Pancakes:
- 1 cup almond flour
- 1 teaspoon baking powder
- ¼ teaspoon salt
- 6 tablespoon extra-virgin olive oil, divided
- 2 large eggs
- Zest and juice of 1 lemon
- ½ teaspoon almond or vanilla extract

For the Berry Sauce:
- 1 cup frozen mixed berries
- 1 tablespoon water or lemon juice, plus more if needed
- ½ teaspoon vanilla extract

Make the Pancakes: 1. In a large bowl, combine the almond flour, baking powder, and salt and whisk to break up any clumps. 2. Add the 4 tablespoons olive oil, eggs, lemon zest and juice, and almond extract and whisk to combine well. 3. In a large skillet, heat 1 tablespoon of olive oil and spoon about 2 tablespoons of batter for each of 4 pancakes. Cook until bubbles begin to form, 4 to 5 minutes, and flip. Cook another 2 to 3 minutes on second side. Repeat with remaining 1 tablespoon olive oil and batter. Make the Berry Sauce 1. In a small saucepan, heat the frozen berries, water, and vanilla extract over medium-high for 3 to 4 minutes, until bubbly, adding more water if mixture is too thick. Using the back of a spoon or fork, mash the berries and whisk until smooth.

Per Serving:
calories: 381 | fat: 35g | protein: 8g | carbs: 12g | fiber: 4g | sodium: 183mg

Mini Spinach Mushroom Quiche Cups

Prep time: 10 minutes | Cook time: 15 minutes | Serves 4

- 1 teaspoon olive oil, plus more for spraying
- 1 cup coarsely chopped mushrooms
- 1 cup fresh baby spinach, shredded
- 4 eggs, beaten
- ½ cup shredded Cheddar cheese
- ½ cup shredded Mozzarella cheese
- ¼ teaspoon salt
- ¼ teaspoon black pepper

1. Lightly spray 4 silicone baking cups with olive oil and set them aside. 2. Heat 1 teaspoon of olive oil in a medium sauté pan over medium heat. Add the mushrooms and cook for 3 to 4 minutes until they soften. 3. Add the spinach and cook for another 1 to 2 minutes until wilted. Remove from heat and set aside. 4. In a medium bowl, whisk together the eggs, Cheddar cheese, Mozzarella cheese, salt, and pepper until well combined. 5. Carefully fold the sautéed mushrooms and spinach into the egg mixture. 6. Pour an equal amount of the mixture into each silicone baking cup, filling them about three-quarters full. 7. Place the baking cups into the air fryer basket and cook at 350ºF (177ºC) for 5 minutes. Stir the mixture gently in each cup, then continue cooking for another 3 to 5 minutes until the eggs are set.

Per Serving:
calories: 156 | fat: 10g | protein: 14g | carbs: 2g | fiber: 1g | sodium: 411mg

Sunshine Overnight Oats

Prep time: 5 minutes | Cook time: 0 minutes | Serves 2

- ⅔ cup vanilla, unsweetened almond milk (not Silk brand)
- ⅓ cup rolled oats
- ¼ cup raspberries
- 1 teaspoon honey
- ¼ teaspoon turmeric
- ⅛ teaspoon ground cinnamon
- Pinch ground cloves

1. In a mason jar, combine the almond milk, oats, raspberries, honey, turmeric, cinnamon, and cloves and shake well. Store in the refrigerator for 8 to 24 hours, then serve cold or heated.

Per Serving:
calories: 82 | fat: 2g | protein: 2g | carbs: 14g | fiber: 3g | sodium: 98mg

Chapter 2 Breakfasts

Turkish Egg Bowl

Prep time: 10 minutes | Cook time: 15 minutes | Serves 2

- 2 tablespoons ghee
- ½–1 teaspoon red chile flakes
- 2 tablespoons extra-virgin olive oil
- 1 cup full-fat goat's or sheep's milk yogurt
- 1 clove garlic, minced
- 1 tablespoon fresh lemon juice
- Salt and black pepper, to taste
- Dash of vinegar
- 4 large eggs
- Optional: pinch of sumac
- 2 tablespoons chopped fresh cilantro or parsley

1. In a skillet, melt the ghee over low heat. Add the chile flakes and let it infuse while you prepare the eggs. Remove from the heat and mix with the extra-virgin olive oil. Set aside. Combine the yogurt, garlic, lemon juice, salt, and pepper. 2. Poach the eggs. Fill a medium saucepan with water and a dash of vinegar. Bring to a boil over high heat. Crack each egg individually into a ramekin or a cup. Using a spoon, create a gentle whirlpool in the water; this will help the egg white wrap around the egg yolk. Slowly lower the egg into the water in the center of the whirlpool. Turn off the heat and cook for 3 to 4 minutes. Use a slotted spoon to remove the egg from the water and place it on a plate. Repeat for all remaining eggs. 3. To assemble, place the yogurt mixture in a bowl and add the poached eggs. Drizzle with the infused oil, and garnish with cilantro. Add a pinch of sumac, if using. Eat warm.

Per Serving:
calories: 576 | fat: 46g | protein: 27g | carbs: 17g | fiber: 4g | sodium: 150mg

Warm Fava Bean Dip with Pita Wedges

Prep time: 5 minutes | Cook time: 10 minutes | Serves 4

- 1½ tablespoons olive oil
- 1 large onion, diced
- 1 large tomato, diced
- 1 clove garlic, crushed
- 1 (15-ounce / 425-g) can fava beans, not drained
- 1 teaspoon ground cumin
- ¼ cup chopped fresh parsley
- ¼ cup lemon juice
- Salt
- Freshly ground black pepper
- Crushed red pepper flakes
- 4 whole-grain pita bread pockets

1. Warm the olive oil in a large skillet over medium-high heat. Add the onion, tomato, and garlic, stirring frequently, and cook for about 3 minutes until the vegetables soften. 2. Pour in the fava beans along with the liquid from the can and bring the mixture to a boil. 3. Reduce the heat to medium, then stir in the cumin, parsley, and lemon juice. Season with salt, black pepper, and crushed red pepper. Let the beans simmer for 5 minutes, stirring occasionally. 4. While the beans are cooking, warm the pitas in a toaster oven or a cast-iron skillet over medium heat. Serve by cutting the pitas into triangles for dipping, or slice them in half and stuff the pockets with the bean mixture.

Per Serving:
calories: 524 | fat: 8g | protein: 32g | carbs: 86g | fiber: 31g | sodium: 394mg

Kagianas

Prep time: 5 minutes | Cook time: 10 minutes | Serves 2

- 2 teaspoons extra virgin olive oil
- 2 tablespoons finely chopped onion (any variety)
- ¼ teaspoon fine sea salt, divided
- 1 medium tomato (any variety), chopped
- 2 eggs
- 1 ounce (28 g) crumbled feta
- ½ teaspoon dried oregano
- 1 teaspoon chopped fresh mint
- Pinch of freshly ground black pepper for serving

1. Heat the olive oil in a small pan placed over medium heat. When the oil begins to shimmer, add the onions along with ⅛ teaspoon sea salt. Sauté for about 3 minutes or until the onions are soft. 2. Add the tomatoes, stir, then reduce the heat to low and simmer for 8 minutes or until the mixture thickens. 3. While the tomatoes are cooking, beat the eggs in a small bowl. 4. When the tomatoes have thickened, pour the eggs into the pan and increase the heat to medium. Continue cooking, using a spatula to stir the eggs and tomatoes continuously, for 2–3 minutes or until the eggs are set. Remove the pan from the heat. 5. Add the feta, oregano, and mint, and stir to combine. 6. Transfer to a plate. Top with a pinch of black pepper and the remaining ⅛ teaspoon sea salt. Serve promptly.

Per Serving:
calories: 156 | fat: 12g | protein: 8g | carbs: 4g | fiber: 1g | sodium: 487mg

Red Pepper, Spinach, and Feta Muffins

Prep time: 10 minutes | Cook time: 22 minutes | Serves 12

- 2 cups all-purpose flour
- ¾ cup whole-wheat flour
- ¼ cup granulated sugar
- 2 teaspoons baking powder
- 1 teaspoon paprika
- ¾ teaspoon salt
- ½ cup extra virgin olive oil
- 2 eggs
- ¾ cup low-fat 2% milk
- ¾ cup crumbled feta
- 1¼ cups fresh baby leaf spinach, thinly sliced
- ⅓ cup jarred red peppers, drained, patted dry, and chopped

1. Preheat the oven to 375°F (190°C) and place 12 muffin liners in a large muffin pan. 2. In a large bowl, mix together the all-purpose flour, whole-wheat flour, sugar, baking powder, paprika, and salt until well combined. 3. In a medium bowl, whisk the olive oil, eggs, and milk until smooth. 4. Pour the wet ingredients into the dry ingredients and stir gently with a wooden spoon until just combined to form a thick dough. 5. Fold in the feta, spinach, and peppers, mixing lightly until evenly distributed. Spoon the mixture evenly into the prepared muffin liners. 6. Bake for 25 minutes, or until a toothpick inserted into the center of a muffin comes out clean. 7. Let the muffins cool in the pan for 10 minutes, then transfer them to a wire rack. Store in an airtight container in the refrigerator for up to 3 days. Allow the muffins to sit at room temperature for 10 minutes before eating.

Per Serving:
calories: 243 | fat: 12g | protein: 6g | carbs: 27g | fiber: 2g | sodium: 306mg

Steel-Cut Oats with Flax, Dates, and Walnuts

Prep time: 5 minutes | Cook time: 5 minutes | Serves 4

- 1 tablespoon light olive oil
- 1 cup steel-cut oats
- 3 cups water
- ⅓ cup chopped pitted dates
- ¼ cup ground flax
- ¼ teaspoon salt
- ½ cup toasted chopped walnuts

1. Add the oil, oats, water, dates, flax, and salt to the Instant Pot®, stirring thoroughly to combine. Close the lid, set the steam release to Sealing, press the Manual button, and set the timer for 5 minutes. 2. Once the timer beeps, allow the pressure to release naturally for 10 minutes, then perform a quick release until the float valve drops. Press the Cancel button, open the lid, and mix in the walnuts. Serve hot.

Per Serving:
calories: 322 | fat: 18g | protein: 10g | carbs: 42g | fiber: 8g | sodium: 150mg

Ricotta and Fruit Bruschetta

Prep time: 5 minutes | Cook time: 0 minutes | Serves 2

- ¼ cup full-fat ricotta cheese
- 1½ teaspoons honey, divided
- 3 drops almond extract
- 2 slices whole-grain bread, toasted
- ½ medium banana, peeled and cut into ¼-inch slices
- ½ medium pear (any variety), thinly sliced
- 2 teaspoons chopped walnuts
- 2 pinches of ground cinnamon

1. In a small bowl, combine the ricotta, ¼ teaspoon honey, and the almond extract. Stir well. 2. Spread 1½ tablespoons of the ricotta mixture over each slice of toast. 3. Divide the pear slices and banana slices equally on top of each slice of toast. 4. Drizzle equal amounts of the remaining honey over each slice, and sprinkle 1 teaspoon of the walnuts over each slice. Top each serving with a pinch of cinnamon.

Per Serving:
calories: 207 | fat: 7g | protein: 8g | carbs: 30g | fiber: 4g | sodium: 162mg

Baked Ricotta with Pears

Prep time: 5 minutes | Cook time: 25 minutes | Serves: 4

- Nonstick cooking spray
- 1 (16-ounce / 454-g) container whole-milk ricotta cheese
- 2 large eggs
- ¼ cup white whole-wheat flour or whole-wheat pastry flour
- 1 tablespoon sugar
- 1 teaspoon vanilla extract
- ¼ teaspoon ground nutmeg
- 1 pear, cored and diced
- 2 tablespoons water
- 1 tablespoon honey

1. Preheat the oven to 400°F(205°C). Spray four 6-ounce ramekins with nonstick cooking spray. 2. In a large bowl, beat together the ricotta, eggs, flour, sugar, vanilla, and nutmeg. Spoon into the ramekins. Bake for 22 to 25 minutes, or until the ricotta is just about set. Remove from the oven and cool slightly on racks. 3. While the ricotta is baking, in a small saucepan over medium heat, simmer the pear in the water for 10 minutes, until slightly softened. Remove from the heat, and stir in the honey. 4. Serve the ricotta ramekins topped with the warmed pear.

Per Serving:
calories: 306 | fat: 17g | protein: 17g | carbs: 21g | fiber: 1g | sodium: 131mg

Savory Farro with Nuts and Dried Fruit

Prep time: 10 minutes | Cook time: 20 minutes | Serves 8

- 16 ounces (454 g) farro, rinsed and drained
- 4½ cups water
- ¼ cup maple syrup
- ¼ teaspoon salt
- 1 cup dried mixed fruit
- ½ cup chopped toasted mixed nuts
- 2 cups almond milk

1. Add the farro, water, maple syrup, and salt to the Instant Pot® and stir well to combine. Secure the lid, set the steam release to Sealing, press the Multigrain button, and set the timer for 20 minutes. Once the cooking time finishes, allow the pressure to release naturally for about 30 minutes. 2. Press the Cancel button, carefully open the lid, and stir in the dried fruit. Close the lid again and let the mixture sit on the Keep Warm setting for 20 minutes. Serve warm with nuts and almond milk.

Per Serving:
calories: 347 | fat: 7g | protein: 9g | carbs: 65g | fiber: 9g | sodium: 145mg

Tuna Tortilla with Roasted Peppers

Prep time: 15 minutes | Cook time: 15 minutes | Serves 4

- 6 large eggs
- ¼ cup olive oil
- 2 small russet potatoes, diced
- 1 small onion, chopped
- 1 roasted red bell pepper, sliced
- 1 (7-ounce / 198-g) can tuna packed in water, drained well and flaked
- 2 plum tomatoes, seeded and diced
- 1 teaspoon dried tarragon

1. Preheat the broiler on high. 2. Crack the eggs into a large bowl and whisk until just blended. In a large oven-safe nonstick or cast-iron skillet, heat the olive oil over medium-low heat. 3. Add the potatoes and cook for about 7 minutes until they start to soften. Add the onion and peppers, and continue to cook for 3 to 5 minutes until they become tender. 4. Stir in the tuna, tomatoes, and tarragon, mixing well, then pour the eggs evenly over the mixture. 5. Cook for 7 to 10 minutes until the eggs bubble from the bottom and the underside is lightly browned. 6. Move the skillet to the oven and place it on one of the top two racks. Broil until the center sets and the top turns golden brown. 7. Slice into wedges and serve warm or at room temperature.

Per Serving:
calories: 247 | fat: 14g | protein: 12g | carbs: 19g | fiber: 2g | sodium: 130mg

Chapter 3

Beans and Grains

Chapter 3 Beans and Grains

Sautéed Lentil Spinach Curry

Prep time: 10 minutes | Cook time: 17 minutes | Serves 4

- 1 tablespoon olive oil
- ½ cup diced onion
- 1 clove garlic, peeled and minced
- 1 cup dried yellow lentils, rinsed and drained
- 4 cups water
- ½ teaspoon ground coriander
- ½ teaspoon ground turmeric
- ½ teaspoon curry powder
- ½ cup diced tomatoes
- 5 ounces (142 g) baby spinach leaves

1. Press the Sauté button on the Instant Pot® and heat oil. Add onion and cook until translucent, about 5 minutes. Add garlic and cook for 30 seconds. Add lentils and toss to combine. Press the Cancel button. 2. Pour in water. Close lid, set steam release to Sealing, press the Manual button, and set time to 6 minutes. When the timer beeps, quick-release the pressure until the float valve drops and open lid. Press the Cancel button. Drain any residual liquid. Stir in coriander, turmeric, curry powder, tomatoes, and spinach. 3. Press the Sauté button, press the Adjust button to change the heat to Less, and simmer uncovered until tomatoes are heated through and spinach has wilted, about 5 minutes. 4. Transfer to a dish and serve.

Per Serving:
calories: 195 | fat: 4g | protein: 13g | carbs: 26g | fiber: 8g | sodium: 111mg

Kale and Chickpea Delight

Prep time: 10 minutes | Cook time: 4 to 6 hours | Serves 6

- 1 to 2 tablespoons rapeseed oil
- ½ teaspoon mustard seeds
- 1 teaspoon cumin seeds
- 1 large onion, diced
- 4 garlic cloves, crushed
- 4 plum tomatoes, finely chopped
- 1 heaped teaspoon coriander seeds, ground
- 1 fresh green chile, chopped
- 1 teaspoon chili powder
- 1 teaspoon turmeric
- 1 teaspoon salt
- 2 (16-ounce / 454-g) cans cooked chickpeas, drained and rinsed
- ¾ cup water
- 7 to 8 ounces (198 to 227 g) kale, chopped
- 1 fresh green chile, sliced, for garnish

1. Heat the oil in a frying pan (or use the sear setting on your slow cooker if available). Once hot, add the mustard seeds followed by the cumin seeds, cooking until they pop and release their aroma. 2. Stir in the diced onion and sauté for 10 minutes, stirring frequently. Add the garlic and cook for a few more minutes, then mix in the tomatoes. Sprinkle in the ground coriander, green chile, chili powder, turmeric, and salt. 3. Add the chickpeas and water, cover, and cook on low for 6 hours or high for 4 hours. 4. Stir in the chopped kale a handful at a time, letting it wilt between additions. Cook for another 10 to 15 minutes until the kale is tender. 5. Garnish with the sliced chile before serving.

Per Serving:
calories: 202 | fat: 6g | protein: 10g | carbs: 30g | fiber: 10g | sodium: 619mg

Moist Greek Yogurt Corn Bread

Prep time: 15 minutes | Cook time: 25 minutes | Serves 4 to 6

- ⅓ cup olive oil, plus extra for greasing
- 1 cup cornmeal
- 1 cup all-purpose flour
- ¼ cup sugar
- ½ teaspoon baking soda
- ½ teaspoon baking powder
- 1 teaspoon sea salt
- 1 cup plain full-fat Greek yogurt
- 1 large egg
- ¼ cup crumbled feta cheese

1. Preheat the oven to 375°F(190°C). Lightly grease an 8-inch square baking dish with olive oil. 2. In a large bowl, stir together the cornmeal, flour, sugar, baking soda, baking powder, and salt until well mixed. Add the yogurt, olive oil, and egg and stir until smooth. Stir in the feta. 3. Pour the batter into the prepared baking dish and bake until a toothpick inserted into the center of the corn bread comes out clean, about 30 minutes. 4. Remove the corn bread from the oven, cut it into 9 squares, and serve.

Per Serving:
calories: 546 | fat: 24g | protein: 11g | carbs: 71g | fiber: 2g | sodium: 584mg

Lentil and Rice Pilaf

Prep time: 5 minutes | Cook time: 50 minutes | Serves 6

- ¼ cup extra-virgin olive oil
- 1 large onion, chopped
- 6 cups water
- 1 teaspoon ground cumin
- 1 teaspoon salt
- 2 cups brown lentils, picked over and rinsed
- 1 cup basmati rice

1. In a medium pot over medium heat, cook the olive oil and onions for 7 to 10 minutes until the edges are browned. 2. Turn the heat to high, add the water, cumin, and salt, and bring this mixture to a boil, boiling for about 3 minutes. 3. Add the lentils and turn the heat to medium-low. Cover the pot and cook for 20 minutes, stirring occasionally. 4. Stir in the rice and cover; cook for an additional 20 minutes. 5. Fluff the rice with a fork and serve warm.

Per Serving:
calories: 397 | fat: 11g | protein: 18g | carbs: 60g | fiber: 18g | sodium: 396mg

Nutty Brown Rice with Cherries and Apricots

Prep time: 10 minutes | Cook time: 55 minutes | Serves 2

- 2 tablespoons olive oil
- 2 green onions, sliced
- ½ cup brown rice
- 1 cup chicken stock
- 4–5 dried apricots, chopped
- 2 tablespoons dried cherries
- 2 tablespoons pecans, toasted and chopped
- Sea salt and freshly ground pepper, to taste

1. Heat the olive oil in a medium saucepan, and add the green onions. 2. Sauté for 1–2 minutes, and add the rice. Stir to coat in oil, then add the stock. 3. Bring to a boil, reduce heat, and cover. Simmer for 50 minutes. 4. Remove the lid, add the apricots, cherries, and pecans, and cover for 10 more minutes. 5. Fluff with a fork to mix the fruit into the rice, season with sea salt and freshly ground pepper, and serve.

Zesty Spanish Rice Bowl

Prep time: 10 minutes | Cook time: 20 minutes | Serves 4

- 2 tablespoons extra-virgin olive oil
- 1 medium onion, finely chopped
- 1 large tomato, finely diced
- 2 tablespoons tomato paste
- 1 teaspoon smoked paprika
- 1 teaspoon salt
- 1½ cups basmati rice
- 3 cups water

1. In a medium pot over medium heat, cook the olive oil, onion, and tomato for 3 minutes. 2. Stir in the tomato paste, paprika, salt, and rice. Cook for 1 minute. 3. Add the water, cover the pot, and turn the heat to low. Cook for 12 minutes. 4. Gently toss the rice, cover, and cook for another 3 minutes.

Per Serving:
calories: 328 | fat: 7g | protein: 6g | carbs: 60g | fiber: 2g | sodium: 651mg

Fava Beans with Ground Meat

Prep time: 15 minutes | Cook time: 6 to 8 hours | Serves 6

- 8 ounces (227 g) raw ground meat
- 1 pound (454 g) dried fava beans, rinsed well under cold water and picked over to remove debris, or 1 (15-ounce/ 425-g) can fava beans, drained and rinsed
- 10 cups water or 5 cups water and 5 cups low-sodium vegetable broth
- 1 small onion, diced
- 1 bell pepper, any color, seeded and diced
- 1 teaspoon sea salt
- 1 teaspoon garlic powder
- 1 teaspoon dried parsley
- 1 teaspoon dried oregano
- 1 teaspoon paprika
- 1 teaspoon cayenne pepper
- ½ teaspoon freshly ground black pepper
- ½ teaspoon dried thyme

1. In a large skillet over medium-high heat, brown the ground meat for 3 to 5 minutes, stirring frequently and breaking it up with a spoon until no longer pink. Drain off any excess grease and transfer the meat to the slow cooker. 2. Add the fava beans, water, onion, bell pepper, salt, garlic powder, parsley, oregano, paprika, cayenne pepper, black pepper, and thyme. Stir everything together until well combined. 3. Cover and cook on Low for 6 to 8 hours, or until the beans are tender.

Per Serving:
calories: 308 | fat: 4g | protein: 26g | carbs: 43g | fiber: 19g | sodium: 417mg

Sautéed Tomato Rice

Prep time: 10 minutes | Cook time: 30 minutes | Serves 8

- 2 tablespoons extra-virgin olive oil
- ½ medium yellow onion, peeled and chopped
- 2 cloves garlic, peeled and minced
- 1 cup chopped sun-dried tomatoes in oil, drained
- 1 tablespoon tomato paste
- 2 cups brown rice
- 2¼ cups water
- ½ cup chopped fresh basil
- ¼ teaspoon salt
- ½ teaspoon ground black pepper

1. Press the Sauté button on the Instant Pot® and add the oil. Once hot, add the onion and cook for about 6 minutes until soft. Stir in the garlic and sun-dried tomatoes, cooking for about 30 seconds until fragrant. Add the tomato paste, rice, and water, stirring thoroughly to combine. Press the Cancel button. 2. Secure the lid, set the steam release to Sealing, press the Manual button, and set the timer for 22 minutes. When the timer finishes, let the pressure release naturally for 10 minutes, then quick-release any remaining pressure. Open the lid and gently fold in the basil. Season with salt and pepper to taste. Serve warm.

Per Serving:
calories: 114 | fat: 4g | protein: 2g | carbs: 18g | fiber: 2g | sodium: 112mg

Amaranth Salad

Prep time: 5 minutes | Cook time: 6 minutes | Serves 4

- 2 cups water
- 1 cup amaranth
- 1 teaspoon dried Greek oregano
- ½ teaspoon salt
- ½ teaspoon ground black pepper
- 1 tablespoon extra-virgin olive oil
- 2 teaspoons red wine vinegar

1. Pour the water and amaranth into the Instant Pot®. Secure the lid, set the steam release to Sealing, press the Manual button, and set the timer for 6 minutes. When the cooking time finishes, quick-release the pressure until the float valve drops. 2. Open the lid and fluff the amaranth with a fork. Stir in the oregano, salt, and pepper until well mixed. Drizzle with olive oil and wine vinegar. Serve hot.

Per Serving:
calories: 93 | fat: 5g | protein: 3g | carbs: 12g | fiber: 3g | sodium: 299mg

Zesty Farro Bowl with Avocado

Prep time: 5 minutes | Cook time: 25 minutes | Serves: 6

- 1 tablespoon plus 2 teaspoons extra-virgin olive oil, divided
- 1 cup chopped onion (about ½ medium onion)
- 2 garlic cloves, minced (about 1 teaspoon)
- 1 carrot, shredded (about 1 cup)
- 2 cups low-sodium or no-salt-added vegetable broth
- 1 cup (6 ounces) uncooked pearled or 10-minute farro
- 2 avocados, peeled, pitted, and sliced
- 1 small lemon
- ¼ teaspoon kosher or sea salt

1. In a medium saucepan over medium-high heat, heat 1 tablespoon of oil. Add the onion and cook for 5 minutes, stirring occasionally. Add the garlic and carrot and cook for 1 minute, stirring frequently. Add the broth and farro, and bring to a boil over high heat. Lower the heat to medium-low, cover, and simmer for about 20 minutes or until the farro is plump and slightly chewy (al dente). 2. Pour the farro into a serving bowl, and add the avocado slices. Using a Microplane or citrus zester, zest the peel of the lemon directly into the bowl of farro. Halve the lemon, and squeeze the juice out of both halves using a citrus juicer or your hands. Drizzle the remaining 2 teaspoons of oil over the bowl, and sprinkle with salt. Gently mix all the ingredients and serve.

Per Serving:
calories: 212 | fat: 11g | protein: 3g | carbs: 29g | fiber: 7g | sodium: 147mg

Flavorful Venetian Pasta with Beans

Prep time: 15 minutes | Cook time: 50 minutes | Serves 2

- 1 cup uncooked borlotti (cranberry) beans or pinto beans
- 3 tablespoons extra virgin olive oil, divided
- 1 small carrot, finely chopped
- ½ medium onion (white or red), finely chopped
- 1 celery stalk, finely chopped
- 1 bay leaf
- 1 tablespoon tomato paste
- 2 cups cold water
- 1 rosemary sprig plus ½ teaspoon chopped fresh rosemary needles
- ¼ teaspoon fine sea salt
- ¼ teaspoon freshly ground black pepper plus more to taste
- 1½ ounces (43 g) uncooked egg fettuccine or other egg noodles
- 1 garlic clove, peeled and finely sliced
- ¼ teaspoon red pepper flakes
- 2 teaspoons grated Parmesan cheese
- Pinch of coarse sea salt, for serving

1. Put the beans in a large bowl and cover them with cold water by about 3 inches (7.5 cm) to allow for expansion. Soak for 12 hours or overnight, then drain and rinse thoroughly. 2. In a medium pot over medium heat, add 2 tablespoons of olive oil. Once the oil shimmers, add the carrot, onions, celery, and bay leaf. Sauté for 3 minutes, then stir in the tomato paste and cook for an additional 2 minutes, stirring constantly. 3. Add the beans, cold water, and a rosemary sprig to the pot. Cover and bring to a boil, then lower the heat to a gentle simmer. Cook for 30 to 40 minutes until the beans are tender but still hold their shape. Remove the rosemary sprig and bay leaf. Scoop out 1 cup of beans using a slotted spoon and set aside. 4. Use an immersion blender to puree the remaining beans in the pot. Return the reserved whole beans to the pot, add sea salt and ¼ teaspoon black pepper, and stir. Increase the heat to medium. Once the mixture starts to bubble, add the pasta and cook for about 3 minutes, or until the pasta is cooked through. 5. As the pasta cooks, heat 1 teaspoon of olive oil in a small pan over medium heat. Add the garlic, red pepper flakes, and chopped rosemary needles. Sauté for 2 minutes, then stir this mixture into the pot of beans. 6. When the pasta is fully cooked, take the pot off the heat and let it rest for 5 minutes. Divide the pasta and beans between 2 plates. Drizzle each serving with 1 teaspoon of olive oil and sprinkle with 1 teaspoon of grated Parmesan. Season with freshly ground black pepper and a pinch of coarse sea salt. This dish is best served immediately, but it can be stored in the refrigerator for up to 2 days.

Per Serving:
calories: 409 | fat: 22g | protein: 12g | carbs: 42g | fiber: 11g | sodium: 763mg

Wild Mushroom Farrotto

Prep time: 15 minutes | Cook time: 20 minutes | Serves 4 to 6

- 1½ cups whole farro
- 3 tablespoons extra-virgin olive oil, divided, plus extra for drizzling
- 12 ounces (340 g) cremini or white mushrooms, trimmed and sliced thin
- ½ onion, chopped fine
- ½ teaspoon table salt
- ¼ teaspoon pepper
- 1 garlic clove, minced
- ¼ ounce dried porcini mushrooms, rinsed and chopped fine
- 2 teaspoons minced fresh thyme or ½ teaspoon dried
- ¼ cup dry white wine
- 2½ cups chicken or vegetable broth, plus extra as needed
- 2 ounces (57 g) Parmesan cheese, grated (1 cup), plus extra for serving
- 2 teaspoons lemon juice
- ½ cup chopped fresh parsley

1. Pulse the farro in a blender about 6 times until roughly half of the grains are broken into smaller pieces. 2. Select the highest Sauté function on the Instant Pot and heat 2 tablespoons of oil until shimmering. Add the cremini mushrooms, onion, salt, and pepper. Partially cover and cook for about 5 minutes until the mushrooms soften and release their liquid. Stir in the farro, garlic, porcini mushrooms, and thyme, cooking until fragrant, about 1 minute. Add the wine and cook until almost evaporated, about 30 seconds. Stir in the broth. 3. Secure the lid and close the pressure release valve. Select the High Pressure Cook function and set the timer for 12 minutes. Once the cooking is complete, turn off the Instant Pot and quick-release the pressure. Carefully open the lid, ensuring the steam escapes away from you. 4. If the consistency is too thick, adjust by stirring in extra hot broth. Alternatively, use the highest Sauté function and stir frequently until the desired consistency is reached. The farrotto should be slightly thickened, and dragging a spoon along the bottom should leave a trail that quickly fills in. Stir in the Parmesan and the remaining 1 tablespoon of oil, mixing vigorously until the farrotto is creamy. Add the lemon juice and season with salt and pepper to taste. Garnish each serving with parsley, extra Parmesan, and a drizzle of olive oil before serving.

Per Serving:
calories: 280 | fat: 10g | protein: 13g | carbs: 35g | fiber: 4g | sodium: 630mg

Endive Boats with Quinoa Salad

Prep time: 10 minutes | Cook time: 3 minutes | Serves 4

- 1 tablespoon walnut oil
- 1 cup quinoa, rinsed and drained
- 2½ cups water
- 2 cups chopped jarred artichoke hearts
- 2 cups diced tomatoes
- ½ small red onion, peeled and thinly sliced
- 2 tablespoons olive oil
- 1 tablespoon balsamic vinegar
- 4 large Belgian endive leaves
- 1 cup toasted pecans

1. Press the Sauté button on the Instant Pot® and heat walnut oil. Add quinoa and toss for 1 minute until slightly browned. Add water and stir. Press the Cancel button. 2. Close lid, set steam release to Sealing, press the Manual button, and set time to 2 minutes. When the timer beeps, let pressure release naturally for 10 minutes. Quick-release any remaining pressure until the float valve drops and open lid. Drain liquid and transfer quinoa to a serving bowl. 3. Add artichoke hearts, tomatoes, onion, olive oil, and vinegar to quinoa and stir to combine. Cover and refrigerate mixture for 1 hour or up to overnight. 4. Place endive leaves on four plates. Top each with ¼ cup quinoa mixture. Sprinkle toasted pecans over the top of each endive boat and serve.

Per Serving:
calories: 536 | fat: 35g | protein: 13g | carbs: 46g | fiber: 13g | sodium: 657mg

Quinoa Salad with Chicken, Chickpeas, and Spinach

Prep time: 15 minutes | Cook time: 18 minutes | Serves 6

- 4 tablespoons olive oil, divided
- 1 medium yellow onion, peeled and chopped
- 2 cloves garlic, peeled and minced
- 4 cups fresh baby spinach leaves
- ½ teaspoon salt
- ¼ teaspoon ground black pepper
- 1½ cups quinoa, rinsed and drained
- 2 cups vegetable broth
- 1⅓ cups water
- 1 tablespoon apple cider vinegar
- 1 (15-ounce / 425-g) can chickpeas, drained and rinsed
- 1 (6-ounce / 170-g) boneless, skinless chicken breast, cooked and shredded

1. Press the Sauté button on the Instant Pot® and heat 2 tablespoons of olive oil. Add the onion and cook for about 3 minutes until tender. Stir in the garlic, spinach, salt, and pepper, and cook for another 3 minutes until the spinach wilts. Transfer the spinach mixture to a large bowl and press the Cancel button. 2. Add the quinoa, broth, and water to the Instant Pot®. Secure the lid, set the steam release to Sealing, press the Rice button, and set the timer for 12 minutes. 3. While the quinoa cooks, add the remaining 2 tablespoons of olive oil, vinegar, chickpeas, and chicken to the spinach mixture. Toss until everything is well coated and set aside. 4. Once the timer beeps, let the pressure release naturally for about 20 minutes. 5. Open the lid and fluff the quinoa with a fork. Press the Cancel button and let it cool for 10 minutes. Transfer the quinoa to the bowl with the chicken mixture and mix thoroughly. Serve warm, at room temperature, or cold.

Per Serving:
calories: 232 | fat: 12g | protein: 14g | carbs: 20g | fiber: 6g | sodium: 463mg

Artichoke Quinoa Delight

Prep time: 10 minutes | Cook time: 26 minutes | Serves 4

- 2 tablespoons light olive oil
- 1 medium yellow onion, peeled and diced
- 2 cloves garlic, peeled and minced
- ½ teaspoon salt
- ½ teaspoon ground black pepper
- 1 cup quinoa, rinsed and drained
- 2 cups vegetable broth
- 1 cup roughly chopped marinated artichoke hearts
- ½ cup sliced green olives
- ½ cup minced fresh flat-leaf parsley
- 2 tablespoons lemon juice

1. Press the Sauté button on the Instant Pot® and heat oil. Add onion and cook until tender, about 5 minutes. Add garlic, salt, and pepper, and cook until fragrant, about 30 seconds. Press the Cancel button. 2. Stir in quinoa and broth. Close lid, set steam release to Sealing, press the Manual button, and set time to 20 minutes. When the timer beeps, let pressure release naturally, about 20 minutes, then open lid. Fluff quinoa with a fork, then stir in remaining ingredients. Serve immediately.

Per Serving:
calories: 270 | fat: 13g | protein: 6g | carbs: 33g | fiber: 4g | sodium: 718mg

Lentil and Spinach Medley

Prep time: 10 minutes | Cook time: 20 minutes | Serves 4

- 1 cup dried yellow lentils, rinsed and drained
- 4 cups water
- 1 tablespoon olive oil
- ½ medium yellow onion, peeled and chopped
- 1 clove garlic, peeled and minced
- ½ teaspoon smoked paprika
- ½ teaspoon ground black pepper
- 1 (15-ounce / 425-g) can diced tomatoes, drained
- 10 ounces (283 g) baby spinach leaves
- ½ cup crumbled feta cheese

1. Add lentils and water to the Instant Pot®. Close lid, set steam release to Sealing, press the Manual button, and set time to 6 minutes. When the timer beeps, quick-release the pressure. Press the Cancel button and open lid. Drain lentils and set aside. Clean pot. 2. Press the Sauté button and heat oil. Add onion and cook until just tender, about 3 minutes. Add garlic, smoked paprika, and pepper, and cook for an additional 30 seconds. Stir in tomatoes, spinach, and lentils. Simmer for 10 minutes. Top with feta and serve.

Per Serving:
calories: 289 | fat: 8g | protein: 21g | carbs: 31g | fiber: 10g | sodium: 623mg

Savory Herbed Lima Beans

Prep time: 10 minutes | Cook time: 6 minutes | Serves 6

- 1 pound (454 g) frozen baby lima beans, thawed
- 2 cloves garlic, peeled and minced
- 2 thyme sprigs
- 1 bay leaf
- 2 tablespoons extra-virgin olive oil
- 3 cups water
- 1 tablespoon chopped fresh dill
- 1 tablespoon chopped fresh tarragon
- 1 tablespoon chopped fresh mint

1. Add lima beans, garlic, thyme, bay leaf, oil, and water to the Instant Pot®. Close lid, set steam release to Sealing, press the Manual button, and set time to 6 minutes. When the timer beeps, quick-release the pressure until the float valve drops. Open lid, remove and discard thyme and bay leaf, and stir well. 2. Stir in dill, tarragon, and mint, and let stand for 10 minutes on the Keep Warm setting before serving.

Per Serving:
calories: 134 | fat: 5g | protein: 5g | carbs: 17g | fiber: 4g | sodium: 206mg

White Beans with Kale

Prep time: 15 minutes | Cook time: 7½ hours | Serves 2

- 1 onion, chopped
- 1 leek, white part only, sliced
- 2 celery stalks, sliced
- 2 garlic cloves, minced
- 1 cup dried white lima beans or cannellini beans, sorted and rinsed
- 2 cups vegetable broth
- ½ teaspoon salt
- ½ teaspoon dried thyme leaves
- ⅛ teaspoon freshly ground black pepper
- 3 cups torn kale

1. In the slow cooker, combine all the ingredients except the kale, stirring well to mix. 2. Cover and cook on low for 7 hours, or until the beans are tender. 3. Stir in the kale until evenly combined. 4. Cover again and cook on high for 30 minutes, or until the kale is tender yet still slightly firm. Serve warm.

Per Serving:
calories: 176 | fat: 1g | protein: 9g | carbs: 36g | fiber: 9g | sodium: 616mg

Garbanzo and Pita No-Bake Casserole

Prep time: 10 minutes | Cook time: 10 minutes | Serves 4

- 4 cups Greek yogurt
- 3 cloves garlic, minced
- 1 teaspoon salt
- 2 (16-ounce/ 454-g) cans garbanzo beans, rinsed and drained
- 2 cups water
- 4 cups pita chips
- 5 tablespoons unsalted butter

1. In a large bowl, whisk the yogurt, garlic, and salt until well combined. Set aside. 2. Place the garbanzo beans and water in a medium pot and bring to a boil. Let the beans boil for about 5 minutes. 3. Pour the garbanzo beans and their cooking liquid into a large casserole dish. 4. Evenly layer the pita chips over the beans, then pour the yogurt sauce over the pita chip layer. 5. In a small saucepan, melt the butter and cook until it browns, about 3 minutes. Drizzle the browned butter over the yogurt sauce. Serve warm.

Per Serving:
calories: 772 | fat: 36g | protein: 39g | carbs: 73g | fiber: 13g | sodium: 1,003mg

Herbed Polenta

Prep time: 10 minutes | Cook time: 3 to 5 hours | Serves 4

- 1 cup stone-ground polenta
- 4 cups low-sodium vegetable stock or low-sodium chicken stock
- 1 tablespoon extra-virgin olive oil
- 1 small onion, minced
- 2 garlic cloves, minced
- 1 teaspoon sea salt
- 1 teaspoon dried parsley
- 1 teaspoon dried oregano
- 1 teaspoon dried thyme
- ½ teaspoon freshly ground black pepper
- ½ cup grated Parmesan cheese

1. In a slow cooker, add the polenta, vegetable stock, olive oil, onion, garlic, salt, parsley, oregano, thyme, and pepper. Stir until everything is well combined. 2. Cover and cook on Low for 3 to 5 hours, stirring occasionally if desired. 3. When ready to serve, stir in the Parmesan cheese until fully incorporated. Serve warm.

Per Serving:
calories: 191 | fat: 9g | protein: 11g | carbs: 18g | fiber: 1g | sodium: 796mg

Mediterranean Bulgur Mix

Prep time: 15 minutes | Cook time: 20 minutes | Serves 6

- 2 tablespoons extra-virgin olive oil
- 1 medium onion, peeled and diced
- ½ cup chopped button mushrooms
- ½ cup golden raisins (sultanas)
- ¼ cup pine nuts
- 2 cups vegetable stock
- 1 teaspoon ground cumin
- ½ teaspoon salt
- ½ teaspoon ground black pepper
- 1 cup medium bulgur wheat
- 1 tablespoon petimezi or honey
- 12 chestnuts, roasted, peeled, and halved
- 1 teaspoon sesame seeds

1. Press the Sauté button on the Instant Pot® and heat oil. Add onion and sauté 3 minutes. Add mushrooms, raisins, and pine nuts and cook 2 minutes. 2. Add stock, cumin, salt, pepper, bulgur, and petimezi. Cook, stirring, for 3 minutes. Add chestnuts, then press the Cancel button. 3. Close lid, set steam release to Sealing, press the Rice button, and set time to 12 minutes. When the timer beeps, quick-release the pressure until the float valve drops and open lid. Stir well, then let stand, uncovered, on the Keep Warm setting for 10 minutes. Sprinkle with sesame seeds and serve.

Per Serving:
calories: 129 | fat: 1g | protein: 3g | carbs: 28g | fiber: 2g | sodium: 219mg

Giant Beans with Tomato and Parsley

Prep time: 10 minutes | Cook time: 54 minutes | Serves 8

- 2 tablespoons light olive oil
- 1 medium white onion, peeled and chopped
- 2 cloves garlic, peeled and minced
- 1 pound (454 g) dried giant beans, soaked overnight and drained
- 2 thyme sprigs
- 1 bay leaf
- 5 cups water
- 1 (15-ounce / 425-g) can diced tomatoes, drained
- 1 (8-ounce / 227-g) can tomato sauce
- ¼ cup chopped fresh flat-leaf parsley
- 2 tablespoons chopped fresh oregano
- 1 tablespoon chopped fresh dill
- ½ cup crumbled feta cheese
- 1 small lemon, cut into 8 wedges

1. Press the Sauté button on the Instant Pot® and heat the oil. Add the onion and sauté until tender, about 3 minutes. Stir in the garlic and cook until fragrant, about 30 seconds. Press the Cancel button. 2. Add the beans, thyme, bay leaf, and water to the Instant Pot®. Secure the lid, set the steam release to Sealing, press the Manual button, and set the timer for 50 minutes. Once the timer beeps, quick-release the pressure until the float valve drops. Open the lid and check if the beans are soft. If they aren't tender, close the lid and cook under pressure for an additional 10 minutes. 3. Stir in the diced tomatoes and tomato sauce. Close the lid and allow the mixture to sit on the Keep Warm setting for 10 minutes to heat through. Remove the bay leaf and discard it. Stir in the herbs, then ladle the soup into bowls. Garnish with feta and lemon slices, and serve hot.

Per Serving:
calories: 241 | fat: 6g | protein: 14g | carbs: 33g | fiber: 10g | sodium: 458mg

Wild Rice and Mushroom Soup

Prep time: 15 minutes | Cook time: 35 minutes | Serves 8

- 2 tablespoons olive oil
- 2 medium carrots, peeled and chopped
- 2 stalks celery, chopped
- 1 medium yellow onion, peeled and chopped
- 2 (8-ounce/ 227-g) containers sliced button mushrooms
- 3 cloves garlic, peeled and minced
- 1 teaspoon dried thyme
- 1 teaspoon dried oregano
- ½ teaspoon salt
- ½ teaspoon ground black pepper
- 1 cup wild rice blend
- 6 cups vegetable broth

1. Press the Sauté button on the Instant Pot® and heat the oil. Add the carrots, celery, and onion, cooking for about 5 minutes until the vegetables are just tender. Add the mushrooms and continue cooking for about 4 minutes until they start to release their juices. 2. Stir in the garlic, thyme, oregano, salt, pepper, and rice, sautéing for about 1 minute until the garlic is fragrant. Press the Cancel button, add the broth, and stir thoroughly. Close the lid, set the steam release to Sealing, press the Manual button, and set the timer for 25 minutes. 3. When the timer beeps, quick-release the pressure until the float valve drops. Open the lid and give everything a good stir. Serve hot.

Per Serving:
calories: 141 | fat: 4g | protein: 4g | carbs: 24g | fiber: 3g | sodium: 722mg

Creamy Lima Bean Soup

Prep time: 10 minutes | Cook time: 17 minutes | Serves 6

- 1 tablespoon olive oil
- 1 small onion, peeled and diced
- 1 clove garlic, peeled and minced
- 2 cups vegetable stock
- ½ cup water
- 2 cups dried lima beans, soaked overnight and drained
- ½ teaspoon salt
- ½ teaspoon ground black pepper
- 2 tablespoons thinly sliced chives

1. Press the Sauté button on the Instant Pot® and heat the oil. Add the onion and cook for about 10 minutes until golden brown. Stir in the garlic and cook for 30 seconds until fragrant. Press the Cancel button. 2. Add the stock, water, and lima beans. Secure the lid, set the steam release to Sealing, press the Manual button, and set the timer for 6 minutes. When the timer beeps, allow the pressure to release naturally for about 20 minutes. 3. Carefully open the lid and purée the soup with an immersion blender or in batches using a regular blender. Season with salt and pepper to taste, and garnish with chives before serving.

Per Serving:
calories: 67 | fat: 2g | protein: 2g | carbs: 9g | fiber: 2g | sodium: 394mg

Date and Pistachio Rice Pilaf

Prep time: 15 minutes | Cook time: 6 minutes | Serves 4 to 6

- 2 tablespoons extra-virgin olive oil, plus extra for drizzling
- 1 shallot, minced
- 1½ teaspoons grated fresh ginger
- ½ teaspoon table salt
- ¼ teaspoon ground coriander
- ¼ teaspoon ground cumin
- ¼ teaspoon pepper
- 1¾ cups water
- 1½ cups cracked freekeh, rinsed
- 3 ounces (85 g) pitted dates, chopped (½ cup)
- ¼ cup shelled pistachios, toasted and coarsely chopped
- 1½ tablespoons lemon juice
- ¼ cup chopped fresh mint

1. Using highest sauté function, heat oil in Instant Pot until shimmering. Add shallot, ginger, salt, coriander, cumin, and pepper and cook until shallot is softened, about 2 minutes. Stir in water and freekeh. 2. Lock lid in place and close pressure release valve. Select high pressure cook function and cook for 4 minutes. Turn off Instant Pot and quick-release pressure. Carefully remove lid, allowing steam to escape away from you. 3. Add dates, pistachios, and lemon juice and gently fluff freekeh with fork to combine. Season with salt and pepper to taste. Transfer to serving dish, sprinkle with mint, and drizzle with extra oil. Serve.

Per Serving:
calories: 280 | fat: 8g | protein: 8g | carbs: 46g | fiber: 9g | sodium: 200mg

Velvety Thyme-Infused Polenta

Prep time: 5 minutes | Cook time: 10 minutes | Serves 6

- 3½ cups water
- ½ cup coarse polenta
- ½ cup fine cornmeal
- 1 cup corn kernels
- 1 teaspoon dried thyme
- 1 teaspoon salt

1. Add all ingredients to the Instant Pot® and stir. 2. Close lid, set steam release to Sealing, press the Manual button, and set time to 10 minutes. When the timer beeps, quick-release the pressure until the float valve drops and open lid. Serve immediately.

Per Serving:
calories: 74 | fat: 1g | protein: 2g | carbs: 14g | fiber: 2g | sodium: 401mg

Spicy Black Beans with Root Veggies

Prep time: 20 minutes | Cook time: 8 hours | Serves 2

- 1 onion, chopped
- 1 leek, white part only, sliced
- 3 garlic cloves, minced
- 1 jalapeño pepper, minced
- 2 Yukon Gold potatoes, peeled and cubed
- 1 parsnip, peeled and cubed
- 1 carrot, sliced
- 1 cup dried black beans, sorted and rinsed
- 2 cups vegetable broth
- 2 teaspoons chili powder
- ½ teaspoon dried marjoram leaves
- ½ teaspoon salt
- ⅛ teaspoon freshly ground black pepper
- ⅛ teaspoon crushed red pepper flakes

1. Place all the ingredients into the slow cooker and stir to combine. 2. Cover and cook on low for 7 to 8 hours until the beans and vegetables are tender. Serve warm.

Per Serving:
calories: 597 | fat: 2g | protein: 27g | carbs: 124g | fiber: 25g | sodium: 699mg

Brown Rice Salad with Zucchini and Tomatoes

Prep time: 5 minutes | Cook time: 22 minutes | Serves 6

- 1 cup brown basmati rice
- 1¼ cups vegetable broth
- 5 tablespoons olive oil, divided
- 2 cups chopped zucchini
- 2 cups sliced cherry tomatoes
- ¼ cup minced red onion
- 2 tablespoons lemon juice
- ¼ teaspoon salt
- ¼ teaspoon ground black pepper
- ¼ cup chopped fresh flat-leaf parsley
- ¼ cup toasted slivered almonds
- ¼ cup crumbled feta cheese

1. Combine the rice, broth, and 1 tablespoon of olive oil in the Instant Pot® and stir thoroughly. Secure the lid, set the steam release to Sealing, press the Manual button, and set the timer for 22 minutes. 2. When the timer finishes, allow the pressure to release naturally for 10 minutes, then quick-release any remaining pressure. Open the lid and fluff the rice with a fork. Transfer the rice to a large bowl and let it cool to room temperature. 3. Add the zucchini, tomatoes, and onion to the rice. In a small bowl, whisk together the remaining 4 tablespoons of olive oil, lemon juice, salt, and pepper. Drizzle the dressing over the rice mixture and toss until evenly combined. Sprinkle with parsley, almonds, and feta. Serve warm or at room temperature.

Per Serving:
calories: 209 | fat: 12g | protein: 5g | carbs: 21g | fiber: 2g | sodium: 380mg

Black Chickpea Snack

Prep time: 11 minutes | Cook time: 9 to 11 hours | Serves 6

- 1 tablespoon rapeseed oil
- 2 teaspoons cumin seeds
- 2 cups dried whole black chickpeas, washed
- 4 cups hot water
- 1 onion, roughly chopped
- 2-inch piece fresh ginger, peeled and roughly chopped
- 4 garlic cloves
- 3 fresh green chiles
- 1 tomato, roughly chopped
- 1 teaspoon turmeric
- 1 teaspoon Kashmiri chili powder
- 1 teaspoon sea salt
- Handful fresh coriander leaves, chopped
- Juice of 1 lemon

1. Heat the oil in a frying pan (or in the slow cooker if you have a sear setting). Add the cumin seeds until they sizzle, then pour them into the cooker. 2. Heat the slow cooker to high, and then add the chickpeas and water. 3. In a blender, purée the onion, ginger, garlic, chiles, and tomato to make a paste. Add it to the cooker, along with the turmeric, chili powder, and salt. 4. Cover and cook for 9 hours on high, or for 11 hours on low. 5. When the chickpeas are cooked, check the seasoning. Add the coriander leaves and lemon juice, and serve.

Per Serving:
calories: 129 | fat: 4g | protein: 5g | carbs: 19g | fiber: 5g | sodium: 525mg

Rice Pilaf

Prep time: 5 minutes | Cook time: 30 minutes | Serves 6

- 2 tablespoons olive oil
- 1 medium onion, diced
- ¼ cup pine nuts
- 1½ cups long-grain brown rice
- 2½ cups hot chicken stock
- 1 cinnamon stick
- ¼ cup raisins
- Sea salt and freshly ground pepper, to taste

1. Heat the olive oil in a large saucepan over medium heat. 2. Sauté the onions and pine nuts for 6–8 minutes, or until the pine nuts are golden and the onion is translucent. 3. Add the rice and sauté for 2 minutes until lightly browned. Pour the chicken stock into the pan and bring to a boil. 4. Add the cinnamon and raisins. 5. Lower the heat, cover the pan, and simmer for 15–20 minutes, or until the rice is tender and the liquid is absorbed. 6. Remove from the heat and fluff with a fork. Season and serve.

Per Serving:
calories: 293 | fat: 10g | protein: 7g | carbs: 45g | fiber: 2g | sodium: 35mg

Chapter 4

Poultry

Chapter 4 Poultry

Coconut Chicken Bites

Prep time: 10 minutes | Cook time: 14 minutes | Serves 4

- 1 pound (454 g) ground chicken
- 2 scallions, finely chopped
- 1 cup chopped fresh cilantro leaves
- ¼ cup unsweetened shredded coconut
- 1 tablespoon hoisin sauce
- 1 tablespoon soy sauce
- 2 teaspoons Sriracha or other hot sauce
- 1 teaspoon toasted sesame oil
- ½ teaspoon kosher salt
- 1 teaspoon black pepper

1. In a large bowl, gently mix the chicken, scallions, cilantro, coconut, hoisin, soy sauce, Sriracha, sesame oil, salt, and pepper until thoroughly combined (the mixture will be wet and sticky). 2. Place a sheet of parchment paper in the air fryer basket. Using a small scoop or teaspoon, drop rounds of the mixture in a single layer onto the parchment paper. 3. Set the air fryer to 350°F (177°C) for 10 minutes, turning the meatballs halfway through the cooking time. Raise the air fryer temperature to 400°F (204°C) and cook for 4 minutes more to brown the outsides of the meatballs. Use a meat thermometer to ensure the meatballs have reached an internal temperature of 165°F (74°C). 4. Transfer the meatballs to a serving platter. Repeat with any remaining chicken mixture.

Per Serving:
calories: 213 | fat: 13g | protein: 21g | carbs: 4g | fiber: 1g | sodium: 501mg

Garlic-Lemon Chicken and Potatoes

Prep time: 10 minutes | Cook time: 45 minutes | Serves 4 to 6

- 1 cup garlic, minced
- 1½ cups lemon juice
- 1 cup plus 2 tablespoons extra-virgin olive oil, divided
- 1½ teaspoons salt, divided
- 1 teaspoon freshly ground black pepper
- 1 whole chicken, cut into 8 pieces
- 1 pound (454 g) fingerling or red potatoes

1. Preheat the oven to 400°F (205°C). 2. In a large bowl, whisk together the garlic, lemon juice, 1 cup of olive oil, 1 teaspoon of salt, and pepper until well combined. 3. Place the chicken in a large baking dish and pour half of the lemon sauce over it. Cover the dish with foil and bake for 20 minutes. 4. Halve the potatoes and toss them with 2 tablespoons of olive oil and 1 teaspoon of salt. Spread them out on a baking sheet and bake for 20 minutes alongside the chicken. 5. Remove both the chicken and potatoes from the oven. Use a spatula to transfer the potatoes to the baking dish with the chicken. Pour the remaining lemon sauce over everything. Bake uncovered for another 25 minutes. 6. Move the chicken and potatoes to a serving dish and drizzle the garlic-lemon sauce from the pan over the top. Serve immediately.

Per Serving:
calories: 748 | fat: 59g | protein: 32g | carbs: 24g | fiber: 2g | sodium: 707mg

Duck with Fennel Root

Prep time: 10 minutes | Cook time: 50 minutes | Serves 6

- ¼ cup olive oil
- 1 whole duck, cleaned
- 3 teaspoon fresh rosemary
- 2 garlic cloves, minced
- Sea salt and freshly ground pepper, to taste
- 3 fennel bulbs, cut into chunks
- ½ cup sherry

1. Preheat the oven to 375°F (190°C) 2. Heat the olive oil in a large stew pot or Dutch oven. 3. Season the duck, including the cavity, with the rosemary, garlic, sea salt, and freshly ground pepper. 4. Place the duck in the oil, and cook it for 10–15 minutes, turning as necessary to brown all sides. 5. Add the fennel bulbs and cook an additional 5 minutes. 6. Pour the sherry over the duck and fennel, cover the pot, and cook in the oven for 30–45 minutes, or until internal temperature of the duck is 150°F (66°C) at its thickest part. 7. Allow duck to sit for 15 minutes before serving.

Per Serving:
calories: 308 | fat: 23g | protein: 17g | carbs: 9g | fiber: 4g | sodium: 112mg

Lemon Chicken

Prep time: 5 minutes | Cook time: 20 to 25 minutes | Serves 4

- 8 bone-in chicken thighs, skin on
- 1 tablespoon olive oil
- 1½ teaspoons lemon-pepper seasoning
- ½ teaspoon paprika
- ½ teaspoon garlic powder
- ¼ teaspoon freshly ground black pepper
- Juice of ½ lemon

1. Preheat the air fryer to 360°F (182°C). 2. In a large bowl, add the chicken and drizzle with olive oil. Sprinkle with lemon-pepper seasoning, paprika, garlic powder, and freshly ground black pepper. Toss until the chicken is evenly coated. 3. Arrange the chicken in a single layer in the air fryer basket, working in batches if needed. Air fry for 20 to 25 minutes, turning the chicken halfway through, until a thermometer inserted into the thickest part reads 165°F (74°C). 4. Place the chicken on a serving platter and squeeze fresh lemon juice over the top before serving.

Per Serving:
calories: 399 | fat: 19g | protein: 56g | carbs: 1g | fiber: 0g | sodium: 367mg

Spinach and Feta Stuffed Chicken Breasts

Prep time: 10 minutes | Cook time: 27 minutes | Serves 4

- 1 (10 ounces / 283 g) package frozen spinach, thawed and drained well
- 1 cup feta cheese, crumbled
- ½ teaspoon freshly ground black pepper
- 4 boneless chicken breasts
- Salt and freshly ground black pepper, to taste
- 1 tablespoon olive oil

1. Make the filling by squeezing as much liquid as possible from the thawed spinach. Roughly chop the spinach and place it in a mixing bowl. Add the feta cheese and freshly ground black pepper, stirring to combine. 2. Prepare the chicken breast by placing it on a cutting board. With one hand, press down to stabilize it. Using a sharp knife, make a small 1-inch incision on the thickest part of the breast. Carefully move the knife inside to create a pocket about 3 inches long, being cautious not to cut through the top, bottom, or other side. If making a smaller pocket is difficult, extend the incision slightly, but be mindful when cooking, as more filling will be exposed. 3. Stuff the chicken by using your fingers to push the spinach-feta mixture into the pocket, spreading it as deep as possible. 4. Preheat the air fryer to 380°F (193°C). 5. Lightly brush or spray the air fryer basket and chicken breasts with olive oil. Place two stuffed chicken breasts into the basket. Cook for 12 minutes, flipping the chicken halfway through. Transfer the cooked chicken to a plate and air fry the remaining two breasts for 12 minutes. Once both batches are cooked, return all four pieces to the air fryer and cook for an additional 3 minutes. The chicken is done when an instant-read thermometer registers 165°F (74°C) in the thickest part of both the chicken and the filling. 6. Let the chicken rest on a cutting board for 2 to 3 minutes. Slice each breast on the bias and serve, fanning out the slices for presentation.

Per Serving:
calories: 476 | fat: 19g | protein: 69g | carbs: 5g | fiber: 2g | sodium: 519mg

Tex-Mex Chicken Roll-Ups

Prep time: 10 minutes | Cook time: 14 to 17 minutes | Serves 8

- 2 pounds (907 g) boneless, skinless chicken breasts or thighs
- 1 teaspoon chili powder
- ½ teaspoon smoked paprika
- ½ teaspoon ground cumin
- Sea salt and freshly ground black pepper, to taste
- 6 ounces (170 g) Monterey Jack cheese, shredded
- 4 ounces (113 g) canned diced green chiles
- Avocado oil spray

1. Place the chicken in a large zip-top bag or between two sheets of plastic wrap. Using a meat mallet or heavy skillet, pound the chicken until it is about ¼ inch thick. 2. In a small bowl, mix the chili powder, smoked paprika, cumin, salt, and pepper. Season both sides of the chicken evenly with the spice blend. 3. Sprinkle Monterey Jack cheese and diced green chiles over each piece of chicken. 4. Roll each piece tightly from the long side, tucking in the ends as you roll. Secure each roll with a toothpick. 5. Preheat the air fryer to 350°F (177°C). Lightly spray the outside of the chicken with avocado oil. Place the chicken in a single layer in the basket, working in batches if needed. Roast for 7 minutes, flip, and cook for another 7 to 10 minutes, until the internal temperature reaches 160°F (71°C). 6. Remove the chicken from the air fryer and let it rest for 5 minutes before serving.

Per Serving:
calories: 220 | fat: 10g | protein: 31g | carbs: 1g | fiber: 0g | sodium: 355mg

Pork Rind Fried Chicken

Prep time: 30 minutes | Cook time: 20 minutes | Serves 4

- ¼ cup buffalo sauce
- 4 (4-ounce / 113-g) boneless, skinless chicken breasts
- ½ teaspoon paprika
- ½ teaspoon garlic powder
- ¼ teaspoon ground black pepper
- 2 ounces (57 g) plain pork rinds, finely crushed

1. Pour the buffalo sauce into a large sealable bowl or bag. Add the chicken and toss until fully coated. Seal the bowl or bag and refrigerate for at least 30 minutes, or up to overnight for more flavor. 2. Take the chicken out of the marinade, leaving any excess sauce on. Season both sides of the chicken thighs with paprika, garlic powder, and pepper. 3. Place the pork rinds in a large bowl. Press each piece of chicken firmly into the pork rinds, ensuring both sides are evenly coated. 4. Put the chicken into the air fryer basket without greasing it. Set the temperature to 400°F (204°C) and cook for 20 minutes, turning the chicken halfway through. The chicken should be golden brown and have an internal temperature of at least 165°F (74°C). Serve warm.

Per Serving:
calories: 217 | fat: 8g | protein: 35g | carbs: 1g | fiber: 0g | sodium: 400mg

Sweet and Tangy Mango Chutney Chicken

Prep time: 10 minutes | Cook time: 6 to 8 hours | Serves 2

- 12 ounces (340 g) boneless, skinless chicken thighs, cut into 1-inch pieces
- ½ cup thinly sliced red onion
- 1 cup canned mango or peaches, drained and diced
- 2 tablespoons golden raisins
- 2 tablespoons apple cider vinegar
- 1 teaspoon minced fresh ginger
- ¼ teaspoon red pepper flakes
- 1 teaspoon curry powder
- ¼ teaspoon ground cinnamon
- ⅛ teaspoon sea salt

1. Put all the ingredients to the slow cooker and gently stir to combine. 2. Cover and cook on low for 6 to 8 hours. The chutney should be thick and sweet and the chicken tender and cooked through.

Per Serving:
calories: 278 | fat: 8g | protein: 35g | carbs: 17g | fiber: 3g | sodium: 320mg

Greek-Style Roast Turkey Breast

Prep time: 10 minutes | Cook time: 7½ hours | Serves 8

- 1 (4-pound / 1.8-kg) turkey breast, trimmed of fat
- ½ cup chicken stock
- 2 tablespoons fresh lemon juice
- 2 cups chopped onions
- ½ cup pitted kalamata olives
- ½ cup oil-packed sun-dried tomatoes, drained and thinly sliced
- 1 clove garlic, minced
- 1 teaspoon dried oregano
- ½ teaspoon ground cinnamon
- ½ teaspoon ground dill
- ¼ teaspoon ground nutmeg
- ¼ teaspoon cayenne pepper
- 1 teaspoon sea salt
- ¼ teaspoon black pepper
- 3 tablespoons all-purpose flour

1. Add the turkey breast, ¼ cup of chicken stock, lemon juice, onions, Kalamata olives, garlic, and sun-dried tomatoes to the slow cooker. Sprinkle with oregano, cinnamon, dill, nutmeg, cayenne pepper, salt, and black pepper. Cover and cook on low for 7 hours. 2. In a small bowl, whisk together the remaining ¼ cup of chicken stock and flour until smooth. Stir this mixture into the slow cooker. Cover and cook on low for another 30 minutes. 3. Serve hot over rice, pasta, potatoes, or your preferred starch.

Per Serving:
calories: 386 | fat: 7g | protein: 70g | carbs: 8g | fiber: 2g | sodium: 601mg

Skillet Greek Turkey and Rice

Prep time: 20 minutes | Cook time: 30 minutes | Serves 2

- 1 tablespoon olive oil
- ½ medium onion, minced
- 2 garlic cloves, minced
- 8 ounces (227 g) ground turkey breast
- ½ cup roasted red peppers, chopped (about 2 jarred peppers)
- ¼ cup sun-dried tomatoes, minced
- 1 teaspoon dried oregano
- ½ cup brown rice
- 1¼ cups low-sodium chicken stock
- Salt
- 2 cups lightly packed baby spinach

1. Warm the olive oil in a sauté pan over medium heat. Add the onion and sauté for 5 minutes until softened. Stir in the garlic and cook for another 30 seconds until fragrant. 2. Add the turkey breast and cook for 7 minutes, using a spoon to break it apart, until it is no longer pink. 3. Stir in the roasted red peppers, sun-dried tomatoes, and oregano until well combined. Add the rice and chicken stock, then bring the mixture to a boil. 4. Cover the pan, reduce the heat to medium-low, and let it simmer for 30 minutes, or until the rice is fully cooked and tender. Season with salt to taste. 5. Add the spinach and stir until it wilts slightly.

Per Serving:
calories: 446 | fat: 17g | protein: 30g | carbs: 49g | fiber: 5g | sodium: 663mg

Zesty Spanish Lemon and Garlic Chicken

Prep time: 10 minutes | Cook time: 15 minutes | Serves 3

- 2 large boneless, skinless chicken breasts
- ¼ cup extra virgin olive oil
- 3 garlic cloves, finely chopped
- 5 tablespoons fresh lemon juice
- Zest of 1 lemon
- ½ cup chopped fresh parsley
- ¼ teaspoon fine sea salt
- Pinch of freshly ground black pepper

1. Slice the chicken crosswise into very thin slices, each about ¼-inch thick. 2. In a pan large enough to hold the chicken in a single layer, heat the olive oil over medium heat. When the olive oil starts to shimmer, add the garlic and sauté for about 30 seconds, then add the chicken. Reduce the heat to medium-low and sauté for about 12 minutes, tossing the chicken breasts periodically until they begin to brown on the edges. 3. Add the lemon zest and lemon juice. Increase the heat to medium and bring to a boil. Cook for about 2 minutes while using a wooden spatula to scrape any browned bits from the bottom of the pan. 4. Add the parsley, stir, then remove the pan from the heat. 5. Transfer the chicken along with any juices to a platter. Season with the sea salt and black pepper, then serve promptly. Store in an airtight container in the refrigerator for up to 2 days.

Per Serving:
calories: 358 | fat: 22g | protein: 35g | carbs: 4g | fiber: 1g | sodium: 269mg

Feta and Spinach Stuffed Chicken Breasts

Prep time: 10 minutes | Cook time: 14 minutes | Serves 4

- 1 cup chopped frozen spinach, thawed and drained well
- ½ cup crumbled feta cheese
- 4 (6-ounce / 170-g) boneless, skinless chicken breasts
- ¼ teaspoon salt
- ¼ teaspoon ground black pepper
- 2 tablespoons light olive oil, divided
- 1 cup water

1. In a small bowl, combine spinach and feta. Slice a pocket into each chicken breast along one side. Stuff one-quarter of the spinach and feta mixture into the pocket of each breast. Season chicken on all sides with salt and pepper. Set aside. 2. Press the Sauté button on the Instant Pot® and add 1 tablespoon oil. Add two chicken breasts and brown on both sides, about 3 minutes per side. Transfer to a plate and repeat with remaining 1 tablespoon oil and chicken. 3. Add water to pot and place rack inside. Place chicken breasts on rack. Close lid, set steam release to Sealing, press the Manual button, and set time to 8 minutes. 4. When the timer beeps, quick-release the pressure until the float valve drops. Press the Cancel button and open lid. Transfer chicken to a serving platter. Serve hot.

Per Serving:
calories: 304 | fat: 17g | protein: 40g | carbs: 2g | fiber: 1g | sodium: 772mg

Savory Chicken and Mushroom Medley

Prep time: 20 minutes | Cook time: 1 hour 30 minutes | Serves 4

- 3 tablespoons extra-virgin olive oil
- 8 pieces chicken, thighs and drumsticks
- 1½ cups garlic cloves, peeled
- 1 large onion, chopped
- 1 pound (454 g) cremini mushrooms, cleaned and cut in half
- 1 teaspoon salt
- 4 cups chicken broth
- Rice or noodles, for serving (optional)

1. In a large pot or Dutch oven over medium heat, heat the olive oil and add chicken, browning on all sides, for about 8 minutes. Remove the chicken and place onto a dish; set aside. 2. Add the garlic, onion, mushrooms, and salt to the pot. Stir and cook for 8 minutes. 3. Add the broth to the pot and stir everything together. Add the chicken back into the pot, cover, and turn the heat to medium-low. Let simmer for 1 hour. 4. Uncover the pot and let simmer for another 10 minutes. 5. Serve with rice or noodles, if desired.

Per Serving:
calories: 521 | fat: 31g | protein: 38g | carbs: 24g | fiber: 3g | sodium: 742mg

One-Pan Parsley Chicken and Potatoes

Prep time: 5 minutes | Cook time: 25 minutes | Serves: 6

- 1½ pounds (680 g) boneless, skinless chicken thighs, cut into 1-inch cubes
- 1 tablespoon extra-virgin olive oil
- 1½ pounds (680 g) Yukon Gold potatoes, unpeeled, cut into ½-inch cubes (about 6 small potatoes)
- 2 garlic cloves, minced (about 1 teaspoon)
- ¼ cup dry white wine or apple cider vinegar
- 1 cup low-sodium or no-salt-added chicken broth
- 1 tablespoon Dijon mustard
- ¼ teaspoon kosher or sea salt
- ¼ teaspoon freshly ground black pepper
- 1 cup chopped fresh flat-leaf (Italian) parsley, including stems
- 1 tablespoon freshly squeezed lemon juice (½ small lemon)

1. Pat the chicken dry using paper towels. Heat the oil in a large skillet over medium-high heat. Add the chicken and cook for about 5 minutes, stirring only once the chicken has browned on one side. Use a slotted spoon to transfer the chicken to a plate; it will still be partially uncooked. Leave the skillet on the stove. 2. Add the potatoes to the skillet and cook for 5 minutes, stirring only after they have turned golden and crispy on one side. Move the potatoes to the side of the skillet and add the garlic, stirring constantly for 1 minute. Pour in the wine and cook for another minute until it has almost evaporated. Add the chicken broth, mustard, salt, pepper, and the chicken pieces you set aside. Increase the heat to high and bring the mixture to a boil. 3. Once it boils, cover the skillet, reduce the heat to medium-low, and cook for 10 to 12 minutes, until the potatoes are tender and the chicken's internal temperature reaches 165°F (74°C) with juices running clear. 4. In the last minute of cooking, stir in the parsley. Remove the skillet from the heat, add the lemon juice, stir to combine, and serve immediately.

Per Serving:
calories: 266 | fat: 7g | protein: 26g | carbs: 22g | fiber: 3g | sodium: 258mg

Flavorful Herb-Marinated Chicken

Prep time: 5 minutes | Cook time: 16 minutes | Serves 4

- ½ cup olive oil
- 2 tablespoon fresh rosemary
- 1 teaspoon minced garlic
- Juice and zest of 1 lemon
- ¼ cup chopped flat-leaf parsley
- Sea salt and freshly ground pepper, to taste
- 4 boneless, skinless chicken breasts

1. Mix all ingredients except the chicken together in a plastic bag or bowl. 2. Place the chicken in the container and shake/stir so the marinade thoroughly coats the chicken. 3. Refrigerate up to 24 hours. 4. Heat a grill to medium heat and cook the chicken for 6–8 minutes a side. Turn only once during the cooking process. 5. Serve with a Greek salad and brown rice.

Per Serving:
calories: 571 | fat: 34g | protein: 61g | carbs: 1g | fiber: 0g | sodium: 126mg

Sumac Chicken with Cauliflower and Carrots

Prep time: 15 minutes | Cook time: 40 minutes | Serves 4

- 3 tablespoons extra-virgin olive oil
- 1 tablespoon ground sumac
- 1 teaspoon kosher salt
- ½ teaspoon ground cumin
- ¼ teaspoon freshly ground black pepper
- 1½ pounds (680 g) bone-in chicken thighs and drumsticks
- 1 medium cauliflower, cut into 1-inch florets
- 2 carrots, peeled and cut into 1-inch rounds
- 1 lemon, cut into ¼-inch-thick slices
- 1 tablespoon lemon juice
- ¼ cup fresh parsley, chopped
- ¼ cup fresh mint, chopped

1. Preheat the oven to 425ºF (220ºC) and line a baking sheet with parchment paper or foil. 2. In a large bowl, whisk the olive oil, sumac, salt, cumin, and black pepper until well blended. Add the chicken, cauliflower, and carrots, tossing until everything is evenly coated with the oil and spices. 3. Spread the chicken, cauliflower, and carrots in a single layer on the prepared baking sheet. Lay the lemon slices on top. Roast for 40 minutes, stirring the vegetables halfway through the cooking time. 4. Once roasted, drizzle the lemon juice over the chicken and vegetables. Garnish with fresh parsley and mint before serving.

Per Serving:
calories: 510 | fat: 38g | protein: 31g | carbs: 13g | fiber: 4g | sodium: 490mg

Chapter 4 Poultry

Tangy Chicken Jalfrezi

Prep time: 15 minutes | Cook time: 15 minutes | Serves 4

Chicken:
- 1 pound (454 g) boneless, skinless chicken thighs, cut into 2 or 3 pieces each
- 1 medium onion, chopped
- 1 large green bell pepper, stemmed, seeded, and chopped
- 2 tablespoons olive oil

Sauce:
- ¼ cup tomato sauce
- 1 tablespoon water
- 1 teaspoon garam masala
- 1 teaspoon ground turmeric
- 1 teaspoon garam masala
- 1 teaspoon kosher salt
- ½ to 1 teaspoon cayenne pepper
- ½ teaspoon kosher salt
- ½ teaspoon cayenne pepper
- Side salad, rice, or naan bread, for serving

1. For the chicken: In a large bowl, combine the chicken, onion, bell pepper, oil, turmeric, garam masala, salt, and cayenne. Stir and toss until well combined. 2. Place the chicken and vegetables in the air fryer basket. Set the air fryer to 350°F (177°C) for 15 minutes, stirring and tossing halfway through the cooking time. Use a meat thermometer to ensure the chicken has reached an internal temperature of 165°F (74°C). 3. Meanwhile, for the sauce: In a small microwave-safe bowl, combine the tomato sauce, water, garam masala, salt, and cayenne. Microwave on high for 1 minute. Remove and stir. Microwave for another minute; set aside. 4. When the chicken is cooked, remove and place chicken and vegetables in a large bowl. Pour the sauce over all. Stir and toss to coat the chicken and vegetables evenly. 5. Serve with rice, naan, or a side salad.

Per Serving:
calories: 224 | fat: 12g | protein: 23g | carbs: 6g | fiber: 2g | sodium: 827mg

Lemon-Infused Chicken with Asparagus

Prep time: 10 minutes | Cook time: 13 minutes | Serves 4

- 2 tablespoons olive oil
- 4 (6-ounce / 170-g) boneless, skinless chicken breasts
- ½ teaspoon ground black pepper
- ¼ teaspoon salt
- ¼ teaspoon smoked paprika
- 2 cloves garlic, peeled and minced
- 2 sprigs thyme
- 2 sprigs oregano
- 1 tablespoon grated lemon zest
- ¼ cup lemon juice
- ¼ cup low-sodium chicken broth
- 1 bunch asparagus, trimmed
- ¼ cup chopped fresh parsley
- 4 lemon wedges

1. Press Sauté on the Instant Pot® and heat oil. Season chicken with pepper, salt, and smoked paprika. Brown chicken on both sides, about 4 minutes per side. Add garlic, thyme, oregano, lemon zest, lemon juice, and chicken broth. Press the Cancel button. 2. Close lid, set steam release to Sealing, press the Manual button, and set time to 5 minutes. 3. When the timer beeps, quick-release the pressure until the float valve drops. Press the Cancel button and open lid. Transfer chicken breasts to a serving platter. Tent with foil to keep warm. 4. Add asparagus to the Instant Pot®. Close lid, set steam release to Sealing, press the Manual button, and set time to 0. When the timer beeps, quick-release the pressure until the float valve drops. Open lid and remove asparagus. Arrange asparagus around chicken and garnish with parsley and lemon wedges. Serve immediately.

Per Serving:
calories: 227 | fat: 11g | protein: 35g | carbs: 0g | fiber: 0g | sodium: 426mg

Grape Chicken Panzanella

Prep time: 10 minutes | Cook time: 5 minutes | Serves: 6

- 3 cups day-old bread (like a baguette, crusty Italian bread, or whole-grain bread), cut into 1-inch cubes
- 5 tablespoons extra-virgin olive oil, divided
- 2 cups chopped cooked chicken breast (about 1 pound / 454 g)
- 1 cup red seedless grapes, halved
- ½ pint grape or cherry tomatoes, halved (about ¾ cup)
- ½ cup Gorgonzola cheese crumbles (about 2 ounces / 57 g)
- ⅓ cup chopped walnuts
- ¼ cup diced red onion (about ⅛ onion)
- 3 tablespoons chopped fresh mint leaves
- ¼ teaspoon freshly ground black pepper
- 1 tablespoon balsamic vinegar
- Zest and juice of 1 small lemon
- 1 teaspoon honey

1. Cover a large, rimmed baking sheet with aluminum foil and set it aside. Adjust an oven rack so it sits about 4 inches below the broiler. Turn the broiler on to high to preheat. 2. In a large serving bowl, drizzle 2 tablespoons of olive oil over the cubed bread. Use your hands to gently toss the bread until it's evenly coated. Spread the bread onto the prepared baking sheet in an even layer. Broil for 2 minutes, then stir the bread cubes. Broil for another 30 to 60 seconds, keeping a close eye to prevent burning. Take the bread out of the oven and set it aside to cool. 3. In the same large bowl, combine the chicken, grapes, tomatoes, Gorgonzola, walnuts, onion, mint, and a pinch of pepper. Add the toasted bread cubes and gently mix everything together. 4. In a small bowl, whisk together the remaining 3 tablespoons of olive oil, vinegar, lemon zest, lemon juice, and honey. Drizzle the dressing over the salad and toss gently to coat all the ingredients. Serve immediately.

Per Serving:
calories: 334 | fat: 21g | protein: 19g | carbs: 19g | fiber: 2g | sodium: 248mg

Lemon Mushroom Chicken Piccata

Prep time: 25 minutes | Cook time: 25 minutes | Serves 4

- 1 pound (454 g) thinly sliced chicken breasts
- 1½ teaspoons salt, divided
- ½ teaspoon freshly ground black pepper
- ¼ cup ground flaxseed
- 2 tablespoons almond flour
- 8 tablespoons extra-virgin olive oil, divided
- 4 tablespoons butter, divided
- 2 cups sliced mushrooms
- ½ cup dry white wine or chicken stock
- ¼ cup freshly squeezed lemon juice
- ¼ cup roughly chopped capers
- Zucchini noodles, for serving
- ¼ cup chopped fresh flat-leaf Italian parsley, for garnish

1. Season the chicken with 1 teaspoon salt and the pepper. On a plate, combine the ground flaxseed and almond flour and dredge each chicken breast in the mixture. Set aside. 2. In a large skillet, heat 4 tablespoons olive oil and 1 tablespoon butter over medium-high heat. Working in batches if necessary, brown the chicken, 3 to 4 minutes per side. Remove from the skillet and keep warm. 3. Add the remaining 4 tablespoons olive oil and 1 tablespoon butter to the skillet along with mushrooms and sauté over medium heat until just tender, 6 to 8 minutes. 4. Add the white wine, lemon juice, capers, and remaining ½ teaspoon salt to the skillet and bring to a boil, whisking to incorporate any little browned bits that have stuck to the bottom of the skillet. Reduce the heat to low and whisk in the final 2 tablespoons butter. 5. Return the browned chicken to skillet, cover, and simmer over low heat until the chicken is cooked through and the sauce has thickened, 5 to 6 more minutes. 6. Serve chicken and mushrooms warm over zucchini noodles, spooning the mushroom sauce over top and garnishing with chopped parsley.

Per Serving:
calories: 596 | fat: 48g | protein: 30g | carbs: 8g | fiber: 4g | sodium: 862mg

Chapter 5
Beef, Pork, and Lamb

Chapter 5 Beef, Pork, and Lamb

Savory Pork Chops with Peppers and Onions

Prep time: 5 minutes | Cook time: 25 minutes | Serves 4

- 4 (4-ounce / 113-g) pork chops, untrimmed
- 1½ teaspoons salt, divided
- 1 teaspoon freshly ground black pepper, divided
- ½ cup extra-virgin olive oil, divided
- 1 red or orange bell pepper, thinly sliced
- 1 green bell pepper, thinly sliced
- 1 small yellow onion, thinly sliced
- 2 teaspoons dried Italian herbs (such as oregano, parsley, or rosemary)
- 2 garlic cloves, minced
- 1 tablespoon balsamic vinegar

1. Season the pork chops with 1 teaspoon salt and ½ teaspoon pepper. 2. In a large skillet, heat ¼ cup olive oil over medium-high heat. Fry the pork chops in the oil until browned and almost cooked through but not fully cooked, 4 to 5 minutes per side, depending on the thickness of chops. Remove from the skillet and cover to keep warm. 3. Pour the remaining ¼ cup olive oil in the skillet and sauté the sliced peppers, onions, and herbs over medium-high heat until tender, 6 to 8 minutes. Add the garlic, stirring to combine, and return the pork to skillet. Cover, reduce the heat to low, and cook for another 2 to 3 minutes, or until the pork is cooked through. 4. Turn off the heat. Using a slotted spoon, transfer the pork, peppers, and onions to a serving platter. Add the vinegar to the oil in the skillet and whisk to combine well. Drizzle the vinaigrette over the pork and serve warm.

Per Serving:
calories: 402 | fat: 31g | protein: 26g | carbs: 4g | fiber: 1g | sodium: 875mg

Stuffed Flank Steak

Prep time: 20 minutes | Cook time: 6 hours | Serves 6

- 2 pounds (907 g) flank steak
- Sea salt and freshly ground pepper, to taste
- 1 tablespoon olive oil
- ¼ cup onion, diced
- 1 clove garlic, minced
- 2 cups baby spinach, chopped
- ½ cup dried tomatoes, chopped
- ½ cup roasted red peppers, diced
- ½ cup almonds, toasted and chopped
- Kitchen twine
- ½ cup chicken stock

1. Lay the flank steak flat on a cutting board and season generously with sea salt and freshly ground pepper. 2. In a medium saucepan, heat the olive oil over medium heat. Add the onion and garlic, and cook for about 5 minutes, stirring frequently, until the onion becomes tender and translucent. 3. Add the spinach, tomatoes, peppers, and chopped almonds to the pan. Cook for another 3 minutes, or until the spinach begins to wilt slightly. 4. Let the tomato and spinach mixture cool to room temperature, then spread it evenly over the seasoned flank steak. 5. Carefully roll up the flank steak and tie it securely with kitchen twine at both ends and in the middle to hold its shape. 6. In the same saucepan, brown the rolled steak for 5 minutes, turning it to sear all sides evenly. 7. Transfer the browned steak to a slow cooker and add the chicken stock. Cover and cook on low for 4 to 6 hours until tender. 8. Once cooked, remove the twine, slice the steak into rounds, and serve warm.

Per Serving:
calories: 287 | fat: 14g | protein: 35g | carbs: 4g | fiber: 2g | sodium: 95mg

Greek Stuffed Tenderloin

Prep time: 10 minutes | Cook time: 10 minutes | Serves 4

- 1½ pounds (680 g) venison or beef tenderloin, pounded to ¼ inch thick
- 3 teaspoons fine sea salt
- 1 teaspoon ground black pepper
- 2 ounces (57 g) creamy goat cheese
- ½ cup crumbled feta cheese (about 2 ounces / 57 g)
- ¼ cup finely chopped onions
- 2 cloves garlic, minced

For Garnish/Serving (Optional):
- Prepared yellow mustard
- Halved cherry tomatoes
- Extra-virgin olive oil
- Sprigs of fresh rosemary
- Lavender flowers

1. Lightly spray the air fryer basket with avocado oil and preheat the air fryer to 400°F (204°C). 2. Season the tenderloin thoroughly on all sides with salt and pepper. 3. In a medium mixing bowl, combine the goat cheese, feta, onions, and garlic. Spread the mixture down the center of the tenderloin. Starting from the end closest to you, roll the tenderloin tightly like a jelly roll. Secure the roll with kitchen twine, tying it firmly along the length. 4. Place the tenderloin in the air fryer basket and cook for 5 minutes. Flip the tenderloin over and air fry for another 5 minutes, or until the internal temperature reads 135°F (57°C) for medium-rare. 5. To serve, smear a line of yellow mustard on a serving platter. Place the tenderloin next to the mustard and add halved cherry tomatoes on the side, if desired. Drizzle with olive oil and garnish with rosemary sprigs and lavender flowers for an optional decorative touch. 6. This dish is best enjoyed fresh. Store any leftovers in an airtight container in the refrigerator for up to 3 days. Reheat in a preheated air fryer at 350°F (177°C) for 4 minutes, or until warmed through.

Per Serving:
calories: 345 | fat: 17g | protein: 43g | carbs: 2g | fiber: 0g | sodium: 676mg

Stuffed Cube Steak Rolls

Prep time: 30 minutes | Cook time: 8 to 10 minutes | Serves 4

- 4 cube steaks (6 ounces / 170 g each)
- 1 (16-ounce / 454-g) bottle Italian dressing
- 1 teaspoon salt
- ½ teaspoon freshly ground black pepper
- ½ cup finely chopped yellow onion
- ½ cup finely chopped green bell pepper
- ½ cup finely chopped mushrooms
- 1 to 2 tablespoons oil

1. In a large resealable bag or airtight storage container, combine the steaks and Italian dressing. Seal the bag and refrigerate to marinate for 2 hours. 2. Remove the steaks from the marinade and place them on a cutting board. Discard the marinade. Evenly season the steaks with salt and pepper. 3. In a small bowl, stir together the onion, bell pepper, and mushrooms. Sprinkle the onion mixture evenly over the steaks. Roll up the steaks, jelly roll-style, and secure with toothpicks. 4. Preheat the air fryer to 400°F (204°C). 5. Place the steaks in the air fryer basket. 6. Cook for 4 minutes. Flip the steaks and spritz them with oil. Cook for 4 to 6 minutes more until the internal temperature reaches 145°F (63°C). Let rest for 5 minutes before serving.

Per Serving:
calories: 364 | fat: 20g | protein: 37g | carbs: 7g | fiber: 1g | sodium: 715mg

Lamb Chops with Fresh Zucchini Slaw

Prep time: 20 minutes | Cook time: 40 minutes | Serves 4

- 4 (8- to 12-ounce/ 227- to 340-g) lamb shoulder chops (blade or round bone), about ¾ inch thick, trimmed
- ¾ teaspoon table salt, divided
- ¾ teaspoon pepper, divided
- 2 tablespoons extra-virgin olive oil, divided
- 1 onion, chopped
- 5 garlic cloves, minced
- ½ cup chicken broth
- 1 bay leaf
- 4 zucchini (6 ounces / 170 g each), sliced lengthwise into ribbons
- 1 teaspoon grated lemon zest plus 1 tablespoon juice
- 2 ounces (57 g) goat cheese, crumbled (½ cup)
- ¼ cup chopped fresh mint
- 2 tablespoons raisins

1. Pat lamb chops dry with paper towels and sprinkle with ½ teaspoon salt and ½ teaspoon pepper. Using highest sauté function, heat 1½ teaspoons oil in Instant Pot for 5 minutes (or until just smoking). Brown half of chops on both sides, 6 to 8 minutes; transfer to plate. Repeat with 1½ teaspoons oil and remaining chops; transfer to plate. 2. Add onion to fat left in pot and cook, using highest sauté function, until softened, about 5 minutes. Stir in garlic and cook until fragrant, about 30 seconds. Stir in broth and bay leaf, scraping up any browned bits. Return chops to pot along with any accumulated juices (chops will overlap). Lock lid in place and close pressure release valve. Select high pressure cook function and cook for 20 minutes. 3. Turn off Instant Pot and let pressure release naturally for 15 minutes. Quick-release any remaining pressure, then carefully remove lid, allowing steam to escape away from you. Transfer chops to serving dish. Gently toss zucchini with lemon zest and juice, remaining 1 tablespoon oil, remaining ¼ teaspoon salt, and remaining ¼ teaspoon pepper in bowl. Arrange zucchini on serving dish with lamb, and sprinkle with goat cheese, mint, and raisins. Serve.

Per Serving:
calories: 390 | fat: 20g | protein: 38g | carbs: 14g | fiber: 2g | sodium: 720mg

Savory Herb Lamb Loin Chops

Prep time: 5 minutes | Cook time: 10 to 12 minutes | Serves 4 to 6

- 3 tablespoons olive oil
- Zest and juice of 1 lemon
- 2 tablespoons pomegranate molasses
- 1 cup finely chopped fresh mint
- ½ cup finely chopped fresh cilantro or parsley
- 2 scallions (green onions), finely chopped
- 6 lamb loin chops
- Freshly ground black pepper, to taste

1. In a small bowl, whisk together the olive oil, lemon zest, lemon juice, pomegranate molasses, mint, parsley, and scallions until well combined. Put the lamb in a large zip-top plastic bag. Add the marinade, seal the bag, and massage the marinade onto all sides of the chops. Refrigerate for at least 1 hour or up to overnight. 2. When ready to cook, heat a grill to medium. 3. Remove the chops from the marinade; discard the marinade. Season with pepper, if desired. Grill the chops for 10 to 12 minutes, turning once, for medium. Let rest for 10 minutes before serving.

Per Serving:
1 cup: calories: 182 | fat: 11g | protein: 10g | carbs: 10g | fiber: 0g | sodium: 46mg

Flank Steak and Blue Cheese Wraps

Prep time: 20 minutes | Cook time: 0 minutes | Serves 6

- 1 cup leftover flank steak, cut into 1-inch slices
- ¼ cup red onion, thinly sliced
- ¼ cup cherry tomatoes, chopped
- ¼ cup low-salt olives, pitted and chopped
- ¼ cup roasted red bell peppers, drained and coarsely chopped
- ¼ cup blue cheese crumbles
- 6 whole-wheat or spinach wraps
- Sea salt and freshly ground pepper, to taste

1. In a small bowl, mix together the flank steak, onion, tomatoes, olives, bell pepper, and blue cheese until well combined. 2. Take each wrap and spread ½ cup of the mixture evenly across the center. Roll the wrap halfway, fold in the ends to secure the filling, and continue rolling tightly like a burrito. 3. Slice diagonally if desired, season to taste, and serve immediately.

Per Serving:
calories: 370 | fat: 26g | protein: 31g | carbs: 1g | fiber: 0g | sodium: 81mg

Greek Meatball Soup

Prep time: 20 minutes | Cook time: 45 minutes | Serves 5

- 1 pound (454 g) ground beef
- ⅓ cup orzo
- 4 large eggs
- 1 onion, finely chopped
- 2 garlic cloves, minced
- 2 tablespoons finely chopped fresh Italian parsley
- Sea salt
- Freshly ground black pepper
- ½ cup all-purpose flour
- 5 to 6 cups chicken broth
- Juice of 2 lemons

1. In a large bowl, combine the ground beef, orzo, 1 egg, onion, garlic, and parsley. Stir until everything is well blended, then season with salt and pepper and mix again. 2. Pour the flour into a small bowl. 3. Shape the meat mixture into golf ball-sized meatballs, then roll each one in the flour, shaking off any excess. Place the meatballs into a stockpot and repeat until all the meat mixture is used. 4. Add enough broth to the pot to cover the meatballs by about 1 inch. Bring the broth to a boil over high heat, then lower the heat, cover, and let it simmer for 30 to 45 minutes until the meatballs are fully cooked. 5. While the meatballs are simmering, whisk the remaining 3 eggs in a small bowl until frothy. Add the lemon juice and whisk until fully combined. 6. Once the meatballs are done, gradually pour 1½ cups of hot broth into the egg mixture while whisking continuously. Pour the egg mixture back into the pot, stirring well. Bring the soup back to a gentle simmer, then remove from the heat and serve immediately.

Per Serving:
calories: 297 | fat: 9g | protein: 27g | carbs: 28g | fiber: 1g | sodium: 155mg

Pepper Steak

Prep time: 30 minutes | Cook time: 16 to 20 minutes | Serves 4

- 1 pound (454 g) cube steak, cut into 1-inch pieces
- 1 cup Italian dressing
- 1½ cups beef broth
- 1 tablespoon soy sauce
- ½ teaspoon salt
- ¼ teaspoon freshly ground black pepper
- ¼ cup cornstarch
- 1 cup thinly sliced bell pepper, any color
- 1 cup chopped celery
- 1 tablespoon minced garlic
- 1 to 2 tablespoons oil

1. Place the beef and Italian dressing in a large resealable bag. Seal the bag and refrigerate for 8 hours to marinate. 2. In a small bowl, whisk together the beef broth, soy sauce, salt, and pepper until well combined. 3. In another small bowl, whisk ¼ cup water with the cornstarch until dissolved. Stir the cornstarch mixture into the beef broth mixture until fully blended. 4. Preheat the air fryer to 375°F (191°C). 5. Pour the broth mixture into a baking pan and place it in the air fryer. Cook for 4 minutes, stir, then cook for another 4 to 5 minutes until the mixture thickens. Remove and set aside. 6. Increase the air fryer temperature to 400°F (204°C) and line the basket with parchment paper. 7. Remove the steak from the marinade, discard the marinade, and place the steak in a medium bowl. Add the bell pepper, celery, and garlic, and stir until combined. 8. Spread the steak and pepper mixture onto the parchment in the basket and lightly spritz with oil. 9. Cook for 4 minutes, shake the basket, and continue cooking for 4 to 7 minutes until the vegetables are tender and the steak reaches an internal temperature of 145°F (63°C). Serve the dish warm with the gravy.

Per Serving:
calories: 302 | fat: 14g | protein: 27g | carbs: 15g | fiber: 1g | sodium: 635mg

Zesty Mustard-Glazed Lamb Chops

Prep time: 5 minutes | Cook time: 14 minutes | Serves 4

- Oil, for spraying
- 1 tablespoon Dijon mustard
- 2 teaspoons lemon juice
- ½ teaspoon dried tarragon
- ¼ teaspoon salt
- ¼ teaspoon freshly ground black pepper
- 4 (1¼-inch-thick) loin lamb chops

1. Preheat the air fryer to 390°F (199°C). Line the air fryer basket with parchment and spray lightly with oil. 2. In a small bowl, mix together the mustard, lemon juice, tarragon, salt, and black pepper. 3. Pat dry the lamb chops with a paper towel. Brush the chops on both sides with the mustard mixture. 4. Place the chops in the prepared basket. You may need to work in batches, depending on the size of your air fryer. 5. Cook for 8 minutes, flip, and cook for another 6 minutes, or until the internal temperature reaches 125°F (52°C) for rare, 145°F (63°C) for medium-rare, or 155°F (68°C) for medium.

Per Serving:
calories: 96 | fat: 4g | protein: 14g | carbs: 0g | fiber: 0g | sodium: 233mg

Wedding Soup

Prep time: 15 minutes | Cook time: 17 minutes | Serves 6

- 3 (1-ounce/ 28-g) slices Italian bread, toasted
- ¾ pound (340 g) 90% lean ground beef
- 1 large egg, beaten
- 1 medium onion, peeled and chopped
- 3 cloves garlic, peeled and minced
- ¼ cup chopped fresh parsley
- 1 tablespoon minced fresh oregano
- 1 tablespoon minced fresh basil
- 1 teaspoon salt
- ½ teaspoon ground black pepper
- ½ cup grated Parmesan cheese, divided
- 2 tablespoons olive oil
- 8 cups low-sodium chicken broth
- 5 ounces (142 g) baby spinach

1. Transfer the browned meatballs to a plate and press the Cancel button. 3. Pour the broth into the pot, stirring to scrape up any browned bits from the bottom. Return the meatballs to the pot and stir gently. Secure the lid, set the steam release to Sealing, press the Manual button, and set the timer for 10 minutes. When the timer goes off, quick-release the pressure until the float valve drops, then open the lid. 4. Add the spinach and stir until it wilts, about 1 minute. Ladle the soup into bowls and sprinkle each serving with the remaining ¼ cup of cheese.

Per Serving:
calories: 270 | fat: 16g | protein: 24g | carbs: 10g | fiber: 1g | sodium: 590mg

Chapter 5 Beef, Pork, and Lamb

Spiced Flank Steak with Harissa Couscous

Prep time: 5 minutes | Cook time: 15 minutes | Serves 4

- 1½ teaspoons coriander seeds
- 1¼ teaspoons ground ginger
- ½ teaspoon ground cumin
- ¾ teaspoon ground cinnamon
- ¼ teaspoon ground cloves
- 1½ pounds (680 g) flank steak
- 3 tablespoons olive oil
- ¾ cup chicken broth
- 1 tablespoon harissa
- ½ cup chopped pitted dried dates
- 1 cup uncooked couscous
- Sea salt
- Freshly ground black pepper
- ¼ cup chopped fresh Italian parsley

1. In a small bowl, combine the coriander, ginger, cumin, cinnamon, and cloves. Rub the steak all over with the seasoning mix. 2. In a large sauté pan, heat the olive oil over medium-high heat. Add the steak and cook for 2 to 3 minutes on each side for medium-rare. Transfer the steak to a plate and set aside to rest for 10 minutes. 3. In the same pan, mix together the meat juices with the broth, harissa, and dates. Bring to a boil over medium-high heat. Add the couscous, remove from the heat, cover, and let stand for 5 minutes. Season with salt and pepper. 4. Cut the steak across the grain into thin strips. 5. Serve the steak with the couscous, garnished with parsley.

Per Serving:
calories: 516 | fat: 16g | protein: 43g | carbs: 49g | fiber: 4g | sodium: 137mg

Asian Glazed Meatballs

Prep time: 15 minutes | Cook time: 10 minutes per batch | Serves 4 to 6

- 1 large shallot, finely chopped
- 2 cloves garlic, minced
- 1 tablespoon grated fresh ginger
- 2 teaspoons fresh thyme, finely chopped
- 1½ cups brown mushrooms, very finely chopped (a food processor works well here)
- 2 tablespoons soy sauce
- Freshly ground black pepper, to taste
- 1 pound (454 g) ground beef
- ½ pound (227 g) ground pork
- 3 egg yolks
- 1 cup Thai sweet chili sauce (spring roll sauce)
- ¼ cup toasted sesame seeds
- 2 scallions, sliced

1. In a bowl, combine the shallot, garlic, ginger, thyme, mushrooms, soy sauce, freshly ground black pepper, ground beef, ground pork, and egg yolks. Mix well until all the ingredients are evenly incorporated. Gently form the mixture into 24 golf ball-sized meatballs. 2. Preheat the air fryer to 380ºF (193ºC). 3. Place the meatballs in the air fryer basket in a single layer, working in batches if needed. Air fry for 8 minutes, turning them halfway through. Drizzle a bit of Thai sweet chili sauce over each meatball, then return the basket to the air fryer and cook for another 2 minutes. Reserve the remaining Thai sweet chili sauce for dipping. 4. Once the meatballs are cooked, sprinkle them with toasted sesame seeds and transfer to a serving platter. Garnish with sliced scallions and serve warm.

Per Serving:
calories: 274 | fat: 11g | protein: 29g | carbs: 14g | fiber: 4g | sodium: 802mg

Hearty Beef, Mushroom, and Green Bean Broth

Prep time: 10 minutes | Cook time: 45 minutes | Serves 4

- 2 tablespoons olive oil
- 1 pound (454 g) chuck or round beef roast, cut into 2-inch pieces
- 1 large onion, diced
- ½ teaspoon sea salt
- ¼ teaspoon freshly ground black pepper
- ½ cup white wine
- 8 cups chicken broth
- 1 pound (454 g) green beans
- 8 ounces (227 g) cremini (baby bella) mushrooms, chopped
- 3 tablespoons tomato paste
- ½ teaspoon dried oregano

1. In a large stockpot, heat the olive oil over medium-high heat. Add the beef and brown, 5 to 7 minutes. Add the onion, salt, and pepper and cook for 5 minutes. Add the wine and cook for 4 minutes. Add the broth, green beans, mushrooms, tomato paste, and oregano and stir to combine. 2. Bring to a boil, reduce the heat to low, cover, and simmer for 35 to 45 minutes, until the meat is cooked through. Serve.

Per Serving:
calories: 307 | fat: 14g | protein: 28g | carbs: 17g | fiber: 5g | sodium: 265mg

Filipino Crispy Pork Belly

Prep time: 20 minutes | Cook time: 30 minutes | Serves 4

- 1 pound (454 g) pork belly
- 3 cups water
- 6 garlic cloves
- 2 tablespoons soy sauce
- 1 teaspoon kosher salt
- 1 teaspoon black pepper
- 2 bay leaves

1. Cut the pork belly into three thick chunks to ensure even cooking. 2. Place the pork, water, garlic, soy sauce, salt, pepper, and bay leaves into the inner pot of an Instant Pot or electric pressure cooker. Seal the lid and cook on high pressure for 15 minutes. Allow the pressure to release naturally for 10 minutes, then manually release any remaining pressure. (If using a regular saucepan, combine all the ingredients, cover, and simmer over low heat for about 1 hour, until the skin side of the pork belly can be pierced easily with a knife.) Carefully transfer the pork to a wire rack set over a rimmed baking sheet and let it drain and dry for 10 minutes. 3. Slice each pork belly chunk into two long strips. Place the strips in the air fryer basket. Air fry at 400ºF (204ºC) for 15 minutes, or until the fat becomes crispy. 4. Serve immediately while hot and crisp.

Per Serving:
calories: 619 | fat: 62g | protein: 12g | carbs: 4g | fiber: 0g | sodium: 743mg

Mediterranean Lamb Burger with Feta

Prep time: 10 minutes | Cook time: 20 minutes | Serves 3 to 4

- 2 teaspoons olive oil
- ⅓ onion, finely chopped
- 1 clove garlic, minced
- 1 pound (454 g) ground lamb
- 2 tablespoons fresh parsley, finely chopped
- 1½ teaspoons fresh oregano, finely chopped
- ½ cup black olives, finely chopped
- ⅓ cup crumbled feta cheese
- ½ teaspoon salt
- Freshly ground black pepper, to taste
- 4 thick pita breads

1. Preheat a medium skillet over medium-high heat on the stovetop. Add the olive oil and cook the onion until tender, but not browned, about 4 to 5 minutes. Add the garlic and cook for another minute. Transfer the onion and garlic to a mixing bowl and add the ground lamb, parsley, oregano, olives, feta cheese, salt and pepper. Gently mix the ingredients together. 2. Divide the mixture into 3 or 4 equal portions and then form the hamburgers, being careful not to over-handle the meat. One good way to do this is to throw the meat back and forth between your hands like a baseball, packing the meat each time you catch it. Flatten the balls into patties, making an indentation in the center of each patty. Flatten the sides of the patties as well to make it easier to fit them into the air fryer basket. 3. Preheat the air fryer to 370ºF (188ºC). 4. If you don't have room for all four burgers, air fry two or three burgers at a time for 8 minutes at 370ºF (188ºC). Flip the burgers over and air fry for another 8 minutes. If you cooked your burgers in batches, return the first batch of burgers to the air fryer for the last two minutes of cooking to re-heat. This should give you a medium-well burger. If you'd prefer a medium-rare burger, shorten the cooking time to about 13 minutes. Remove the burgers to a resting plate and let the burgers rest for a few minutes before dressing and serving. 5. While the burgers are resting, toast the pita breads in the air fryer for 2 minutes. Tuck the burgers into the toasted pita breads, or wrap the pitas around the burgers and serve with a tzatziki sauce or some mayonnaise.

Per Serving:

calories: 380 | fat: 21g | protein: 28g | carbs: 20g | fiber: 2g | sodium: 745mg

Pork Milanese

Prep time: 10 minutes | Cook time: 12 minutes | Serves 4

- 4 (1-inch) boneless pork chops
- Fine sea salt and ground black pepper, to taste
- 2 large eggs
- ¾ cup powdered Parmesan cheese
- Chopped fresh parsley, for garnish
- Lemon slices, for serving

1. Spray the air fryer basket with avocado oil. Preheat the air fryer to 400ºF (204ºC). 2. Place the pork chops between 2 sheets of plastic wrap and pound them with the flat side of a meat tenderizer until they're ¼ inch thick. Lightly season both sides of the chops with salt and pepper. 3. Lightly beat the eggs in a shallow bowl. Divide the Parmesan cheese evenly between 2 bowls and set the bowls in this order: Parmesan, eggs, Parmesan. Dredge a chop in the first bowl of Parmesan, then dip it in the eggs, and then dredge it again in the second bowl of Parmesan, making sure both sides and all edges are well coated. Repeat with the remaining chops. 4. Place the chops in the air fryer basket and air fry for 12 minutes, or until the internal temperature reaches 145ºF (63ºC), flipping halfway through. 5. Garnish with fresh parsley and serve immediately with lemon slices. Store leftovers in an airtight container in the refrigerator for up to 3 days. Reheat in a preheated 390ºF (199ºC) air fryer for 5 minutes, or until warmed through.

Per Serving:

calories: 349 | fat: 14g | protein: 50g | carbs: 3g | fiber: 0g | sodium: 464mg

Braised Short Ribs with Fennel and Pickled Grapes

Prep time: 20 minutes | Cook time: 55 minutes | Serves 4

- 1½ pounds (680 g) boneless beef short ribs, trimmed and cut into 2-inch pieces
- 1 teaspoon table salt, divided
- 1 tablespoon extra-virgin olive oil
- 1 fennel bulb, 2 tablespoons fronds chopped, stalks discarded, bulb halved, cored, and sliced into 1-inch-thick wedges
- 1 onion, halved and sliced ½ inch thick
- 4 garlic cloves, minced
- 2 teaspoons fennel seeds
- ½ cup chicken broth
- 1 sprig fresh rosemary
- ¼ cup red wine vinegar
- 1 tablespoon sugar
- 4 ounces (113 g) seedless red grapes, halved (½ cup)

1. Pat the short ribs dry with paper towels and season with ½ teaspoon salt. Set the Instant Pot® to the highest Sauté function and heat the oil for about 5 minutes, or until it just starts smoking. Brown the short ribs on all sides for 6 to 8 minutes, then transfer them to a plate. 2. Add the fennel wedges, onion, and ¼ teaspoon salt to the remaining fat in the pot. Cook on the highest Sauté setting until the vegetables soften and turn lightly browned, about 5 minutes. Stir in the garlic and fennel seeds and cook until fragrant, about 30 seconds. Add the broth and rosemary sprig, scraping up any browned bits from the bottom. Nestle the short ribs into the vegetable mixture and pour in any juices that accumulated on the plate. Secure the lid, close the pressure release valve, and select the high-pressure cook function for 35 minutes. 3. While the ribs cook, microwave the vinegar, sugar, and remaining ¼ teaspoon salt in a bowl until it simmers, about 1 minute. Add the grapes and let them sit, stirring occasionally, for 20 minutes. Drain the grapes and return them to the bowl. (You can refrigerate drained grapes for up to a week.) 4. After the ribs finish cooking, turn off the Instant Pot and allow the pressure to release naturally for 15 minutes. Quick-release any remaining pressure and carefully open the lid, keeping the steam away from you. Transfer the short ribs to a serving dish, tent them with foil, and let them rest. 5. Strain the braising liquid through a fine-mesh strainer into a fat separator. Discard the rosemary sprig and add the vegetables to the serving dish with the ribs. Let the liquid settle for 5 minutes, then pour ¾ cup of the defatted liquid over the short ribs and vegetables, discarding the remaining liquid. Sprinkle the dish with the grapes and fennel fronds. Serve warm.

Per Serving:

calories: 310 | fat: 17g | protein: 24g | carbs: 15g | fiber: 3g | sodium: 750mg

Chapter 5 Beef, Pork, and Lamb

Beef Brisket with Onions

Prep time: 10 minutes | Cook time: 6 hours | Serves 6

- 1 large yellow onion, thinly sliced
- 2 garlic cloves, smashed and peeled
- 1 first cut of beef brisket (4 pounds / 1.8 kg), trimmed of excess fat
- Coarse sea salt
- Black pepper
- 2 cups chicken broth
- 2 tablespoons chopped fresh parsley leaves, for serving

1. Place the onion and garlic into the slow cooker. 2. Season the brisket generously with salt and pepper, then place it fat-side up in the slow cooker. 3. Pour the broth into the slow cooker, cover, and cook on high for about 6 hours, or until the brisket is fork-tender. 4. Transfer the brisket to a cutting board and slice it thinly across the grain. 5. Serve the brisket with the onions and a spoonful of the cooking liquid, garnished with fresh parsley.

Per Serving:
calories: 424 | fat: 16g | protein: 67g | carbs: 4g | fiber: 1g | sodium: 277mg

Parmesan-Crusted Filet Mignon

Prep time: 20 minutes | Cook time: 13 minutes | Serves 4

- 1 pound (454 g) filet mignon
- Sea salt and ground black pepper, to taste
- ½ teaspoon cayenne pepper
- 1 teaspoon dried basil
- 1 teaspoon dried rosemary
- 1 teaspoon dried thyme
- 1 tablespoon sesame oil
- 1 small-sized egg, well-whisked
- ½ cup Parmesan cheese, grated

1. Season the filet mignon with salt, black pepper, cayenne pepper, basil, rosemary, and thyme. Brush with sesame oil. 2. Put the egg in a shallow plate. Now, place the Parmesan cheese in another plate. 3. Coat the filet mignon with the egg; then lay it into the Parmesan cheese. Set the air fryer to 360°F (182°C). 4. Cook for 10 to 13 minutes or until golden. Serve with mixed salad leaves and enjoy!

Per Serving:
calories: 252 | fat: 13g | protein: 32g | carbs: 1g | fiber: 0g | sodium: 96mg

Chapter 6
Fish and Seafood

Chapter 6 Fish and Seafood

Crispy Flounder Fillets

Prep time: 10 minutes | Cook time: 5 to 8 minutes | Serves 4

- 1 egg white
- 1 tablespoon water
- 1 cup panko bread crumbs
- 2 tablespoons extra-light virgin olive oil
- 4 (4-ounce / 113-g) flounder fillets
- Salt and pepper, to taste
- Oil for misting or cooking spray

1. Preheat the air fryer to 390°F (199°C). 2. Beat together egg white and water in shallow dish. 3. In another shallow dish, mix panko crumbs and oil until well combined and crumbly (best done by hand). 4. Season flounder fillets with salt and pepper to taste. Dip each fillet into egg mixture and then roll in panko crumbs, pressing in crumbs so that fish is nicely coated. 5. Spray the air fryer basket with nonstick cooking spray and add fillets. Air fry at 390°F (199°C) for 3 minutes. 6. Spray fish fillets but do not turn. Cook 2 to 5 minutes longer or until golden brown and crispy. Using a spatula, carefully remove fish from basket and serve.

Per Serving:
calories: 252 | fat: 10g | protein: 19g | carbs: 19g | fiber: 1g | sodium: 212mg

Salmon Cakes with Bell Pepper and Lemon Yogurt

Prep time: 15 minutes | Cook time: 15 minutes | Serves 4

- ¼ cup whole-wheat bread crumbs
- ¼ cup mayonnaise
- 1 large egg, beaten
- 1 tablespoon chives, chopped
- 1 tablespoon fresh parsley, chopped
- Zest of 1 lemon
- ¾ teaspoon kosher salt, divided
- ¼ teaspoon freshly ground black pepper
- 2 (5- to 6-ounce / 142- to 170-g) cans no-salt boneless/skinless salmon, drained and finely flaked
- ½ bell pepper, diced small
- 2 tablespoons extra-virgin olive oil, divided
- 1 cup plain Greek yogurt
- Juice of 1 lemon

1. In a large bowl, mix together the bread crumbs, mayonnaise, egg, chives, parsley, lemon zest, ½ teaspoon salt, and black pepper until well combined. Add the salmon and bell pepper, stirring gently to incorporate. Form the mixture into 8 evenly sized patties. 2. Heat 1 tablespoon of olive oil in a large skillet over medium-high heat. Add half the patties and cook for 4 to 5 minutes until the bottoms are golden brown, lowering the heat to medium if needed to prevent burning. Flip the patties and cook for another 4 to 5 minutes until golden on both sides. Repeat with the remaining 1 tablespoon of olive oil and the rest of the patties. 3. In a small bowl, whisk together the yogurt, lemon juice, and the remaining ¼ teaspoon salt. Serve the salmon cakes warm with the yogurt sauce on the side.

Per Serving:
calories: 330 | fat: 23g | protein: 21g | carbs: 9g | fiber: 1g | sodium: 385mg

Garlic Basil Prawns with Tomatoes

Prep time: 10 minutes | Cook time: 10 minutes | Serves 4

- 2 tablespoons olive oil
- 1¼ pounds (567 g) shrimp, peeled and deveined
- 3 cloves garlic, minced
- ⅛ teaspoon crushed red pepper flakes
- ¾ cup dry white wine
- 1½ cups grape tomatoes
- ¼ cup finely chopped fresh basil, plus more for garnish
- ¾ teaspoon salt
- ½ teaspoon freshly ground black pepper

1. Heat the olive oil in a medium skillet over medium-high heat. Add the shrimp and cook about 1 minute on each side, until just cooked through. Transfer the shrimp to a plate, leaving the oil in the pan. 2. Add the garlic and red pepper flakes to the oil in the pan and cook, stirring, for 30 seconds. Stir in the wine and cook until it is reduced by about half. Add the tomatoes and cook, stirring, for 3 to 4 minutes more, until the tomatoes begin to break down. Stir in the basil, salt, pepper, and the reserved shrimp. Cook 1 to 2 minutes more, until heated through. Serve hot, garnished with the remaining basil.

Per Serving:
calories: 282 | fat: 10g | protein: 33g | carbs: 7g | fiber: 1g | sodium: 299mg

Pan-fried Fresh Sardines

Prep time: 5 minutes | Cook time: 5 minutes | Serves 4

- Avocado oil
- 1½ pounds (680 g) whole fresh sardines, scales removed
- 1 teaspoon salt
- 1 teaspoon freshly ground black pepper
- 2 cups flour

1. Preheat a deep skillet over medium heat and pour in enough oil to create a depth of about 1 inch. 2. Season the fish fillets with salt and pepper. 3. Coat the fish thoroughly in flour, making sure all sides are evenly covered. 4. Carefully place the fish into the hot oil, one piece at a time, being sure not to overcrowd the skillet. 5. Fry the fish for about 3 minutes per side, or until it turns golden brown and crispy on all sides. Serve immediately while warm.

Per Serving:
calories: 581 | fat: 20g | protein: 48g | carbs: 48g | fiber: 2g | sodium: 583mg

Italian Fish

Prep time: 10 minutes | Cook time: 3 minutes | Serves 4

- 1 (14½-ounce / 411-g) can diced tomatoes
- ¼ teaspoon dried minced onion
- ¼ teaspoon onion powder
- ¼ teaspoon dried minced garlic
- ¼ teaspoon garlic powder
- ¼ teaspoon dried basil
- ¼ teaspoon dried parsley
- ⅛ teaspoon dried oregano
- ¼ teaspoon sugar
- ⅛ teaspoon dried lemon granules, crushed
- ⅛ teaspoon chili powder
- ⅛ teaspoon dried red pepper flakes
- 1 tablespoon grated Parmesan cheese
- 4 (4-ounce / 113-g) cod fillets, rinsed and patted dry

1. Add the tomatoes, minced onion, onion powder, minced garlic, garlic powder, basil, parsley, oregano, sugar, lemon granules, chili powder, red pepper flakes, and cheese to the Instant Pot® and stir to combine. Place the fillets on top of the tomato mixture, folding the thin tail ends under to ensure even thickness. Spoon some of the tomato mixture over the fillets. 2. Close the lid, set the steam release to Sealing, press the Manual button, and set the timer for 3 minutes. When the timer finishes, quick-release the pressure until the float valve drops, then carefully open the lid. Serve immediately while hot.

Per Serving:
calories: 116 | fat: 3g | protein: 20g | carbs: 5g | fiber: 2g | sodium: 400mg

Shrimp Saganaki with Feta

Prep time: 10 minutes | Cook time: 35 minutes | Serves 2

- 1¼ pounds (567 g) raw medium shrimp (about 20), peeled and deveined
- ¼ teaspoon fine sea salt
- ¼ teaspoon freshly ground black pepper
- 4 tablespoons extra virgin olive oil, divided
- 5 garlic cloves, minced
- ¼ cup ouzo (anise-flavored liquor)
- ½ large onion (any variety), chopped
- 1 small hot chili, sliced
- 1 teaspoon red pepper flakes
- 14 ounces (397 g) canned crushed tomatoes or whole tomatoes chopped in a food processor
- 1 teaspoon dried oregano, divided
- 3 ounces (85 g) crumbled feta, divided
- 1 tablespoon chopped fresh basil

1. Preheat the oven to 400°F (205°C). Pat the shrimp dry with paper towels, then season with the sea salt and black pepper. 2. Add 2 tablespoons of the olive oil to a large skillet over medium-high heat. When the oil begins to shimmer, add the shrimp and sauté for about 2 minutes and then add the garlic and sauté for 1 more minute or until the shrimp turn pink. 3. Add the ouzo and sauté for 2 minutes or until the alcohol has evaporated. Remove the pan from the heat and set aside. 4. Add the remaining 2 tablespoons of olive oil to a medium pot or saucepan placed over medium heat. When the olive oil begins to shimmer, add the onions and sauté for 5 minutes or until translucent. Add the sliced chili and red pepper flakes and sauté for 2 more minutes. Add the tomatoes, cover, and simmer for 7 minutes or until the sauce thickens. 5. Pour the tomato sauce into an oven-proof casserole dish or cast-iron skillet large enough to hold the shrimp in a single layer. Sprinkle ½ teaspoon of the oregano and half of the feta over the sauce, then place the shrimp on top of the sauce, lightly pressing each shrimp into the sauce. Sprinkle the remaining feta and oregano over the shrimp. 6. Transfer to the oven and bake for 15 minutes, then top with the chopped basil. Store covered in the refrigerator for up to 2 days.

Per Serving:
calories: 652 | fat: 38g | protein: 66g | carbs: 15g | fiber: 5g | sodium: 704mg

Herb-Crusted River Trout

Prep time: 10 minutes | Cook time: 3 minutes | Serves 4

- 4 (½-pound / 227-g) fresh river trout, rinsed and patted dry
- 1 teaspoon salt, divided
- 1 teaspoon white wine vinegar
- ½ cup water
- ½ cup minced fresh flat-leaf parsley
- 2 tablespoons chopped fresh oregano
- 1 teaspoon fresh thyme leaves
- 1 small shallot, peeled and minced
- 2 tablespoons olive oil
- ½ teaspoon lemon juice

1. Sprinkle trout with ¾ teaspoon salt inside and out. Combine vinegar and water, pour into the Instant Pot®, and place rack inside. Place trout on rack. 2. Close lid, set steam release to Sealing, press the Manual button, and set time to 3 minutes. When the timer beeps, let pressure release naturally for 3 minutes. Quick-release any remaining pressure until the float valve drops and then open lid. 3. Transfer fish to a serving plate. Peel and discard skin from fish. Remove and discard the heads if desired. 4. In a small bowl, mix together parsley, oregano, thyme, shallot, olive oil, lemon juice, and remaining ¼ teaspoon salt. Pour evenly over fish. Serve immediately.

Per Serving:
calories: 344 | fat: 18g | protein: 45g | carbs: 1g | fiber: 0g | sodium: 581mg

Paprika-Spiced Fish

Prep time: 5 minutes | Cook time: 10 minutes | Serves 4

- 4 (5-ounce / 142-g) sea bass fillets
- ½ teaspoon salt
- 1 tablespoon smoked paprika
- 3 tablespoons unsalted butter
- Lemon wedges

1. Season both sides of the fish evenly with salt, then sprinkle with paprika. 2. Preheat a skillet over high heat and melt the butter until it begins to sizzle. 3. Place the fish in the skillet and cook for 4 minutes per side, or until the fish is cooked through and lightly browned. 4. Transfer the fish to a serving dish and squeeze fresh lemon juice over the top. Serve immediately.

Per Serving:
calories: 257 | fat: 34g | protein: 34g | carbs: 1g | fiber: 1g | sodium: 416mg

Shrimp and Asparagus Risotto

Prep time: 15 minutes | Cook time: 20 minutes | Serves 4

- ¼ cup extra-virgin olive oil, divided
- 8 ounces (227 g) asparagus, trimmed and cut on bias into 1-inch lengths
- ½ onion, chopped fine
- ¼ teaspoon table salt
- 1½ cups Arborio rice
- 3 garlic cloves, minced
- ½ cup dry white wine
- 3 cups chicken or vegetable broth, plus extra as needed
- 1 pound (454 g) large shrimp (26 to 30 per pound), peeled and deveined
- 2 ounces (57 g) Parmesan cheese, grated (1 cup)
- 1 tablespoon lemon juice
- 1 tablespoon minced fresh chives

1. Using the highest Sauté function on the Instant Pot®, heat 1 tablespoon of oil until shimmering. Add the asparagus, partially cover, and cook for about 4 minutes until just crisp-tender. Use a slotted spoon to transfer the asparagus to a bowl and set aside. 2. In the now-empty pot, add the onion, 2 tablespoons of oil, and salt. Cook on the highest Sauté function for about 5 minutes until the onion is softened. Stir in the rice and garlic, cooking for about 3 minutes until the grains are translucent around the edges. Add the wine and cook for about 1 minute until it has almost evaporated. 3. Stir in the broth, scraping up any rice stuck to the bottom of the pot. Secure the lid, close the pressure release valve, select the high-pressure cook function, and set the timer for 7 minutes. 4. Turn off the Instant Pot® and quick-release the pressure. Carefully open the lid, directing the steam away from you. Stir the shrimp and asparagus into the risotto, cover, and let it sit for 5 to 7 minutes until the shrimp are opaque throughout. 5. Stir in the Parmesan and the remaining 1 tablespoon of oil, mixing vigorously until the risotto becomes creamy. If needed, adjust the consistency with extra hot broth. Add the lemon juice and season with salt and pepper to taste. Garnish each serving with chives before serving.

Per Serving:
calories: 707 | fat: 24g | protein: 45g | carbs: 76g | fiber: 5g | sodium: 360mg

Wild Rice and Orange Salmon Bowl

Prep time: 20 minutes | Cook time: 18 minutes | Serves 4

- 1 cup wild rice, picked over and rinsed
- 3 tablespoons extra-virgin olive oil, divided
- 1½ teaspoon table salt, for cooking rice
- 2 oranges, plus ⅛ teaspoon grated orange zest
- 4 (6-ounce / 170-g) skinless salmon fillets, 1½ inches thick
- 1 teaspoon ground dried Aleppo pepper
- ½ teaspoon table salt
- 1 small shallot, minced
- 1 tablespoon red wine vinegar
- 2 teaspoons Dijon mustard
- 1 teaspoon honey
- 2 carrots, peeled and shredded
- ¼ cup chopped fresh mint

1. Combine 6 cups water, rice, 1 tablespoon oil, and 1½ teaspoons salt in Instant Pot. Lock lid in place and close pressure release valve. Select high pressure cook function and cook for 15 minutes. Turn off Instant Pot and let pressure release naturally for 15 minutes. Quick-release any remaining pressure, then carefully remove lid, allowing steam to escape away from you. Drain rice and set aside to cool slightly. Wipe pot clean with paper towels. 2. Add ½ cup water to now-empty Instant Pot. Fold sheet of aluminum foil into 16 by 6-inch sling. Slice 1 orange ¼ inch thick and shingle widthwise in 3 rows across center of sling. Sprinkle flesh side of salmon with Aleppo pepper and ½ teaspoon salt, then arrange skinned side down on top of orange slices. Using sling, lower salmon into Instant Pot; allow narrow edges of sling to rest along sides of insert. Lock lid in place and close pressure release valve. Select high pressure cook function and cook for 3 minutes. 3. Meanwhile, cut away peel and pith from remaining 1 orange. Quarter orange, then slice crosswise into ¼-inch pieces. Whisk remaining 2 tablespoons oil, shallot, vinegar, mustard, honey, and orange zest together in large bowl. Add rice, orange pieces, carrots, and mint, and gently toss to combine. Season with salt and pepper to taste. 4. Turn off Instant Pot and quick-release pressure. Carefully remove lid, allowing steam to escape away from you. Using sling, transfer salmon to large plate. Gently lift and tilt fillets with spatula to remove orange slices. Serve salmon with salad.

Per Serving:
calories: 690 | fat: 34g | protein: 43g | carbs: 51g | fiber: 5g | sodium: 770mg

Flavorful Scallops with Dandelion Greens

Prep time: 5 minutes | Cook time: 15 minutes | Serves 4

- 3 tablespoons olive oil, divided
- 2 cloves garlic, thinly sliced
- 1 pound (454 g) dandelion greens
- 1 cup low-sodium chicken broth or water
- ½ teaspoon kosher salt, divided
- ¼ teaspoon ground black pepper, divided
- 1 cup chopped fresh mint
- 1 cup chopped fresh flat-leaf parsley
- 1 pound (454 g) scallops, muscle tabs removed
- Lemon wedges, for serving

1. In a large skillet over medium-high heat, warm 1 tablespoon of the oil. Cook the garlic until softened, about 2 minutes. Add the dandelion greens and broth or water and bring to a boil. Cover and cook until the greens are wilted, 2 minutes. Season with ¼ teaspoon of the salt and ⅛ teaspoon of the pepper. Cover and cook until the greens are tender, 5 to 10 minutes. Stir in the mint and parsley. 2. Meanwhile, pat the scallops dry and season with the remaining ¼ teaspoon salt and the remaining ⅛ teaspoon pepper. In a large nonstick skillet over medium heat, warm 1 tablespoon of the oil. Add the scallops in a single layer and cook without disturbing until browned, 1 to 2 minutes. Add the remaining 1 tablespoon oil to the skillet, flip the scallops, and cook until browned on the other side, 1 to 2 minutes. Serve the scallops over the braised greens and with the lemon wedges.

Per Serving:
calories: 235 | fat: 12g | protein: 18g | carbs: 17g | fiber: 5g | sodium: 850mg

Spiced Moroccan Tuna Steaks

Prep time: 10 minutes | Cook time: 6 to 8 minutes | Serves 4

- 2 tablespoons finely chopped cilantro
- 2 tablespoons finely chopped parsley
- 6 cloves garlic, minced
- ½ teaspoon unrefined sea salt or salt
- ½ teaspoon paprika
- 1 lemon, juiced and zested
- 3 tablespoons extra-virgin olive oil
- 4 tuna steaks (4 ounces / 113 g each)

1. In a medium bowl, mix the cilantro, parsley, garlic, salt, paprika, and lemon juice and zest together. Whisk in the olive oil. 2. Place the fish in a glass baking dish and pour half of the chermoula sauce over the top. Cover with plastic wrap and allow to marinate for 1 hour. 3. Preheat grill to medium-high heat. 4. Grill the fish, turning once, until firm, 6 to 8 minutes. Transfer to a platter, spread with the remaining chermoula sauce, and let stand for 5 minutes to absorb the flavors.

Per Serving:
calories: 217 | fat: 11g | protein: 25g | carbs: 3g | fiber: 0g | sodium: 335mg

Stuffed Shrimp

Prep time: 20 minutes | Cook time: 12 minutes per batch | Serves 4

- 16 tail-on shrimp, peeled and deveined (last tail section intact)
- ¾ cup crushed panko bread
Stuffing:
- 2 (6-ounce / 170-g) cans lump crab meat
- 2 tablespoons chopped shallots
- 2 tablespoons chopped green onions
- 2 tablespoons chopped celery
- 2 tablespoons chopped green bell pepper
- ½ cup crushed saltine crackers
- crumbs
- Oil for misting or cooking spray
- 1 teaspoon Old Bay Seasoning
- 1 teaspoon garlic powder
- ¼ teaspoon ground thyme
- 2 teaspoons dried parsley flakes
- 2 teaspoons fresh lemon juice
- 2 teaspoons Worcestershire sauce
- 1 egg, beaten

1. Rinse the shrimp thoroughly. Remove the tail section (shell) from 4 shrimp, discard the shells, and finely chop the meat. 2. For the remaining 12 shrimp, cut a deep slit along the back so the meat opens flat, being careful not to cut all the way through. 3. Preheat the air fryer to 360°F (182°C). 4. In a large bowl, combine the chopped shrimp with all the stuffing ingredients, stirring until well mixed. 5. Divide the stuffing mixture into 12 equal portions, each about 2 tablespoons. 6. Place a portion of stuffing onto the back of each butterflied shrimp, shaping it into a ball or oblong form and pressing firmly so the stuffing sticks and adheres well to the shrimp. 7. Carefully roll each stuffed shrimp in panko crumbs and mist lightly with oil or cooking spray. 8. Place 6 shrimp in the air fryer basket and air fry at 360°F (182°C) for 10 minutes. Mist with additional oil or spray and cook for another 2 minutes, or until the stuffing is cooked through and crispy on the outside. 9. Repeat the process to cook the remaining shrimp. Serve warm.

Per Serving:
calories: 223 | fat: 4g | protein: 24g | carbs: 24g | fiber: 2g | sodium: 758mg

Italian Tuna Roast

Prep time: 15 minutes | Cook time: 21 to 24 minutes | Serves 8

- Cooking spray
- 1 tablespoon Italian seasoning
- ⅛ teaspoon ground black pepper
- 1 tablespoon extra-light olive oil
- 1 teaspoon lemon juice
- 1 tuna loin (approximately 2 pounds / 907 g, 3 to 4 inches thick)

1. Spray baking dish with cooking spray and place in air fryer basket. Preheat the air fryer to 390°F (199°C). 2. Mix together the Italian seasoning, pepper, oil, and lemon juice. 3. Using a dull table knife or butter knife, pierce top of tuna about every half inch: Insert knife into top of tuna roast and pierce almost all the way to the bottom. 4. Spoon oil mixture into each of the holes and use the knife to push seasonings into the tuna as deeply as possible. 5. Spread any remaining oil mixture on all outer surfaces of tuna. 6. Place tuna roast in baking dish and roast at 390°F (199°C) for 20 minutes. Check temperature with a meat thermometer. Cook for an additional 1 to 4 minutes or until temperature reaches 145°F (63°C). 7. Remove basket from the air fryer and let tuna sit in the basket for 10 minutes.

Per Serving:
calories: 178 | fat: 7g | protein: 26g | carbs: 0g | fiber: 0g | sodium: 44mg

Salmon with Tarragon-Dijon Sauce

Prep time: 5 minutes | Cook time: 15 minutes | Serves 4

- 1¼ pounds (567 g) salmon fillet (skin on or removed), cut into 4 equal pieces
- ¼ cup avocado oil mayonnaise
- ¼ cup Dijon or stone-ground mustard
- Zest and juice of ½ lemon
- 2 tablespoons chopped fresh tarragon or 1 to 2 teaspoons dried tarragon
- ½ teaspoon salt
- ¼ teaspoon freshly ground black pepper
- 4 tablespoons extra-virgin olive oil, for serving

1. Preheat the oven to 425°F (220°C). Line a baking sheet with parchment paper. 2. Place the salmon pieces, skin-side down, on a baking sheet. 3. In a small bowl, whisk together the mayonnaise, mustard, lemon zest and juice, tarragon, salt, and pepper. Top the salmon evenly with the sauce mixture. 4. Bake until slightly browned on top and slightly translucent in the center, 10 to 12 minutes, depending on the thickness of the salmon. Remove from the oven and leave on the baking sheet for 10 minutes. Drizzle each fillet with 1 tablespoon olive oil before serving.

Per Serving:
calories: 343 | fat: 23g | protein: 30g | carbs: 4g | fiber: 1g | sodium: 585mg

Chili-Spiced Trout with Sautéed Salad

Prep time: 10 minutes | Cook time: 30 minutes | Serves 4

- 2 pounds (907 g) rainbow trout fillets (about 6 fillets)
- Salt
- Ground white pepper
- 1 tablespoon extra-virgin olive oil
- 1 pound (454 g) asparagus
- 4 medium golden potatoes, thinly sliced
- 1 scallion, thinly sliced, green and white parts separated
- 1 garlic clove, finely minced
- 1 large carrot, thinly sliced
- 2 Roma tomatoes, chopped
- 8 pitted kalamata olives, chopped
- ¼ cup ground cumin
- 2 tablespoons dried parsley
- 2 tablespoons paprika
- 1 tablespoon vegetable bouillon seasoning
- ½ cup dry white wine

1. Lightly season the fish with salt and white pepper and set aside. 2. In a large sauté pan or skillet, heat the oil over medium heat. Add and stir in the asparagus, potatoes, the white part of the scallions, and garlic to the hot oil. Cook and stir for 5 minutes, until fragrant. Add the carrot, tomatoes, and olives; continue to cook for 5 to 7 minutes, until the carrots are slightly tender. 3. Sprinkle the cumin, parsley, paprika, and vegetable bouillon seasoning over the pan. Season with salt. Stir to incorporate. Put the trout on top of the vegetables and add the wine to cover the vegetables. 4. Reduce the heat to low, cover, and cook for 5 to 7 minutes, until the fish flakes easily with a fork and juices run clear. Top with scallion greens and serve.

Per Serving:
calories: 493 | fat: 19g | protein: 40g | carbs: 41g | fiber: 7g | sodium: 736mg

Shrimp with Arugula Pesto and Zucchini Noodles

Prep time: 20 minutes | Cook time: 5 minutes | Serves 2

- 3 cups lightly packed arugula
- ½ cup lightly packed basil leaves
- 3 medium garlic cloves
- ¼ cup walnuts
- 3 tablespoons olive oil
- 2 tablespoons grated Parmesan cheese
- 1 tablespoon freshly squeezed lemon juice
- Salt
- Freshly ground black pepper
- 1 (10-ounce / 283-g) package zucchini noodles
- 8 ounces (227 g) cooked, shelled shrimp
- 2 Roma tomatoes, diced

1. In a food processor with a chopping blade, combine the arugula, basil, garlic, walnuts, olive oil, Parmesan cheese, and lemon juice. Process until smooth, scraping down the sides as needed. Season the pesto with salt and pepper to taste. 2. Heat a sauté pan over medium heat. Add the pesto, zucchini noodles, and shrimp, tossing to coat everything evenly in the sauce. Cook just until the shrimp and noodles are warmed through; avoid overcooking to keep the zucchini firm. 3. Taste and adjust the seasoning with more salt and pepper if necessary. Garnish with diced tomatoes and serve immediately.

Per Serving:
calories: 434 | fat: 30g | protein: 33g | carbs: 15g | fiber: 5g | sodium: 412mg

Herb Halibut in Parchment

Prep time: 15 minutes | Cook time: 15 minutes | Serves 4

- ½ cup zucchini, diced small
- 1 shallot, minced
- 4 (5-ounce / 142-g) halibut fillets (about 1 inch thick)
- 4 teaspoons extra-virgin olive oil
- ¼ teaspoon kosher salt
- ⅛ teaspoon freshly ground black pepper
- 1 lemon, sliced into ⅛-inch-thick rounds
- 8 sprigs of thyme

1. Preheat the oven to 450°F (235°C). Combine the zucchini and shallots in a medium bowl. 2. Cut 4 (15-by-24-inch) pieces of parchment paper. Fold each sheet in half horizontally. Draw a large half heart on one side of each folded sheet, with the fold along the center of the heart. Cut out the heart, open the parchment, and lay it flat. 3. Place a fillet near the center of each parchment heart. Drizzle 1 teaspoon olive oil on each fillet. Sprinkle with salt and pepper. Top each fillet with lemon slices and 2 sprigs of thyme. Sprinkle each fillet with one-quarter of the zucchini and shallot mixture. Fold the parchment over. 4. Starting at the top, fold the edges of the parchment over, and continue all the way around to make a packet. Twist the end tightly to secure. 5. Arrange the 4 packets on a baking sheet. Bake for about 15 minutes. Place on plates; cut open. Serve immediately.

Per Serving:
calories: 190 | fat: 7g | protein: 27g | carbs: 5g | fiber: 1g | sodium: 170mg

Lemon Mahi-Mahi

Prep time: 5 minutes | Cook time: 14 minutes | Serves 2

- Oil, for spraying
- 2 (6-ounce / 170-g) mahi-mahi fillets
- 1 tablespoon lemon juice
- 1 tablespoon olive oil
- ¼ teaspoon salt
- ¼ teaspoon freshly ground black pepper
- 1 tablespoon chopped fresh dill
- 2 lemon slices

1. Line the air fryer basket with parchment paper and lightly spray it with oil. 2. Place the mahi-mahi fillets into the prepared basket. 3. In a small bowl, whisk together the lemon juice and olive oil. Brush this mixture evenly over the surface of the fillets. 4. Season the mahi-mahi with salt and black pepper, then sprinkle with fresh dill. 5. Air fry at 400°F (204°C) for 12 to 14 minutes, depending on the thickness of the fillets, until the fish flakes easily with a fork. 6. Transfer the fillets to serving plates, place a lemon slice on top of each, and serve immediately.

Per Serving:
calories: 218 | fat: 8g | protein: 32g | carbs: 3g | fiber: 1g | sodium: 441mg

Spicy Creole Crayfish

Prep time: 10 minutes | Cook time: 3 to 4 hours | Serves 2

- 1½ cups diced celery
- 1 large yellow onion, chopped
- 2 small bell peppers, any colors, chopped
- 1 (8-ounce / 227-g) can tomato sauce
- 1 (28-ounce / 794-g) can whole tomatoes, broken up, with the juice
- 1 clove garlic, minced
- ½ teaspoon sea salt
- ¼ teaspoon black pepper
- 6 drops hot pepper sauce (like tabasco)
- 1 pound (454 g) precooked crayfish meat

1. Place the celery, onion, and bell peppers in the slow cooker. Add the tomato sauce, tomatoes, and garlic. Sprinkle with the salt and pepper and add the hot sauce. 2. Cover and cook on high for 3 to 4 hours or on low for 6 to 8 hours. 3. About 30 minutes before the cooking time is completed, add the crayfish. 4. Serve hot.

Per Serving:
calories: 334 | fat: 4g | protein: 43g | carbs: 34g | fiber: 13g | sodium: 659mg

One-Pot Shrimp Fried Rice

Prep time: 10 minutes | Cook time: 25 minutes | Serves 4

Shrimp:
- 1 teaspoon cornstarch
- ½ teaspoon kosher salt
- ¼ teaspoon black pepper

Rice:
- 2 cups cold cooked rice
- 1 cup frozen peas and carrots, thawed
- ¼ cup chopped green onions (white and green parts)

Eggs:
- 2 large eggs, beaten
- ¼ teaspoon kosher salt

- 1 pound (454 g) jumbo raw shrimp (21 to 25 count), peeled and deveined
- 3 tablespoons toasted sesame oil
- 1 tablespoon soy sauce
- ½ teaspoon kosher salt
- 1 teaspoon black pepper
- ¼ teaspoon black pepper

1. For the shrimp: In a small bowl, whisk together the cornstarch, salt, and pepper. Place the shrimp in a large bowl and sprinkle with the seasoned cornstarch. Toss until the shrimp are well coated and set aside. 2. For the rice: In a baking pan, combine the rice, peas and carrots, green onions, sesame oil, soy sauce, salt, and pepper. Toss until all the ingredients are evenly mixed. 3. Place the pan in the air fryer basket. Set the air fryer to 350°F (177°C) and cook for 15 minutes, stirring the rice halfway through to ensure even cooking. 4. After 15 minutes, place the shrimp on top of the rice. Cook in the air fryer at 350°F (177°C) for 5 minutes. 5. For the eggs: While the shrimp cooks, beat the eggs with salt and pepper in a medium bowl. 6. Open the air fryer and pour the beaten eggs evenly over the shrimp and rice. Set the air fryer to 350°F (177°C) and cook for another 5 minutes. 7. Remove the pan from the air fryer and stir everything thoroughly to break up the rice and combine the eggs and shrimp. Serve warm.

Per Serving:
calories: 364 | fat: 15g | protein: 30g | carbs: 28g | fiber: 3g | sodium: 794mg

Garlicky Broiled Sardines

Prep time: 5 minutes | Cook time: 3 minutes | Serves 4

- 4 (3¼-ounce / 92-g) cans sardines (about 16 sardines), packed in water or olive oil
- 2 tablespoons extra-virgin olive oil (if sardines are packed in water)
- 4 garlic cloves, minced
- ½ teaspoon red pepper flakes
- ½ teaspoon salt
- ¼ teaspoon freshly ground black pepper

1. Preheat the broiler and line a baking dish with aluminum foil. Arrange the sardines in a single layer on the foil. 2. In a small bowl, mix together the olive oil (if using), garlic, and red pepper flakes. Spoon the mixture over each sardine, then season with salt and pepper. 3. Broil the sardines for 2 to 3 minutes, until they are sizzling and cooked through. 4. To serve, place 4 sardines on each plate and drizzle with any remaining garlic mixture left in the baking dish.

Per Serving:
calories: 197 | fat: 11g | protein: 23g | carbs: 1g | fiber: 0g | sodium: 574mg

Herb-Infused Trout with Parsley

Prep time: 10 minutes | Cook time: 3 minutes | Serves 4

- 4 (½-pound / 227-g) river trout, rinsed and patted dry
- ¾ teaspoon salt, divided
- 4 cups torn lettuce leaves, divided
- 1 teaspoon white wine vinegar
- ½ cup water
- ½ cup minced fresh flat-leaf parsley
- 1 small shallot, peeled and minced
- 2 tablespoons olive oil mayonnaise
- ½ teaspoon lemon juice
- ¼ teaspoon sugar
- 2 tablespoons toasted sliced almonds

1. Season trout with ½ teaspoon salt inside and out. Put 3 cups lettuce leaves in the bottom of the Instant Pot®. Arrange trout over lettuce and top trout with remaining 1 cup lettuce. Stir vinegar into water and pour into pot. 2. Close lid, set steam release to Sealing, press the Manual button, and set time to 3 minutes. When the timer beeps, quick-release the pressure until the float valve drops and open lid. 3. Use a spatula to move fish to a serving plate. Peel and discard skin from fish. Remove and discard fish heads if desired. 4. In a small bowl, mix together parsley, shallot, mayonnaise, lemon juice, sugar, and remaining ¼ teaspoon salt. Evenly divide among the fish, spreading it over them. Sprinkle toasted almonds over the sauce. Serve immediately.

Per Serving:
calories: 159 | fat: 9g | protein: 15g | carbs: 4g | fiber: 1g | sodium: 860mg

Chili Tilapia

Prep time: 5 minutes | Cook time: 20 minutes | Serves 4

- 4 tilapia fillets, boneless
- 1 teaspoon chili flakes
- 1 teaspoon dried oregano
- 1 tablespoon avocado oil
- 1 teaspoon mustard

1. Season the tilapia fillets by rubbing them with chili flakes, dried oregano, avocado oil, and mustard. 2. Place the fillets in the air fryer basket. Cook at 360°F (182°C) for 10 minutes on each side until the fish is cooked through and flakes easily with a fork. Serve hot.

Per Serving:
calories: 146 | fat: 6g | protein: 23g | carbs: 1g | fiber: 0g | sodium: 94mg

Herb-Crusted Tilapia Fingers

Prep time: 15 minutes | Cook time: 9 minutes | Serves 4

- 1 pound (454 g) tilapia fillet
- ½ cup coconut flour
- 2 eggs, beaten
- ½ teaspoon ground paprika
- 1 teaspoon dried oregano
- 1 teaspoon avocado oil

1. Cut the tilapia fillets into fingers and sprinkle with ground paprika and dried oregano. 2. Then dip the tilapia fingers in eggs and coat in the coconut flour. 3. Sprinkle fish fingers with avocado oil and cook in the air fryer at 370°F (188°C) for 9 minutes.

Per Serving:
calories: 187 | fat: 9g | protein: 26g | carbs: 2g | fiber: 1g | sodium: 92mg

Sicilian Baked Cod with Herbed Breadcrumbs

Prep time: 5 minutes | Cook time: 25 minutes | Serves 4

- 2 tablespoons olive oil, divided
- 1 medium red onion, halved and cut into half circles
- 1 tablespoon red wine vinegar
- ¾ teaspoon salt, divided, plus more for seasoning
- ¼ teaspoon freshly ground black pepper, plus more for seasoning
- ½ teaspoon anchovy paste
- 3 tablespoons dried breadcrumbs
- 2 tablespoons chopped flat-leaf parsley
- 2 tablespoons chopped fresh mint leaves
- 2 tablespoons chopped fresh basil leaves
- 4 (6-ounce / 170-g) cod fillets
- ½ cup dry white wine

1. Preheat the oven to 400°F (205°C). 2. In a medium skillet over medium-high heat, warm 1 tablespoon of olive oil. Add the onion and cook, stirring often, until softened, about 5 minutes. Stir in the vinegar and season with salt and pepper. Cook for another 30 seconds, then spread the onions evenly in a baking dish large enough to hold the fish in a single layer. 3. In the same skillet, heat the remaining 1 tablespoon of olive oil over low heat. Add the anchovy paste and cook, stirring, for 1 minute. Add the breadcrumbs and toss to coat them in the oil. Transfer the breadcrumbs to a bowl and let them cool slightly. Stir in the parsley, mint, basil, ¼ teaspoon salt, and a pinch of pepper. 4. Lay the fish fillets over the onions in the dish and season with the remaining ½ teaspoon of salt and ¼ teaspoon of pepper. Sprinkle the breadcrumb mixture evenly over the fillets. Pour the wine into the dish. 5. Bake for 10 to 15 minutes, depending on the thickness of the fillets, until the fish is cooked through. Add a little more wine or water during baking if the dish begins to dry out. Serve hot.

Per Serving:
calories: 299 | fat: 10g | protein: 40g | carbs: 8g | fiber: 1g | sodium: 652mg

Ouzo Mussels

Prep time: 10 minutes | Cook time: 15 minutes | Serves 4

- 1 tablespoon olive oil
- 2 shallots, chopped
- 4 cloves garlic, sliced
- 1 pound (454 g) mussels, scrubbed and debearded
- 1 cup low-sodium chicken broth or water
- ½ cup ouzo
- Grated peel of 1 lemon
- 2 tablespoons chopped fresh flat-leaf parsley

1. Heat the oil in a large pot over medium heat. Add the shallots and garlic, cooking until they soften, about 5 minutes. 2. Turn up the heat to high and add the mussels, broth (or water), and ouzo. Cover the pot, bring the mixture to a boil, and cook for about 8 minutes, or until the mussels open. 3. Discard any mussels that remain closed. Sprinkle the dish with lemon peel and parsley. Serve the mussels hot with their broth.

Per Serving:
calories: 238 | fat: 6g | protein: 16g | carbs: 22g | fiber: 0g | sodium: 344mg

Crunchy Almond-Coated Salmon

Prep time: 10 minutes | Cook time: 12 minutes | Serves 4

- ¼ cup olive oil
- 1 tablespoon honey
- ¼ cup breadcrumbs
- ½ cup finely chopped almonds, lightly toasted
- ½ teaspoon dried thyme
- Sea salt and freshly ground pepper, to taste
- 4 salmon steaks

1. Preheat the oven to 350°F (180°C). 2. Combine the olive oil with the honey. (Soften the honey in the microwave for 15 seconds, if necessary, for easier blending.) 3. In a shallow dish, combine the breadcrumbs, almonds, thyme, sea salt, and freshly ground pepper. 4. Coat the salmon steaks with the olive oil mixture, then the almond mixture. 5. Place on a baking sheet brushed with olive oil and bake 8–12 minutes, or until the almonds are lightly browned and the salmon is firm.

Per Serving:
calories: 634 | fat: 34g | protein: 69g | carbs: 12g | fiber: 2g | sodium: 289mg

Tuna Steaks with Olive Tapenade

Prep time: 10 minutes | Cook time: 10 minutes | Serves 4

- 4 (6-ounce / 170-g) ahi tuna steaks
- 1 tablespoon olive oil

Olive Tapenade:
- ½ cup pitted kalamata olives
- 1 tablespoon olive oil
- 1 tablespoon chopped fresh parsley
- Salt and freshly ground black pepper, to taste
- ½ lemon, sliced into 4 wedges
- 1 clove garlic
- 2 teaspoons red wine vinegar
- 1 teaspoon capers, drained

1. Preheat the air fryer to 400°F (204°C). 2. Drizzle the tuna steaks with olive oil, then season them with salt and black pepper. Place the tuna steaks in a single layer in the air fryer basket. Air fry for 10 minutes, turning the steaks halfway through, until the fish is firm to the touch. 3. For the tapenade: In a food processor with a metal blade, combine the olives, olive oil, parsley, garlic, vinegar, and capers. Pulse until finely chopped, scraping down the sides of the bowl as needed. 4. Spoon the tapenade over the cooked tuna steaks and serve immediately with lemon wedges.

Per Serving:
calories: 269 | fat: 9g | protein: 42g | carbs: 2g | fiber: 1g | sodium: 252mg

Pan-Fried Spicy Mussels with Tomato and Basil

Prep time: 20 minutes | Cook time: 5½ hours | Serves 4

- 3 tablespoons olive oil
- 4 cloves garlic, minced
- 3 shallot cloves, minced
- 8 ounces (227 g) mushrooms, diced
- 1 (28-ounce / 794-g) can diced tomatoes, with the juice
- ¾ cup white wine
- 2 tablespoons dried oregano
- ½ tablespoon dried basil
- ½ teaspoon black pepper
- 1 teaspoon paprika
- ¼ teaspoon red pepper flakes
- 3 pounds (1.4 kg) mussels

1. In a large sauté pan, heat the olive oil over medium-high heat. Cook the garlic, shallots, and mushrooms for 2 to 3 minutes, until the garlic is just a bit brown and fragrant. Scrape the entire contents of the pan into the slow cooker. 2. Add the tomatoes and white wine to the slow cooker. Sprinkle with the oregano, basil, black pepper, paprika, and red pepper flakes. 3. Cover and cook on low for 4 to 5 hours, or on high for 2 to 3 hours. The mixture is done cooking when mushrooms are fork tender. 4. Clean and debeard the mussels. Discard any open mussels. 5. Increase the heat on the slow cooker to high once the mushroom mixture is done. Add the cleaned mussels to the slow cooker and secure the lid tightly. Cook for 30 more minutes. 6. To serve, ladle the mussels into bowls with plenty of broth. Discard any mussels that didn't open up during cooking. Serve hot, with crusty bread for sopping up the sauce.

Per Serving:
calories: 470 | fat: 19g | protein: 44g | carbs: 24g | fiber: 5g | sodium: 897mg

Chapter 7
Vegetables and Sides

Chapter 7 Vegetables and Sides

Cauliflower with Lemon Tahini Sauce

Prep time: 10 minutes | Cook time: 20 minutes | Serves 2

- ½ large head cauliflower, stemmed and broken into florets (about 3 cups)
- 1 tablespoon olive oil
- 2 tablespoons tahini
- 2 tablespoons freshly squeezed lemon juice
- 1 teaspoon harissa paste
- Pinch salt

1. Preheat the oven to 400°F(205°C) and set the rack to the lowest position. Line a sheet pan with parchment paper or foil. 2. Toss the cauliflower florets with the olive oil in a large bowl and transfer to the sheet pan. Reserve the bowl to make the tahini sauce. 3. Roast the cauliflower for 15 minutes, turning it once or twice, until it starts to turn golden. 4. In the same bowl, combine the tahini, lemon juice, harissa, and salt. 5. When the cauliflower is tender, remove it from the oven and toss it with the tahini sauce. Return to the sheet pan and roast for 5 minutes more.

Per Serving:
calories: 205 | fat: 15g | protein: 7g | carbs: 15g | fiber: 7g | sodium: 161mg

Blackened Zucchini with Kimchi-Herb Sauce

Prep time: 10 minutes | Cook time: 15 minutes | Serves 2

- 2 medium zucchini, ends trimmed (about 6 ounces / 170 g each)
- 2 tablespoons olive oil
- ½ cup kimchi, finely chopped
- ¼ cup finely chopped fresh cilantro
- ¼ cup finely chopped fresh flat-leaf parsley, plus more for garnish
- 2 tablespoons rice vinegar
- 2 teaspoons Asian chili-garlic sauce
- 1 teaspoon grated fresh ginger
- Kosher salt and freshly ground black pepper, to taste

1. Brush the zucchini with half of the olive oil, then place it in the air fryer basket. Air fry at 400°F (204°C) for about 15 minutes, turning the zucchini halfway through, until the outside is lightly charred and the inside is tender. 2. While the zucchini cooks, mix the remaining 1 tablespoon of olive oil, kimchi, cilantro, parsley, vinegar, chili-garlic sauce, and ginger in a small bowl until well combined. 3. Once the zucchini is done, transfer it to a colander and allow it to cool for 5 minutes. Using your fingers, pinch and tear the zucchini into bite-size pieces, letting them drop back into the colander. Season with salt and pepper, toss gently, and let it sit for another 5 minutes to drain any excess liquid. 4. Arrange the zucchini on a plate over the prepared kimchi sauce and sprinkle with additional parsley before serving.

Per Serving:
calories: 172 | fat: 15g | protein: 4g | carbs: 8g | fiber: 3g | sodium: 102mg

Garlic-Mint Zucchini Bites

Prep time: 5 minutes | Cook time: 10 minutes | Serves 4

- 3 large green zucchini
- 3 tablespoons extra-virgin olive oil
- 1 large onion, chopped
- 3 cloves garlic, minced
- 1 teaspoon salt
- 1 teaspoon dried mint

1. Cut the zucchini into ½-inch cubes. 2. In a large skillet over medium heat, cook the olive oil, onions, and garlic for 3 minutes, stirring constantly. 3. Add the zucchini and salt to the skillet and toss to combine with the onions and garlic, cooking for 5 minutes. 4. Add the mint to the skillet, tossing to combine. Cook for another 2 minutes. Serve warm.

Per Serving:
calories: 147 | fat: 11g | protein: 4g | carbs: 12g | fiber: 3g | sodium: 607mg

Indian Eggplant Bharta

Prep time: 15 minutes | Cook time: 20 minutes | Serves 4

- 1 medium eggplant
- 2 tablespoons vegetable oil
- ½ cup finely minced onion
- ½ cup finely chopped fresh tomato
- 2 tablespoons fresh lemon juice
- 2 tablespoons chopped fresh cilantro
- ½ teaspoon kosher salt
- ⅛ teaspoon cayenne pepper

1. Coat the eggplant evenly with vegetable oil and place it in the air fryer basket. Set the air fryer to 400°F (204°C) and cook for 20 minutes, or until the skin is blistered and charred. 2. Remove the eggplant and transfer it to a resealable plastic bag. Seal the bag and set it aside for 15 to 20 minutes to allow the eggplant to finish cooking in the residual heat. 3. Once cooled, remove the eggplant from the bag and place it in a large bowl. Peel off and discard the charred skin. Roughly mash the eggplant flesh. Stir in the onion, tomato, lemon juice, cilantro, salt, and cayenne, mixing well to combine.

Per Serving:
calories: 105 | fat: 7g | protein: 2g | carbs: 11g | fiber: 5g | sodium: 295mg

Braised Whole Cauliflower with North African Spices

Prep time: 15 minutes | Cook time: 10 minutes | Serves 4

- 2 tablespoons extra-virgin olive oil
- 6 garlic cloves, minced
- 3 anchovy fillets, rinsed and minced (optional)
- 2 teaspoons ras el hanout
- ⅛ teaspoon red pepper flakes
- 1 (28-ounce / 794-g) can whole peeled tomatoes, drained with juice reserved, chopped coarse
- 1 large head cauliflower (3 pounds / 1.4 kg)
- ½ cup pitted brine-cured green olives, chopped coarse
- ¼ cup golden raisins
- ¼ cup fresh cilantro leaves
- ¼ cup pine nuts, toasted

1. Set the Instant Pot to the highest sauté function and cook the oil, garlic, anchovies (if using), ras el hanout, and pepper flakes until fragrant, about 3 minutes. Turn off the Instant Pot and stir in the tomatoes and reserved juice. 2. Trim the outer leaves of the cauliflower and cut the stem flush with the bottom florets. Using a paring knife, make a 4-inch-deep cross in the stem. Carefully place the cauliflower stem-side down into the pot and spoon some of the sauce over the top. Lock the lid in place, close the pressure release valve, and select the high-pressure cook function. Cook for 3 minutes. 3. Turn off the Instant Pot and quick-release the pressure. Carefully remove the lid, allowing the steam to escape away from you. Use tongs and a slotted spoon to transfer the cauliflower to a serving dish and cover with aluminum foil. Stir the olives and raisins into the sauce and cook using the highest sauté function for about 5 minutes, until the sauce thickens slightly. Season with salt and pepper to taste. Cut the cauliflower into wedges, spoon some sauce over the top, and garnish with cilantro and pine nuts. Serve with the remaining sauce on the side.

Per Serving:
calories: 265 | fat: 16g | protein: 8g | carbs: 29g | fiber: 9g | sodium: 319mg

Nutty Freekeh Pilaf with Walnuts

Prep time: 15 minutes | Cook time: 15 minutes | Serves 4

- 2½ cups freekeh
- 3 tablespoons extra-virgin olive oil, divided
- 2 medium onions, diced
- ¼ teaspoon ground cinnamon
- ¼ teaspoon ground allspice
- 5 cups chicken stock
- ½ cup chopped walnuts
- Salt
- Freshly ground black pepper
- ½ cup plain, unsweetened, full-fat Greek yogurt
- 1½ teaspoons freshly squeezed lemon juice
- ½ teaspoon garlic powder

1. In a small bowl, soak the freekeh covered in cold water for 5 minutes. Drain and rinse the freekeh, then rinse one more time. 2. In a large sauté pan or skillet, heat 2 tablespoons oil, then add the onions and cook until fragrant. Add the freekeh, cinnamon, and allspice. Stir periodically for 1 minute. 3. Add the stock and walnuts and season with salt and pepper. Bring to a simmer. 4. Cover and reduce the heat to low. Cook for 15 minutes. Once freekeh is tender, remove from the heat and allow to rest for 5 minutes. 5. In a small bowl, combine the yogurt, lemon juice, and garlic powder. You may need to add salt to bring out the flavors. Add the yogurt mixture to the freekeh and serve immediately.

Per Serving:
calories: 653 | fat: 25g | protein: 23g | carbs: 91g | fiber: 12g | sodium: 575mg

White Beans with Rosemary, Sage, and Garlic

Prep time: 10 minutes | Cook time: 10 minutes | Serves 2

- 1 tablespoon olive oil
- 2 garlic cloves, minced
- 1 (15-ounce / 425-g) can white cannellini beans, drained and rinsed
- ¼ teaspoon dried sage
- 1 teaspoon minced fresh rosemary (from 1 sprig) plus 1 whole fresh rosemary sprig
- ½ cup low-sodium chicken stock
- Salt

1. Heat olive oil in a sauté pan over medium-high heat. Add the garlic and sauté for 30 seconds until fragrant. 2. Stir in the beans, sage, both minced and whole rosemary, and chicken stock. Bring the mixture to a boil. 3. Lower the heat to medium and simmer the beans for about 10 minutes, or until most of the liquid has evaporated. If you prefer a thicker consistency, mash some of the beans with a fork. 4. Season with salt to taste and remove the rosemary sprig before serving.

Per Serving:
calories: 155 | fat: 7g | protein: 6g | carbs: 17g | fiber: 8g | sodium: 153mg

Parmesan Garlic Cauliflower

Prep time: 5 minutes | Cook time: 40 minutes | Serves 4

- 1 large head cauliflower (about 6 to 7 inches/15.25 to 17.5cm in diameter), washed
- 2 garlic cloves, minced
- ⅓ cup extra virgin olive oil
- 1 teaspoon kosher salt
- ¼ cup grated Parmesan cheese
- Freshly ground black pepper to taste

1. Preheat the oven to 400ºF (205ºC). 2. In a large bowl, combine the cauliflower and garlic. Toss to combine, then add the olive oil and mix well, ensuring the florets are thoroughly coated in the oil. 3. Spread the cauliflower florets in a single layer on a large sheet pan, and drizzle any remaining olive oil over the florets. (Make sure the florets are closely grouped.) 4. Transfer to the oven. Bake for 30–40 minutes or until the florets are golden brown and tender, then carefully remove the pan from the oven. 5. Promptly sprinkle the kosher salt, Parmesan cheese, and black pepper over the top of the florets. Store in the refrigerator for up to 4 days.

Per Serving:
calories: 251 | fat: 20g | protein: 7g | carbs: 11g | fiber: 4g | sodium: 649mg

Braised Fennel

Prep time: 10 minutes | Cook time: 50 minutes | Serves 4

- 2 large fennel bulbs
- ¼ cup extra-virgin avocado oil or ghee, divided
- 1 small shallot or red onion
- 1 clove garlic, sliced
- 4 to 6 thyme sprigs
- 1 small bunch fresh parsley, leaves and stalks separated
- 1 cup water
- 3 tablespoons fresh lemon juice
- Salt and black pepper, to taste
- ¼ cup extra-virgin olive oil, to drizzle

1. Cut off the fennel stalks where they attach to the bulb, saving the stalks for later. Slice the fennel bulb in half, trim the tough bottom, and cut it into wedges. 2. Heat a saucepan with 2 tablespoons of avocado oil over medium-high heat. Add the shallot, garlic, thyme sprigs, parsley stalks, and fennel stalks, sautéing for about 5 minutes. Add the water, bring it to a boil, then lower the heat and simmer for 10 minutes. Remove from the heat, let sit for 10 minutes, and strain the stock, discarding the aromatics. 3. Preheat the oven to 350°F (180°C) for fan-assisted or 400°F (205°C) for conventional settings. 4. Heat an ovenproof skillet with the remaining 2 tablespoons of avocado oil over medium-high heat. Add the fennel wedges and sear until caramelized, about 5 minutes, turning them once. Pour the strained stock and lemon juice over the fennel, then season with salt and pepper. Cover loosely with aluminum foil and bake for about 30 minutes. The fennel should be easily pierced with a knife when done. 5. Once cooked, remove from the oven and sprinkle with chopped parsley. Drizzle with olive oil before serving. Let cool to room temperature before refrigerating any leftovers for up to 5 days.

Per Serving:
calories: 225 | fat: 20g | protein: 2g | carbs: 12g | fiber: 5g | sodium: 187mg

Fragrant Rice Pilaf with Dill

Prep time: 15 minutes | Cook time: 25 minutes | Serves 6

- 2 tablespoons olive oil
- 1 carrot, finely chopped (about ¾ cup)
- 2 leeks, halved lengthwise, washed, well drained, and sliced in half-moons
- ½ teaspoon salt
- ¼ teaspoon freshly ground black pepper
- 2 tablespoons chopped fresh dill
- 1 cup low-sodium vegetable broth or water
- ½ cup basmati rice

1. In a 2-or 3-quart saucepan, heat the olive oil over medium heat. Add the carrot, leeks, salt, pepper, and 1 tablespoon of the dill. Cover and cook for 6 to 8 minutes, stirring once, to soften all the vegetables but not brown them. 2. Add the broth or water and bring to a boil. Stir in the rice, reduce the heat to maintain a simmer, cover, and cook for 15 minutes. Remove from the heat; let stand, covered, for 10 minutes. 3. Fluff the rice with fork. Stir in the remaining 1 tablespoon dill and serve.

Per Serving:
1 cup: calories: 100 | fat: 7g | protein: 2g | carbs: 11g | fiber: 4g | sodium: 209mg

Moroccan-Style Couscous

Prep time: 10 minutes | Cook time: 5 minutes | Serves 2

- 1 tablespoon olive oil
- ¾ cup couscous
- ¼ teaspoon garlic powder
- ¼ teaspoon salt
- ¼ teaspoon cinnamon
- 1 cup water
- 2 tablespoons raisins
- 2 tablespoons minced dried apricots
- 2 teaspoons minced fresh parsley

1. Heat the olive oil in a saucepan over medium-high heat. Add the couscous, garlic powder, salt, and cinnamon, stirring for 1 minute to lightly toast the couscous and spices. 2. Pour in the water, add the raisins and apricots, and bring the mixture to a boil. 3. Once boiling, cover the pot and turn off the heat. Let the couscous sit for 4 to 5 minutes, then fluff with a fork. Stir in the parsley and adjust the seasoning with additional salt or spices if desired.

Per Serving:
calories: 338 | fat: 8g | protein: 9g | carbs: 59g | fiber: 4g | sodium: 299mg

Pine Nut and Currant Cabbage Rolls

Prep time: 15 minutes | Cook time: 2 hours | Serves 4

- 1 large head green cabbage, cored
- 1 tablespoon olive oil
- 1 large yellow onion, chopped
- 3 cups cooked pearl barley
- 3 ounces (85 g) feta cheese, crumbled
- ½ cup dried currants
- 2 tablespoons pine nuts, toasted
- 2 tablespoons chopped fresh flat-leaf parsley
- ½ teaspoon sea salt
- ½ teaspoon black pepper
- ½ cup apple juice
- 1 tablespoon apple cider vinegar
- 1 (15-ounce / 425-g) can crushed tomatoes, with the juice

1. Steam the cabbage head in a large pot over boiling water for 8 minutes. Remove to a cutting board and let cool slightly. 2. Remove 16 leaves from the cabbage head (reserve the rest of the cabbage for another use). Cut off the raised portion of the center vein of each cabbage leaf (do not cut out the vein). 3. Heat the oil in a large nonstick lidded skillet over medium heat. Add the onion, cover, and cook 6 minutes, or until tender. Remove to a large bowl. 4. Stir the barley, feta cheese, currants, pine nuts, and parsley into the onion mixture. Season with ¼ teaspoon of the salt and ¼ teaspoon of the pepper. 5. Place cabbage leaves on a work surface. On 1 cabbage leaf, spoon about ⅓ cup of the barley mixture into the center. Fold in the edges of the leaf over the barley mixture and roll the cabbage leaf up as if you were making a burrito. Repeat for the remaining 15 cabbage leaves and filling. 6. Arrange the cabbage rolls in the slow cooker. 7. Combine the remaining ¼ teaspoon salt, ¼ teaspoon pepper, the apple juice, apple cider vinegar, and tomatoes. Pour the apple juice mixture evenly over the cabbage rolls. 8. Cover and cook on high 2 hours or on low for 6 to 8 hours. Serve hot.

Per Serving:
calories: 394 | fat: 12g | protein: 12g | carbs: 66g | fiber: 16g | sodium: 560mg

Caesar Whole Cauliflower

Prep time: 20 minutes | Cook time: 30 minutes | Serves 2 to 4

- 3 tablespoons olive oil
- 2 tablespoons red wine vinegar
- 2 tablespoons Worcestershire sauce
- 2 tablespoons grated Parmesan cheese
- 1 tablespoon Dijon mustard
- 4 garlic cloves, minced
- 4 oil-packed anchovy fillets, drained and finely minced
- Kosher salt and freshly ground black pepper, to taste
- 1 small head cauliflower (about 1 pound / 454 g), green leaves trimmed and stem trimmed flush with the bottom of the head
- 1 tablespoon roughly chopped fresh flat-leaf parsley (optional)

1. In a liquid measuring cup, whisk together the olive oil, vinegar, Worcestershire sauce, Parmesan, mustard, garlic, anchovies, and salt and pepper to taste. Place the cauliflower head upside down on a cutting board and use a paring knife to cut an "x" through the entire length of the core. Transfer the cauliflower to a large bowl and pour half of the dressing over it. Turn the cauliflower to coat it evenly, then let it rest, stem-side up, in the dressing for at least 10 minutes, or up to 30 minutes, to allow the dressing to seep into the cauliflower. 2. Place the cauliflower, stem-side down, into the air fryer basket and air fry at 340°F (171°C) for 25 minutes. Drizzle the remaining dressing over the cauliflower and increase the temperature to 400°F (204°C), air frying for about 5 minutes more, or until the top is golden brown and the core is tender. 3. Remove the basket from the air fryer and transfer the cauliflower to a large plate. Optionally, sprinkle with parsley and serve hot.

Per Serving:
calories: 187 | fat: 15g | protein: 5g | carbs: 9g | fiber: 2g | sodium: 453mg

Gorgonzola Sweet Potato Burgers

Prep time: 10 minutes | Cook time: 15 minutes | Serves: 4

- 1 large sweet potato (about 8 ounces / 227 g)
- 2 tablespoons extra-virgin olive oil, divided
- 1 cup chopped onion (about ½ medium onion)
- 1 cup old-fashioned rolled oats
- 1 large egg
- 1 tablespoon balsamic vinegar
- 1 tablespoon dried oregano
- 1 garlic clove
- ¼ teaspoon kosher or sea salt
- ½ cup crumbled Gorgonzola or blue cheese (about 2 ounces / 57 g)
- Salad greens or 4 whole-wheat rolls, for serving (optional)

1. Pierce the sweet potato all over with a fork and microwave on high for 4 to 5 minutes, or until tender in the center. Allow it to cool slightly, then slice it in half. 2. While the sweet potato cooks, heat 1 tablespoon of oil in a large skillet over medium-high heat. Add the onion and cook for about 5 minutes, stirring occasionally. 3. Once the sweet potato has cooled, scoop the flesh out of the skin and transfer it to a food processor. Add the cooked onion, oats, egg, vinegar, oregano, garlic, and salt. Process until smooth. Add the cheese and pulse a few times to combine. Using your hands, form the mixture into four burger patties, each about ½ cup in size. Flatten each patty to about ¾ inch thick and set them on a plate. 4. Wipe the skillet with a paper towel, then heat the remaining 1 tablespoon of oil over medium-high heat until hot, about 2 minutes. Add the patties to the skillet and lower the heat to medium. Cook the burgers for 5 minutes, flip them with a spatula, and cook for another 5 minutes. Serve as is or on salad greens or whole-wheat rolls.

Per Serving:
calories: 337 | fat: 16g | protein: 13g | carbs: 38g | fiber: 6g | sodium: 378mg

Garlicky Swiss Chard and White Bean Medley

Prep time: 15 minutes | Cook time: 15 minutes | Serves 4

- 2 tablespoons olive oil
- 1 medium onion, chopped
- 1 bell pepper, diced
- 2 cloves garlic, minced
- 1 large bunch of Swiss chard, tough stems removed, cut into bite-size pieces
- 2 cups white beans, cooked
- Sea salt and freshly ground pepper, to taste

1. Heat the oil in a large skillet over medium-high heat. Add the onion and pepper and cook for 5 minutes until soft. 2. Add the garlic, stir, and add the Swiss chard. Cook for 10 minutes until greens are tender. 3. Add the beans, stir until heated through, and season with sea salt and freshly ground pepper. 4. Serve immediately.

Per Serving:
calories: 212 | fat: 7g | protein: 10g | carbs: 28g | fiber: 7g | sodium: 66mg

Spiced Eggplant with Harissa Yogurt

Prep time: 10 minutes | Cook time: 15 minutes | Serves 2

- 1 medium eggplant (about ¾ pound / 340 g), cut crosswise into ½-inch-thick slices and quartered
- 2 tablespoons vegetable oil
- Kosher salt and freshly ground black pepper, to taste
- ½ cup plain yogurt (not Greek)
- 2 tablespoons harissa paste
- 1 garlic clove, grated
- 2 teaspoons honey

1. In a bowl, toss together the eggplant and oil, season with salt and pepper, and toss to coat evenly. Transfer to the air fryer and air fry at 400°F (204°C), shaking the basket every 5 minutes, until the eggplant is caramelized and tender, about 15 minutes. 2. Meanwhile, in a small bowl, whisk together the yogurt, harissa, and garlic, then spread onto a serving plate. 3. Pile the warm eggplant over the yogurt and drizzle with the honey just before serving.

Per Serving:
calories: 247 | fat: 16g | protein: 5g | carbs: 25g | fiber: 8g | sodium: 34mg

Beet and Watercress Salad with Orange Zest

Prep time: 20 minutes | Cook time: 8 minutes | Serves 4

- 2 pounds (907 g) beets, scrubbed, trimmed, and cut into ¾-inch pieces
- ½ cup water
- 1 teaspoon caraway seeds
- ½ teaspoon table salt
- 1 cup plain Greek yogurt
- 1 small garlic clove, minced to paste
- 5 ounces (142 g) watercress, torn into bite-size pieces
- 1 tablespoon extra-virgin olive oil, divided, plus extra for drizzling
- 1 tablespoon white wine vinegar, divided
- 1 teaspoon grated orange zest plus 2 tablespoons juice
- ¼ cup hazelnuts, toasted, skinned, and chopped
- ¼ cup coarsely chopped fresh dill
- Coarse sea salt

1. Combine beets, water, caraway seeds, and table salt in Instant Pot. Lock lid in place and close pressure release valve. Select high pressure cook function and cook for 8 minutes. Turn off Instant Pot and quick-release pressure. Carefully remove lid, allowing steam to escape away from you. 2. Using slotted spoon, transfer beets to plate; set aside to cool slightly. Combine yogurt, garlic, and 3 tablespoons beet cooking liquid in bowl; discard remaining cooking liquid. In large bowl toss watercress with 2 teaspoons oil and 1 teaspoon vinegar. Season with table salt and pepper to taste. 3. Spread yogurt mixture over surface of serving dish. Arrange watercress on top of yogurt mixture, leaving 1-inch border of yogurt mixture. Add beets to now-empty large bowl and toss with orange zest and juice, remaining 2 teaspoons vinegar, and remaining 1 teaspoon oil. Season with table salt and pepper to taste. Arrange beets on top of watercress mixture. Drizzle with extra oil and sprinkle with hazelnuts, dill, and sea salt. Serve.

Per Serving:
calories: 240 | fat: 15g | protein: 9g | carbs: 19g | fiber: 5g | sodium: 440mg

Kale with Lemon-Tahini Dressing

Prep time: 5 minutes | Cook time: 15 minutes | Serves 2 to 4

- ¼ cup tahini
- ¼ cup fresh lemon juice
- 2 tablespoons olive oil
- 1 teaspoon sesame seeds
- ½ teaspoon garlic powder
- ¼ teaspoon cayenne pepper
- 4 cups packed torn kale leaves (stems and ribs removed and leaves torn into palm-size pieces; about 4 ounces / 113 g)
- Kosher salt and freshly ground black pepper, to taste

1. In a large bowl, whisk together the tahini, lemon juice, olive oil, sesame seeds, garlic powder, and cayenne until smooth. Add the kale leaves, season with salt and black pepper, and toss in the dressing until completely coated. Transfer the kale leaves to a cake pan. 2. Place the pan in the air fryer and roast at 350ºF (177ºC), stirring every 5 minutes, until the kale is wilted and the top is lightly browned, about 15 minutes. Remove the pan from the air fryer and serve warm.

Per Serving:
calories: 221 | fat: 21g | protein: 5g | carbs: 8g | fiber: 3g | sodium: 32mg

Glazed Carrots

Prep time: 10 minutes | Cook time: 8 to 10 minutes | Serves 4

- 2 teaspoons honey
- 1 teaspoon orange juice
- ½ teaspoon grated orange rind
- ⅛ teaspoon ginger
- 1 pound (454 g) baby carrots
- 2 teaspoons olive oil
- ¼ teaspoon salt

1. In a small bowl, combine the honey, orange juice, grated rind, and ginger, and set aside. 2. Toss the carrots with the oil and salt, ensuring they are well coated, then transfer them to the air fryer basket. 3. Roast at 390ºF (199ºC) for 5 minutes. Shake the basket to stir the carrots, then cook for an additional 2 to 4 minutes until they are just barely tender. 4. Transfer the carrots to a baking pan. 5. Stir the honey mixture to combine, then pour the glaze over the carrots and toss to coat. 6. Roast at 360ºF (182ºC) for 1 minute, or just until the carrots are heated through.

Per Serving:
calories: 71 | fat: 2g | protein: 1g | carbs: 12g | fiber: 3g | sodium: 234mg

Eggplant Caponata

Prep time: 20 minutes | Cook time: 5 minutes | Serves 8

- ¼ cup extra-virgin olive oil
- ¼ cup white wine
- 2 tablespoons red wine vinegar
- 1 teaspoon ground cinnamon
- 1 large eggplant, peeled and diced
- 1 medium onion, peeled and diced
- 1 medium green bell pepper, seeded and diced
- 1 medium red bell pepper, seeded and diced
- 2 cloves garlic, peeled and minced
- 1 (14½-ounce / 411-g) can diced tomatoes
- 3 stalks celery, diced
- ½ cup chopped oil-cured olives
- ½ cup golden raisins
- 2 tablespoons capers, rinsed and drained
- ½ teaspoon salt
- ½ teaspoon ground black pepper

1. Add all ingredients to the Instant Pot® and stir well to combine. Close the lid, set the steam release valve to Sealing, press the Manual button, and set the cooking time to 5 minutes. 2. When the timer beeps, quick-release the pressure until the float valve drops. Carefully open the lid, stir the mixture, and serve warm or at room temperature.

Per Serving:
calories: 90 | fat: 1g | protein: 2g | carbs: 17g | fiber: 4g | sodium: 295mg

Braised Greens with Olives and Walnuts

Prep time: 5 minutes | Cook time: 20 minutes | Serves 4

- 8 cups fresh greens (such as kale, mustard greens, spinach, or chard)
- 2 to 4 garlic cloves, finely minced
- ½ cup roughly chopped pitted green or black olives
- ½ cup roughly chopped shelled walnuts
- ¼ cup extra-virgin olive oil
- 2 tablespoons red wine vinegar
- 1 to 2 teaspoons freshly chopped herbs such as oregano, basil, rosemary, or thyme

1. Remove the tough stems from the greens and chop them into bite-sized pieces. Place the greens into a large skillet or pot with high sides. 2. Set the heat to high, then add the minced garlic and enough water to just cover the greens. Bring the mixture to a boil, then reduce the heat to low and simmer until the greens are tender and most of the liquid has evaporated. If the greens begin to burn, add a bit more water. For delicate greens like spinach, this will take about 5 minutes, while heartier greens like chard may take up to 20 minutes. Once cooked, remove from the heat and stir in the olives and walnuts. 3. In a small bowl, whisk together the olive oil, vinegar, and herbs. Drizzle this mixture over the cooked greens and toss gently to coat. Serve warm.

Per Serving:
calories: 254 | fat: 25g | protein: 4g | carbs: 6g | fiber: 3g | sodium: 137mg

Lightened-Up Eggplant Parmigiana

Prep time: 10 minutes | Cook time: 1 hour 20 minutes | Serves 3

- 2 medium globe eggplants, sliced into ¼-inch rounds
- 2 tablespoons extra virgin olive oil, divided
- 1 teaspoon fine sea salt, divided
- 1 medium onion (any variety), diced
- 1 garlic clove, finely chopped
- 20 ounces (567g) canned crushed tomatoes or tomato purée
- 3 tablespoons chopped fresh basil, divided
- ¼ teaspoon freshly ground black pepper
- 7 ounces (198 g) low-moisture mozzarella, thinly sliced or grated
- 2 ounces (57 g) grated Parmesan cheese

1. Line an oven rack with aluminum foil and preheat the oven to 350°F (180°C). 2. Place the eggplant slices in a large bowl, tossing them with 1 tablespoon of olive oil and ½ teaspoon of sea salt. Arrange the slices in a single layer on the prepared oven rack. Roast the eggplant in the middle position of the oven for 15–20 minutes, or until soft. 3. While the eggplant is roasting, heat the remaining tablespoon of olive oil in a medium pan over medium heat. Once the oil begins to shimmer, add the onions and sauté for 5 minutes. Add the garlic and sauté for another minute. Stir in the crushed tomatoes, 1½ tablespoons of basil, the remaining ½ teaspoon of sea salt, and black pepper. Reduce the heat to low and simmer for 15 minutes, then remove from the heat. 4. Once the eggplant is done, remove it from the oven and start assembling the dish. Spread ½ cup of the tomato sauce over the bottom of an 11 × 7-inch (30 × 20 cm) casserole dish. Arrange a third of the eggplant slices in a single layer, overlapping them slightly if necessary. Layer half of the mozzarella on top, followed by ¾ cup of the tomato sauce and 2½ tablespoons of grated Parmesan cheese. Repeat the layering process with the remaining eggplant, sauce, and cheese, and then top with the remaining sauce. Sprinkle the remaining 1½ tablespoons of basil over the top. 5. Bake for 40–45 minutes, or until browned and bubbly. Remove from the oven and let sit for 10 minutes before cutting into 6 equal pieces. Serve warm. Store covered in the refrigerator for up to 3 days.

Per Serving:
calories: 453 | fat: 28g | protein: 28g | carbs: 26g | fiber: 4g | sodium: 842mg

Whole Roasted Garlic

Prep time: 5 minutes | Cook time: 20 minutes | Makes 12 cloves

- 1 medium head garlic
- 2 teaspoons avocado oil

1. Remove any hanging excess peel from the garlic but leave the cloves covered. Cut off ¼ of the head of garlic, exposing the tips of the cloves. 2. Drizzle with avocado oil. Place the garlic head into a small sheet of aluminum foil, completely enclosing it. Place it into the air fryer basket. 3. Adjust the temperature to 400°F (204°C) and air fry for 20 minutes. If your garlic head is a bit smaller, check it after 15 minutes. 4. When done, garlic should be golden brown and very soft. 5. To serve, cloves should pop out and easily be spread or sliced. Store in an airtight container in the refrigerator up to 5 days. You may also freeze individual cloves on a baking sheet, then store together in a freezer-safe storage bag once frozen.

Per Serving:
calories: 8 | fat: 1g | protein: 0g | carbs: 0g | fiber: 0g | sodium: 0mg

Herb-Infused Fasolakia

Prep time: 10 minutes | Cook time: 6 to 8 hours | Serves 6

- 2 pounds (907 g) green beans, trimmed
- 1 (15-ounce / 425-g) can no-salt-added diced tomatoes, with juice
- 1 large onion, chopped
- 4 garlic cloves, chopped
- Juice of 1 lemon
- 1 teaspoon dried dill
- 1 teaspoon ground cumin
- 1 teaspoon dried oregano
- 1 teaspoon sea salt
- ½ teaspoon freshly ground black pepper
- ¼ cup feta cheese, crumbled

1. In a slow cooker, combine the green beans, tomatoes and their juice, onion, garlic, lemon juice, dill, cumin, oregano, salt, and pepper. Stir to mix well. 2. Cover the cooker and cook for 6 to 8 hours on Low heat. 3. Top with feta cheese for serving.

Per Serving:
calories: 94 | fat: 2g | protein: 5g | carbs: 18g | fiber: 7g | sodium: 497mg

Spinach and Paneer Cheese

Prep time: 15 minutes | Cook time: 2 to 4 hours | Serves 6

- 2 pounds (907 g) fresh spinach
- 1½-inch piece fresh ginger, roughly chopped
- 5 garlic cloves, whole
- 2 fresh green chiles, roughly chopped
- 1 onion, roughly chopped
- 1 teaspoon salt
- ½ teaspoon turmeric
- 4 tomatoes, finely chopped
- 1 to 2 tablespoons cornstarch to thicken (if required)
- 4 tablespoons butter
- 1 teaspoon cumin seeds
- 3 garlic cloves, minced
- 1 tablespoon dried fenugreek leaves
- 2 tablespoons rapeseed oil
- 12 ounces (340 g) paneer, cut into cubes

1. Set the slow cooker to high and add the spinach, ginger, garlic, chiles, onion, salt, turmeric, and tomatoes. 2. Cover and cook on high for 3 hours or on low for 6 hours. 3. Once cooked, use an immersion blender or food processor to purée the greens until smooth and glossy. The goal is to achieve a thick, vibrant green purée. If the consistency is too watery, reduce the mixture on the stove to thicken, or use the boil function on your slow cooker to evaporate excess liquid. If needed, you can also thicken it by adding a sprinkle of cornstarch. 4. Heat the butter in a pan and add the cumin seeds, cooking until they sizzle. Next, add the minced garlic and stir until it lightly browns. Remove from the heat and stir in the dried fenugreek leaves. Pour this mixture into the saag in the slow cooker and whisk to combine. 5. In the same pan, fry the paneer cubes in a little oil until golden brown. Stir the fried paneer into the saag. Replace the lid and let everything sit for another 10 minutes before serving.

Per Serving:
calories: 252 | fat: 17g | protein: 10g | carbs: 20g | fiber: 6g | sodium: 682mg

Spiced Yogurt Beets with Hazelnuts

Prep time: 5 minutes | Cook time: 40 minutes | Serves 4

- 4 or 5 beets, peeled
- ¼ cup hazelnuts
- ½ cup low-fat plain Greek yogurt
- 1 tablespoon honey
- 1 tablespoon chopped fresh mint
- 1 teaspoon ground cinnamon
- ¼ teaspoon ground cumin
- ⅛ teaspoon ground black pepper

1. Place racks in the upper and lower thirds of the oven. Preheat the oven to 400°F(205°C). 2. Place the beets on a 12' × 12' piece of foil. Fold the foil over the beets, and seal the sides. Bake until the beets are tender enough to be pierced by a fork, about 40 minutes. Remove from the oven, carefully open the packet, and let cool slightly. When cool enough to handle, slice the beets into ¼'-thick rounds. 3. Meanwhile, toast the hazelnuts on a small baking sheet until browned and fragrant, about 5 minutes. Using a paper towel or kitchen towel, rub the skins off. Coarsely chop the nuts and set aside. 4. In a medium bowl, stir together the yogurt, honey, mint, cinnamon, cumin, and pepper. 5. Serve the beets with a dollop of the spiced yogurt and a sprinkle of the nuts.

Per Serving:
calories: 126 | fat: 6g | protein: 5g | carbs: 15g | fiber: 4g | sodium: 74mg

Potato Vegetable Hash

Prep time: 20 minutes | Cook time: 5 to 7 hours | Serves 4

- 1½ pounds (680 g) red potatoes, diced
- 8 ounces (227 g) green beans, trimmed and cut into ½-inch pieces
- 4 ounces (113 g) mushrooms, chopped
- 1 large tomato, chopped
- 1 large zucchini, diced
- 1 small onion, diced
- 1 red bell pepper, seeded and chopped
- ⅓ cup low-sodium vegetable broth
- 1 teaspoon sea salt
- ½ teaspoon garlic powder
- ½ teaspoon freshly ground black pepper
- ¼ teaspoon red pepper flakes
- ¼ cup shredded cheese of your choice (optional)

1. In a slow cooker, combine the potatoes, green beans, mushrooms, tomato, zucchini, onion, bell pepper, vegetable broth, salt, garlic powder, black pepper, and red pepper flakes. Stir everything together to mix well. 2. Cover the slow cooker and cook on Low heat for 5 to 7 hours. 3. When ready to serve, garnish with cheese, if desired.

Per Serving:
calories: 183 | fat: 1g | protein: 7g | carbs: 41g | fiber: 8g | sodium: 642mg

Zucchini Fritters

Prep time: 10 minutes | Cook time: 10 minutes | Serves 4

- 2 zucchini, grated (about 1 pound / 454 g)
- 1 teaspoon salt
- ¼ cup almond flour
- ¼ cup grated Parmesan cheese
- 1 large egg
- ¼ teaspoon dried thyme
- ¼ teaspoon ground turmeric
- ¼ teaspoon freshly ground black pepper
- 1 tablespoon olive oil
- ½ lemon, sliced into wedges

1. Preheat the air fryer to 400°F (204°C). Cut a piece of parchment paper to fit just slightly smaller than the base of the air fryer. 2. Place the zucchini in a large colander, sprinkle with salt, and let it sit for 5 to 10 minutes. Afterward, squeeze out as much liquid as possible and transfer the zucchini to a large mixing bowl. Add the almond flour, Parmesan, egg, thyme, turmeric, and black pepper. Mix gently until all ingredients are fully incorporated. 3. Form the mixture into 8 patties and arrange them on the parchment paper. Lightly brush each patty with olive oil. Air fry for 10 minutes, turning the patties halfway through, until golden brown. Serve warm with lemon wedges.

Per Serving:
calories: 78 | fat: 6g | protein: 4g | carbs: 2g | fiber: 0g | sodium: 712mg

Crunchy Stone Age Loaf

Prep time: 10 minutes | Cook time: 1 hour | Serves 14

- ½ cup flaxseeds
- ½ cup chia seeds
- ½ cup sesame seeds
- ¼ cup pumpkin seeds
- ¼ cup sunflower seeds
- ½ cup whole almonds, chopped
- ½ cup blanched hazelnuts, chopped
- ½ cup pecans or walnuts
- 1 teaspoon salt, or to taste
- 1 teaspoon coarse black pepper
- 4 large eggs
- ½ cup extra-virgin olive oil or melted ghee

1. Preheat the oven to 285°F (140°C) fan assisted or 320°F (160°C) conventional. Line a loaf pan with parchment paper. 2. In a mixing bowl, combine all of the dry ingredients. Add the eggs and olive oil and stir through until well combined. Pour the dough into the loaf pan. Transfer to the oven and bake for about 1 hour or until the top is crisp. 3. Remove from the oven and let cool slightly in the pan before transferring to a wire rack to cool completely before slicing. Store at room temperature for up to 3 days loosely covered with a kitchen towel, refrigerate for up to 10 days, or freeze for up to 3 months.

Per Serving:
calories: 251 | fat: 23g | protein: 7g | carbs: 7g | fiber: 5g | sodium: 192mg

Spiced Squash with Halloumi

Prep time: 20 minutes | Cook time: 15 minutes | Serves 4

- 3 tablespoons extra-virgin olive oil, divided
- 2 tablespoons lemon juice
- 2 garlic cloves, minced, divided
- ⅛ teaspoon plus ½ teaspoon table salt, divided
- 8 ounces (227 g) Brussels sprouts, trimmed, halved, and sliced very thin
- 1 (8-ounce / 227-g) block halloumi cheese, sliced crosswise into ¾-inch-thick slabs
- 4 scallions, white parts minced, green parts sliced thin on bias
- ½ teaspoon ground cardamom
- ¼ teaspoon ground cumin
- ⅛ teaspoon cayenne pepper
- 2 pounds (907 g) butternut squash, peeled, seeded, and cut into 1-inch pieces
- ½ cup chicken or vegetable broth
- 2 teaspoons honey
- ¼ cup dried cherries
- 2 tablespoons roasted pepitas

1. Whisk 1 tablespoon oil, lemon juice, ¼ teaspoon garlic, and ⅛ teaspoon salt together in bowl. Add Brussels sprouts and toss to coat; let sit until ready to serve. 2. Using highest sauté function, heat remaining 2 tablespoons oil in Instant Pot until shimmering. Arrange halloumi around edges of pot and cook until browned, about 3 minutes per side; transfer to plate. Add scallion whites to fat left in pot and cook until softened, about 2 minutes. Stir in remaining garlic, cardamom, cumin, and cayenne and cook until fragrant, about 30 seconds. Stir in squash, broth, and remaining ½ teaspoon salt. Lock lid in place and close pressure release valve. Select high pressure cook function and cook for 6 minutes. 3. Turn off Instant Pot and quick-release pressure. Carefully remove lid, allowing steam to escape away from you. Using highest sauté function, continue to cook squash mixture, stirring occasionally until liquid is almost completely evaporated, about 5 minutes. Turn off Instant Pot. Using potato masher, mash squash until mostly smooth. Season with salt and pepper to taste. 4. Spread portion of squash over bottom of individual serving plates. Top with Brussels sprouts and halloumi. Drizzle with honey and sprinkle with cherries, pepitas, and scallion greens. Serve.

Per Serving:
calories: 337 | fat: 13g | protein: 24g | carbs: 38g | fiber: 8g | sodium: 534mg

Chapter 8
Vegetarian Mains

Chapter 8 Vegetarian Mains

Baked Tofu with Sun-Dried Tomatoes and Artichokes

Prep time: 15 minutes | Cook time: 30 minutes | Serves 4

- 1 (16-ounce / 454-g) package extra-firm tofu, drained and patted dry, cut into 1-inch cubes
- 2 tablespoons extra-virgin olive oil, divided
- 2 tablespoons lemon juice, divided
- 1 tablespoon low-sodium soy sauce or gluten-free tamari
- 1 onion, diced
- ½ teaspoon kosher salt
- 2 garlic cloves, minced
- 1 (14-ounce / 397-g) can artichoke hearts, drained
- 8 sun-dried tomato halves packed in oil, drained and chopped
- ¼ teaspoon freshly ground black pepper
- 1 tablespoon white wine vinegar
- Zest of 1 lemon
- ¼ cup fresh parsley, chopped

1. Preheat the oven to 400°F (205°C) and line a baking sheet with foil or parchment paper. 2. In a bowl, mix together the tofu, 1 tablespoon of olive oil, 1 tablespoon of lemon juice, and soy sauce. Let the tofu marinate for 15 to 30 minutes. After marinating, arrange the tofu in a single layer on the prepared baking sheet and bake for 20 minutes, flipping once, until lightly golden brown. 3. While the tofu bakes, heat the remaining 1 tablespoon of olive oil in a large skillet or sauté pan over medium heat. Add the onion and salt, and sauté for 5 to 6 minutes until translucent. Stir in the garlic and cook for 30 seconds. Add the artichoke hearts, sun-dried tomatoes, and black pepper, and sauté for an additional 5 minutes. Pour in the white wine vinegar and remaining 1 tablespoon of lemon juice, deglazing the pan by scraping up any brown bits. Remove from heat and stir in the lemon zest and parsley. Gently fold in the baked tofu and serve.

Per Serving:
calories: 230 | fat: 14g | protein: 14g | carbs: 13g | fiber: 5g | sodium: 500mg

Savory Broccoli Crust Pizza

Prep time: 15 minutes | Cook time: 12 minutes | Serves 4

- 3 cups riced broccoli, steamed and drained well
- 1 large egg
- ½ cup grated vegetarian Parmesan cheese
- 3 tablespoons low-carb Alfredo sauce
- ½ cup shredded Mozzarella cheese

1. In a large bowl, mix broccoli, egg, and Parmesan. 2. Cut a piece of parchment to fit your air fryer basket. Press out the pizza mixture to fit on the parchment, working in two batches if necessary. Place into the air fryer basket. 3. Adjust the temperature to 370°F (188°C) and air fry for 5 minutes. 4. The crust should be firm enough to flip. If not, add 2 additional minutes. Flip crust. 5. Top with Alfredo sauce and Mozzarella. Return to the air fryer basket and cook an additional 7 minutes or until cheese is golden and bubbling. Serve warm.

Per Serving:
calories: 87 | fat: 2g | protein: 11g | carbs: 5g | fiber: 1g | sodium: 253mg

Tangy Asparagus and Broccoli

Prep time: 25 minutes | Cook time: 22 minutes | Serves 4

- ½ pound (227 g) asparagus, cut into 1½-inch pieces
- ½ pound (227 g) broccoli, cut into 1½-inch pieces
- 2 tablespoons olive oil
- Salt and white pepper, to taste
- ½ cup vegetable broth
- 2 tablespoons apple cider vinegar

1. Arrange the vegetables in a single layer in the lightly greased air fryer basket. Drizzle the olive oil over the top of the vegetables. 2. Sprinkle with salt and white pepper to taste. 3. Air fry at 380°F (193°C) for 15 minutes, shaking the basket halfway through the cooking time. 4. In a saucepan, add ½ cup of vegetable broth and bring to a rapid boil. Add the vinegar and cook for 5 to 7 minutes, or until the sauce has reduced by half. 5. Spoon the sauce over the warm vegetables and serve immediately. Bon appétit!

Per Serving:
calories: 93 | fat: 7g | protein: 3g | carbs: 6g | fiber: 3g | sodium: 89mg

Caprese Eggplant Stacks

Prep time: 5 minutes | Cook time: 12 minutes | Serves 4

- 1 medium eggplant, cut into ¼-inch slices
- 2 large tomatoes, cut into ¼-inch slices
- 4 ounces (113 g) fresh Mozzarella, cut into ½-ounce / 14-g slices
- 2 tablespoons olive oil
- ¼ cup fresh basil, sliced

1. In a baking dish, arrange four slices of eggplant at the bottom. Top each eggplant slice with a slice of tomato, followed by a slice of Mozzarella, then another eggplant slice. Repeat the layering as necessary. 2. Drizzle with olive oil, cover the dish with foil, and place it in the air fryer basket. 3. Set the air fryer to 350°F (177°C) and bake for 12 minutes. 4. Once done, the eggplant should be tender. Garnish with fresh basil before serving.

Per Serving:
calories: 97 | fat: 7g | protein: 2g | carbs: 8g | fiber: 4g | sodium: 11mg

Crispy Eggplant Rounds

Prep time: 15 minutes | Cook time: 10 minutes | Serves 4

- 1 large eggplant, ends trimmed, cut into ½-inch slices
- ½ teaspoon salt
- 2 ounces (57 g) Parmesan 100% cheese crisps, finely ground
- ½ teaspoon paprika
- ¼ teaspoon garlic powder
- 1 large egg

1. Sprinkle the eggplant rounds with salt and place them on a kitchen towel for 30 minutes to draw out excess water. After 30 minutes, pat the rounds dry with a paper towel. 2. In a medium bowl, combine the cheese crisps, paprika, and garlic powder. In another medium bowl, whisk the egg. Dip each eggplant round in the egg, then press gently into the cheese crisps to coat both sides. 3. Place the coated eggplant rounds in an ungreased air fryer basket. Set the air fryer to 400°F (204°C) and air fry for 10 minutes, turning the rounds halfway through. The eggplant should be golden and crispy when done. Serve warm.

Per Serving:
calories: 113 | fat: 5g | protein: 7g | carbs: 10g | fiber: 4g | sodium: 567mg

Creamy Farrotto with Asparagus and Mushrooms

Prep time: 20 minutes | Cook time: 45 minutes | Serves 2

- 1½ ounces (43 g) dried porcini mushrooms
- 1 cup hot water
- 3 cups low-sodium vegetable stock
- 2 tablespoons olive oil
- ½ large onion, minced (about 1 cup)
- 1 garlic clove
- 1 cup diced mushrooms (about 4 ounces / 113-g)
- ¾ cup farro
- ½ cup dry white wine
- ½ teaspoon dried thyme
- 4 ounces (113 g) asparagus, cut into ½-inch pieces (about 1 cup)
- 2 tablespoons grated Parmesan cheese
- Salt

1. Soak the dried mushrooms in the hot water for about 15 minutes. When they're softened, drain the mushrooms, reserving the liquid. (I like to strain the liquid through a coffee filter in case there's any grit.) Mince the porcini mushrooms. 2. Add the mushroom liquid and vegetable stock to a medium saucepan and bring it to a boil. Reduce the heat to low just to keep it warm. 3. Heat the olive oil in a Dutch oven over high heat. Add the onion, garlic, and mushrooms, and sauté for 10 minutes. 4. Add the farro to the Dutch oven and sauté it for 3 minutes to toast. 5. Add the wine, thyme, and one ladleful of the hot mushroom and chicken stock. Bring it to a boil while stirring the farro. Do not cover the pot while the farro is cooking. 6. Reduce the heat to medium. When the liquid is absorbed, add another ladleful or two at a time to the pot, stirring occasionally, until the farro is cooked through. Keep an eye on the heat, to make sure it doesn't cook too quickly. 7. When the farro is al dente, add the asparagus and another ladleful of stock. Cook for another 3 to 5 minutes, or until the asparagus is softened. 8. Stir in Parmesan cheese and season with salt.

Per Serving:
calories: 341 | fat: 16g | protein: 13g | carbs: 26g | fiber: 5g | sodium: 259mg

Herb and Cheese Filled Portobellos

Prep time: 10 minutes | Cook time: 8 minutes | Serves 4

- 3 ounces (85 g) cream cheese, softened
- ½ medium zucchini, trimmed and chopped
- ¼ cup seeded and chopped red bell pepper
- 1½ cups chopped fresh spinach leaves
- 4 large portobello mushrooms, stems removed
- 2 tablespoons coconut oil, melted
- ½ teaspoon salt

1. In a medium bowl, mix cream cheese, zucchini, pepper, and spinach. 2. Drizzle mushrooms with coconut oil and sprinkle with salt. Scoop ¼ zucchini mixture into each mushroom. 3. Place mushrooms into ungreased air fryer basket. Adjust the temperature to 400°F (204°C) and air fry for 8 minutes. Portobellos will be tender and tops will be browned when done. Serve warm.

Per Serving:
calories: 151 | fat: 13g | protein: 4g | carbs: 6g | fiber: 2g | sodium: 427mg

Linguine with Roasted Brussels Sprouts

Prep time: 10 minutes | Cook time: 25 minutes | Serves 4

- 8 ounces (227 g) whole-wheat linguine
- ⅓ cup, plus 2 tablespoons extra-virgin olive oil, divided
- 1 medium sweet onion, diced
- 2 to 3 garlic cloves, smashed
- 8 ounces (227 g) Brussels sprouts, chopped
- ½ cup chicken stock, as needed
- ⅓ cup dry white wine
- ½ cup shredded Parmesan cheese
- 1 lemon, cut in quarters

1. Bring a large pot of water to a boil and cook the pasta according to package directions. Drain, reserving 1 cup of the pasta water. Mix the cooked pasta with 2 tablespoons of olive oil, then set aside. 2. In a large sauté pan or skillet, heat the remaining ⅓ cup of olive oil on medium heat. Add the onion to the pan and cook for about 5 minutes, until softened. Add the smashed garlic cloves and cook for 1 minute, until fragrant. 3. Add the Brussels sprouts and cook covered for 15 minutes. Add chicken stock as needed to prevent burning. Once Brussels sprouts have wilted and are fork-tender, add white wine and cook down for about 7 minutes, until reduced. 4. Add the pasta to the skillet and add the pasta water as needed. 5. Serve with the Parmesan cheese and lemon for squeezing over the dish right before eating.

Per Serving:
calories: 502 | fat: 31g | protein: 15g | carbs: 50g | fiber: 9g | sodium: 246mg

Crispy Mediterranean Pan-Style Pizza

Prep time: 5 minutes | Cook time: 8 minutes | Serves 2

- 1 cup shredded Mozzarella cheese
- ¼ medium red bell pepper, seeded and chopped
- ½ cup chopped fresh spinach leaves
- 2 tablespoons chopped black olives
- 2 tablespoons crumbled feta cheese

1. Sprinkle Mozzarella into an ungreased round nonstick baking dish in an even layer. Add remaining ingredients on top. 2. Place dish into air fryer basket. Adjust the temperature to 350°F (177°C) and bake for 8 minutes, checking halfway through to avoid burning. Top of pizza will be golden brown and the cheese melted when done. 3. Remove dish from fryer and let cool 5 minutes before slicing and serving.

Per Serving:
calories: 108 | fat: 1g | protein: 20g | carbs: 5g | fiber: 3g | sodium: 521mg

Quinoa with Almonds and Cranberries

Prep time: 15 minutes | Cook time: 0 minutes | Serves 4

- 2 cups cooked quinoa
- ⅓ teaspoon cranberries or currants
- ¼ cup sliced almonds
- 2 garlic cloves, minced
- 1¼ teaspoons salt
- ½ teaspoon ground cumin
- ½ teaspoon turmeric
- ¼ teaspoon ground cinnamon
- ¼ teaspoon freshly ground black pepper

1. In a large bowl, combine the quinoa, cranberries, almonds, garlic, salt, cumin, turmeric, cinnamon, and pepper. Toss everything together to mix well. Serve as is or alongside roasted cauliflower for a complete dish.

Per Serving:
calories: 194 | fat: 6g | protein: 7g | carbs: 31g | fiber: 4g | sodium: 727mg

Tortellini with Roasted Red Pepper Sauce

Prep time: 15 minutes | Cook time: 10 minutes | Serves 4

- 1 (16-ounce / 454-g) container fresh cheese tortellini (usually green and white pasta)
- 1 (16-ounce / 454-g) jar roasted red peppers, drained
- 1 teaspoon garlic powder
- ¼ cup tahini
- 1 tablespoon red pepper oil (optional)

1. Bring a large pot of water to a boil and cook the tortellini according to package directions. 2. In a blender, combine the red peppers with the garlic powder and process until smooth. Once blended, add the tahini until the sauce is thickened. If the sauce gets too thick, add up to 1 tablespoon red pepper oil (if using). 3. Once tortellini are cooked, drain and leave pasta in colander. Add the sauce to the bottom of the empty pot and heat for 2 minutes. Then, add the tortellini back into the pot and cook for 2 more minutes. Serve and enjoy!

Per Serving:
calories: 350 | fat: 11g | protein: 12g | carbs: 46g | fiber: 4g | sodium: 192mg

Eggplants Stuffed with Walnuts and Feta

Prep time: 10 minutes | Cook time: 55 minutes | Serves 6

- 3 medium eggplants, halved lengthwise
- 2 teaspoons salt, divided
- ¼ cup olive oil, plus 2 tablespoons, divided
- 2 medium onions, diced
- 1½ pints cherry or grape tomatoes, halved
- ¾ cup roughly chopped walnut pieces
- 2¼ teaspoons ground cinnamon
- 1½ teaspoons dried oregano
- ½ teaspoon freshly ground black pepper
- ¼ cup whole-wheat breadcrumbs
- ⅔ cup (about 3 ounces / 85 g) crumbled feta cheese

1. Scoop out the flesh of the eggplants, leaving a ½-inch thick border of flesh in the skins. Dice the removed flesh and place it in a colander set over the sink. Sprinkle 1½ teaspoons of salt over the diced eggplant and the inside of the eggplant shells. Let stand for 30 minutes. Rinse both the shells and diced eggplant under cold water, then pat dry with paper towels. 2. Heat ¼ cup of olive oil in a large skillet over medium heat. Add the eggplant shells, skin-side down, and cook for about 4 minutes, until browned and softened. Flip the shells over and cook on the cut side for another 4 minutes, until golden brown and tender. Transfer the shells to a plate lined with paper towels to drain. 3. Drain all but 1 to 2 tablespoons of oil from the skillet and heat over medium-high heat. Add the onions and sauté for about 3 minutes until they begin to soften. Add the diced eggplant, tomatoes, walnuts, cinnamon, oregano, ¼ cup of water, the remaining ½ teaspoon of salt, and the pepper. Cook, stirring occasionally, for about 8 minutes, until the vegetables are golden brown and softened. 4. Preheat the broiler to high. 5. In a small bowl, combine the breadcrumbs and 1 tablespoon of olive oil. 6. Arrange the eggplant shells cut-side up on a large, rimmed baking sheet. Brush each shell with about ½ teaspoon of olive oil. Broil for about 5 minutes, until the shells are tender and just starting to turn golden brown. Remove from the broiler and reduce the oven temperature to 375°F (190°C). 7. Spoon the sautéed vegetable mixture into the eggplant shells, dividing the mixture equally between them. Sprinkle the breadcrumbs on top of each filled shell, followed by the cheese, dividing equally. Bake in the oven for about 35 minutes, or until the filling is heated through and the topping is golden brown and crisp.

Per Serving:
calories: 274 | fat: 15g | protein: 7g | carbs: 34g | fiber: 13g | sodium: 973mg

Stuffed Pepper Stew

Prep time: 20 minutes | Cook time: 50 minutes | Serves 2

- 2 tablespoons olive oil
- 2 sweet peppers, diced (about 2 cups)
- ½ large onion, minced
- 1 garlic clove, minced
- 1 teaspoon oregano
- 1 tablespoon gluten-free vegetarian Worcestershire sauce
- 1 cup low-sodium vegetable stock
- 1 cup low-sodium tomato juice
- ¼ cup brown lentils
- ¼ cup brown rice
- Salt

1. In a Dutch oven, heat olive oil over medium-high heat. Add the sweet peppers and onion, sautéing for about 10 minutes, until the peppers are softened and the onion begins to turn golden. 2. Stir in the garlic, oregano, and Worcestershire sauce, cooking for an additional 30 seconds. Then, add the vegetable stock, tomato juice, lentils, and rice. 3. Bring the mixture to a boil, then cover and reduce the heat to medium-low. Simmer for 45 minutes, or until the rice is tender and the lentils have softened. Season with salt to taste.

Per Serving:
calories: 379 | fat: 16g | protein: 11g | carbs: 53g | fiber: 7g | sodium: 392mg

Quinoa Lentil Balls with Tomato Sauce

Prep time: 25 minutes | Cook time: 45 minutes | Serves 4

For the Meatballs:
- Olive oil cooking spray
- 2 large eggs, beaten
- 1 tablespoon no-salt-added tomato paste
- ½ teaspoon kosher salt
- ½ cup grated Parmesan cheese
- ½ onion, roughly chopped
- ¼ cup fresh parsley
- 1 garlic clove, peeled
- 1½ cups cooked lentils
- 1 cup cooked quinoa

For the Tomato Sauce:
- 1 tablespoon extra-virgin olive oil
- 1 onion, minced
- ½ teaspoon dried oregano
- ½ teaspoon kosher salt
- 2 garlic cloves, minced
- 1 (28-ounce / 794-g) can no-salt-added crushed tomatoes
- ½ teaspoon honey
- ¼ cup fresh basil, chopped

Make the Meatballs: 1. Preheat the oven to 400°F (205°C). Lightly grease a 12-cup muffin pan with olive oil cooking spray. 2. In a large bowl, whisk together the eggs, tomato paste, and salt until fully combined. Mix in the Parmesan cheese. 3. In a food processor, add the onion, parsley, and garlic. Process until minced. Add to the egg mixture and stir together. Add the lentils to the food processor and process until puréed into a thick paste. Add to the large bowl and mix together. Add the quinoa and mix well. 4. Form balls, slightly larger than a golf ball, with ¼ cup of the quinoa mixture. Place each ball in a muffin pan cup. Note: The mixture will be somewhat soft but should hold together. 5. Bake 25 to 30 minutes, until golden brown. Make the Tomato Sauce: 6. Heat the olive oil in a large saucepan over medium heat. Add the onion, oregano, and salt and sauté until light golden brown, about 5 minutes. Add the garlic and cook for 30 seconds. 7. Stir in the tomatoes and honey. Increase the heat to high and cook, stirring often, until simmering, then decrease the heat to medium-low and cook for 10 minutes. Remove from the heat and stir in the basil. Serve with the meatballs.

Per Serving:
3 meatballs: calories: 360 | fat: 10g | protein: 20g | carbs: 48g | fiber: 14g | sodium: 520mg

Hearty Mediterranean Farro Bowl

Prep time: 15 minutes | Cook time: 10 minutes | Serves 4 to 6

- ⅓ cup extra-virgin olive oil
- ½ cup chopped red bell pepper
- ⅓ cup chopped red onions
- 2 garlic cloves, minced
- 1 cup zucchini, cut in ½-inch slices
- ½ cup canned chickpeas, drained and rinsed
- ½ cup coarsely chopped artichokes
- 3 cups cooked farro
- Salt
- Freshly ground black pepper
- ¼ cup sliced olives, for serving (optional)
- ½ cup crumbled feta cheese, for serving (optional)
- 2 tablespoons fresh basil, chiffonade, for serving (optional)
- 3 tablespoons balsamic reduction, for serving (optional)

1. In a large sauté pan or skillet, heat the oil over medium heat and sauté the pepper, onions, and garlic for about 5 minutes, until tender. 2. Add the zucchini, chickpeas, and artichokes, then stir and continue to sauté vegetables, approximately 5 more minutes, until just soft. 3. Stir in the cooked farro, tossing to combine and cooking enough to heat through. Season with salt and pepper and remove from the heat. 4. Transfer the contents of the pan into the serving vessels or bowls. 5. Top with olives, feta, and basil (if using). Drizzle with balsamic reduction (if using) to finish.

Per Serving:
calories: 367 | fat: 20g | protein: 9g | carbs: 51g | fiber: 9g | sodium: 87mg

Pistachio Mint Pesto Pasta

Prep time: 10 minutes | Cook time: 10 minutes | Serves 4

- 8 ounces (227 g) whole-wheat pasta
- 1 cup fresh mint
- ½ cup fresh basil
- ⅓ cup unsalted pistachios, shelled
- 1 garlic clove, peeled
- ½ teaspoon kosher salt
- Juice of ½ lime
- ⅓ cup extra-virgin olive oil

1. Cook the pasta according to the package directions. Drain, reserving ½ cup of the pasta water, and set aside. 2. In a food processor, add the mint, basil, pistachios, garlic, salt, and lime juice. Process until the pistachios are coarsely ground. Add the olive oil in a slow, steady stream and process until incorporated. 3. In a large bowl, mix the pasta with the pistachio pesto; toss well to incorporate. If a thinner, more saucy consistency is desired, add some of the reserved pasta water and toss well.

Per Serving:
calories: 420 | fat: 3g | protein: 11g | carbs: 48g | fiber: 2g | sodium: 150mg

Sheet Pan Roasted Chickpeas and Vegetables with Harissa Yogurt

Prep time: 10 minutes | Cook time: 30 minutes | Serves 2

- 4 cups cauliflower florets (about ½ small head)
- 2 medium carrots, peeled, halved, and then sliced into quarters lengthwise
- 2 tablespoons olive oil, divided
- ½ teaspoon garlic powder, divided
- ½ teaspoon salt, divided
- 2 teaspoons za'atar spice mix, divided
- 1 (15-ounce / 425-g) can chickpeas, drained, rinsed, and patted dry
- ¾ cup plain Greek yogurt
- 1 teaspoon harissa spice paste

1. Preheat the oven to 400°F (205°C) and position the rack in the middle. Line a sheet pan with foil or parchment paper. 2. In a large bowl, toss the cauliflower and carrots with 1 tablespoon of olive oil, ¼ teaspoon of garlic powder, ¼ teaspoon of salt, and 1 teaspoon of za'atar. Mix well to coat. 3. Arrange the seasoned vegetables in a single layer on one half of the sheet pan. 4. In the same bowl, add the chickpeas and season with the remaining 1 tablespoon of olive oil, ¼ teaspoon of garlic powder, ¼ teaspoon of salt, and the remaining za'atar. Stir to combine. 5. Spread the chickpeas on the other half of the sheet pan. 6. Roast for 30 minutes or until the vegetables are tender and the chickpeas are starting to turn golden. Flip the vegetables halfway through and stir the chickpeas to ensure even cooking. 7. If you prefer crispy chickpeas, they may need a few more minutes. Remove the vegetables when they are done, and leave the chickpeas in the oven until they reach your desired level of crispiness. 8. While the vegetables are roasting, mix the yogurt and harissa in a small bowl. Taste and add more harissa if desired.

Per Serving:
calories: 467 | fat: 23g | protein: 18g | carbs: 54g | fiber: 15g | sodium: 632mg

Rustic Vegetable and Brown Rice Bowl

Prep time: 15 minutes | Cook time: 20 minutes | Serves 4

- Nonstick cooking spray
- 2 cups broccoli florets
- 2 cups cauliflower florets
- 1 (15-ounce / 425-g) can chickpeas, drained and rinsed
- 1 cup carrots sliced 1 inch thick
- 2 to 3 tablespoons extra-virgin olive oil, divided
- Salt
- Freshly ground black pepper
- 2 to 3 tablespoons sesame seeds, for garnish
- 2 cups cooked brown rice
- For the Dressing:
- 3 to 4 tablespoons tahini
- 2 tablespoons honey
- 1 lemon, juiced
- 1 garlic clove, minced
- Salt
- Freshly ground black pepper

1. Preheat the oven to 400°F (205°C) and spray two baking sheets with cooking spray. 2. Spread the broccoli and cauliflower on the first baking sheet, and the chickpeas and carrots on the second. Drizzle half of the oil over each sheet and season with salt and pepper. Place both sheets in the oven. 3. Roast the carrots and chickpeas for 10 minutes, leaving the carrots slightly crisp, and the broccoli and cauliflower for 20 minutes, until tender. Stir both sheets halfway through cooking. 4. For the dressing, combine the tahini, honey, lemon juice, and garlic in a small bowl. Season with salt and pepper, and set aside. 5. Divide the rice into individual bowls, layer with the roasted vegetables, and drizzle the dressing over the top.

Per Serving:
calories: 454 | fat: 18g | protein: 12g | carbs: 62g | fiber: 11g | sodium: 61mg

Vegetable Burgers

Prep time: 10 minutes | Cook time: 12 minutes | Serves 4

- 8 ounces (227 g) cremini mushrooms
- 2 large egg yolks
- ½ medium zucchini, trimmed and chopped
- ¼ cup peeled and chopped yellow onion
- 1 clove garlic, peeled and finely minced
- ½ teaspoon salt
- ¼ teaspoon ground black pepper

1. Add all ingredients into a food processor and pulse 20 times until finely chopped and well combined. 2. Divide the mixture into four equal portions and shape each into a burger patty. Place the patties in an ungreased air fryer basket. Set the air fryer to 375°F (191°C) and air fry for 12 minutes, turning the burgers halfway through. They should be browned and firm when done. 3. Remove the burgers from the air fryer and place them on a large plate. Let them cool for 5 minutes before serving.

Per Serving:
calories: 50 | fat: 3g | protein: 3g | carbs: 4g | fiber: 1g | sodium: 299mg

Spiced Crispy Mediterranean Chickpeas

Prep time: 15 minutes | Cook time: 15 minutes | Serves 4

- 1 tablespoon extra-virgin olive oil
- ½ medium onion, chopped
- 3 garlic cloves, chopped
- 2 teaspoons smoked paprika
- ¼ teaspoon ground cumin
- 4 cups halved cherry tomatoes
- 2 (15-ounce / 425-g) cans chickpeas, drained and rinsed
- ½ cup plain, unsweetened, full-fat Greek yogurt, for serving
- 1 cup crumbled feta, for serving

1. Preheat the oven to 425°F (220°C). 2. In an oven-safe sauté pan or skillet, heat the oil over medium heat and sauté the onion and garlic. Cook for about 5 minutes, until softened and fragrant. Stir in the paprika and cumin and cook for 2 minutes. Stir in the tomatoes and chickpeas. 3. Bring to a simmer for 5 to 10 minutes before placing in the oven. 4. Roast in oven for 25 to 30 minutes, until bubbling and thickened. To serve, top with Greek yogurt and feta.

Per Serving:
calories: 412 | fat: 15g | protein: 20g | carbs: 51g | fiber: 13g | sodium: 444mg

Chapter 9

Salads

Chapter 9 Salads

Tuscan Bread and Tomato Salad

Prep time: 10 minutes | Cook time: 20 minutes | Serves 6

- 4 ounces (113 g) sourdough bread, cut into 1' slices
- 3 tablespoons extra-virgin olive oil, divided
- 2 tablespoons red wine vinegar
- 2 cloves garlic, mashed to a paste
- 1 teaspoon finely chopped fresh oregano or ½ teaspoon dried
- 1 teaspoon fresh thyme leaves
- ½ teaspoon Dijon mustard
- Pinch of kosher salt
- Few grinds of ground black pepper
- 2 pounds (907 g) ripe tomatoes (mixed colors)
- 6 ounces (170 g) fresh mozzarella pearls
- 1 cucumber, cut into ½'-thick half-moons
- 1 small red onion, thinly sliced
- 1 cup baby arugula
- ½ cup torn fresh basil

1. Coat a grill rack or grill pan with olive oil and prepare to medium-high heat. 2. Brush 1 tablespoon of the oil all over the bread slices. Grill the bread on both sides until grill marks appear, about 2 minutes per side. Cut the bread into 1' cubes. 3. In a large bowl, whisk together the vinegar, garlic, oregano, thyme, mustard, salt, pepper, and the remaining 2 tablespoons oil until emulsified. 4. Add the bread, tomatoes, mozzarella, cucumber, onion, arugula, and basil. Toss to combine and let sit for 10 minutes to soak up the flavors.

Per Serving:
calories: 219 | fat: 12g | protein: 10g | carbs: 19g | fiber: 3g | sodium: 222mg

Dakos (Cretan Salad)

Prep time: 7 minutes | Cook time: 00 minutes | Serves 1

- 1 medium ripe tomato (any variety)
- 2 whole-grain crispbreads or rusks (or 1 slice toasted whole-grain, wheat, or barley bread)
- 1 tablespoon plus 1 teaspoon extra virgin olive oil
- Pinch of kosher salt
- 1½ ounces (43 g) crumbled feta
- 2 teaspoons capers, drained
- 2 Kalamata olives, pitted
- Pinch of dried oregano

1. Slice a thin round off the bottom of the tomato. Hold the tomato by the stem and grate it over a plate using the largest holes of a grater. Continue grating until only the skin remains, then discard the skin. Use a fine mesh strainer to drain the liquid from the grated tomato. 2. Arrange the crisps on a plate, placing them next to each other. Sprinkle a few drops of water over the crisps, then drizzle 1 tablespoon of olive oil on top. Layer the grated tomato evenly over the crisps, ensuring they are well-covered. 3. Sprinkle kosher salt over the tomato, then layer the crumbled feta cheese on top. Add the capers and olives, sprinkle with oregano, and drizzle with the remaining 1 teaspoon of olive oil. Serve immediately. (This dish is best enjoyed fresh.)

Per Serving:
calories: 346 | fat: 24g | protein: 12g | carbs: 21g | fiber: 4g | sodium: 626mg

Tangy Italian Cabbage Slaw

Prep time: 10 minutes | Cook time: 0 minutes | Serves 6

- 1 cup shredded green cabbage
- ½ cup shredded red cabbage
- ½ cup shredded carrot
- 1 small yellow bell pepper, seeded and cut into thin strips
- ¼ cup sliced red onion or shallot
- 2 tablespoons olive oil
- 3 tablespoons red wine vinegar
- ¼ teaspoon celery seeds

1. In a large bowl, mix all the ingredients. Refrigerate until chilled before serving.

Per Serving:
calories: 62 | fat: 4g | protein: 1g | carbs: 5g | fiber: 1g | sodium: 14mg

Spinach Arugula Nectarine Salad

Prep time: 15 minutes | Cook time: 0 minutes | Serves 6

- 1 (7-ounce / 198-g) package baby spinach and arugula blend
- 3 tablespoons fresh lemon juice
- 5 tablespoons olive oil
- ⅛ teaspoon salt
- Pinch (teaspoon) sugar
- Freshly ground black pepper, to taste
- ½ red onion, thinly sliced
- 3 ripe nectarines, pitted and sliced into wedges
- 1 cucumber, peeled, seeded, and sliced
- ½ cup crumbled feta cheese

1. Place the spinach-arugula blend in a large bowl. 2. In a small bowl, whisk together the lemon juice, olive oil, salt, and sugar and season with pepper. Taste and adjust the seasonings. 3. Add the dressing to the greens and toss. Top with the onion, nectarines, cucumber, and feta. 4. Serve immediately.

Per Serving:
1 cup: calories: 178 | fat: 14g | protein: 4g | carbs: 11g | fiber: 2g | sodium: 193mg

Citrusy Spinach Salad

Prep time: 10 minutes | Cook time: 5 minutes | Serves 4

- 1 large ripe tomato
- 1 medium red onion
- ½ teaspoon fresh lemon zest
- 3 tablespoons balsamic vinegar
- ¼ cup extra-virgin olive oil
- ½ teaspoon salt
- 1 pound (454 g) baby spinach, washed, stems removed

1. Cut the tomato into ¼-inch dice and slice the onion into thin, long strips. 2. In a small bowl, whisk the lemon zest, balsamic vinegar, olive oil, and salt until fully combined. 3. Add the spinach, diced tomatoes, and sliced onions to a large bowl. Drizzle the dressing over the salad and gently toss until everything is evenly coated.

Per Serving:
calories: 172 | fat: 14g | protein: 4g | carbs: 10g | fiber: 4g | sodium: 389mg

Tangy Four-Bean Salad

Prep time: 20 minutes | Cook time: 0 minutes | Serves 4

- ½ cup white beans, cooked
- ½ cup black-eyed peas, cooked
- ½ cup fava beans, cooked
- ½ cup lima beans, cooked
- 1 red bell pepper, diced
- 1 small bunch flat-leaf parsley, chopped
- 2 tablespoons olive oil
- 1 teaspoon ground cumin
- Juice of 1 lemon
- Sea salt and freshly ground pepper, to taste

1. You can cook the beans a day or two in advance to speed up the preparation of this dish. 2. Combine all ingredients in a large bowl and mix well. Season to taste. 3. Allow to sit for 30 minutes, so the flavors can come together before serving.

Per Serving:
calories: 189 | fat: 7g | protein: 8g | carbs: 24g | fiber: 7g | sodium: 14mg

Yellow and White Hearts of Palm Salad

Prep time: 10 minutes | Cook time: 0 minutes | Serves 4

- 2 (14-ounce / 397-g) cans hearts of palm, drained and cut into ½-inch-thick slices
- 1 avocado, cut into ½-inch pieces
- 1 cup halved yellow cherry tomatoes
- ½ small shallot, thinly sliced
- ¼ cup coarsely chopped flat-leaf parsley
- 2 tablespoons low-fat mayonnaise
- 2 tablespoons extra-virgin olive oil
- ¼ teaspoon salt
- ⅛ teaspoon freshly ground black pepper

1. In a large bowl, combine the hearts of palm, avocado, tomatoes, shallot, and parsley, tossing gently to mix. 2. In a small bowl, whisk together the mayonnaise, olive oil, salt, and pepper until smooth. Pour the dressing over the salad and stir gently until everything is evenly coated.

Per Serving:
calories: 192 | fat: 15g | protein: 5g | carbs: 14g | fiber: 7g | sodium: 841mg

Crunchy Pita and Veggie Salad

Prep time: 10 minutes | Cook time: 0 minutes | Serves 4

For the Dressing:
- ½ cup lemon juice
- ½ cup olive oil
- 1 small clove garlic, minced
- 1 teaspoon salt
- ½ teaspoon ground sumac
- ¼ teaspoon freshly ground black pepper

For the Salad:
- 2 cups shredded romaine lettuce
- 1 large or 2 small cucumbers, seeded and diced
- 2 medium tomatoes, diced
- ½ cup chopped fresh flat-leaf parsley leaves
- ¼ cup chopped fresh mint leaves
- 1 small green bell pepper, diced
- 1 bunch scallions, thinly sliced
- 2 whole-wheat pita bread rounds, toasted and broken into quarter-sized pieces
- Ground sumac for garnish

1. To make the dressing, whisk together the lemon juice, olive oil, garlic, salt, sumac, and pepper in a small bowl. 2. To make the salad, in a large bowl, combine the lettuce, cucumber, tomatoes, parsley, mint, bell pepper, scallions, and pita bread. Toss to combine. Add the dressing and toss again to coat well. 3. Serve immediately sprinkled with sumac.

Per Serving:
calories: 359 | fat: 27g | protein: 6g | carbs: 29g | fiber: 6g | sodium: 777mg

Tricolor Tomato Salad

Prep time: 10 minutes | Cook time: 0 minutes | Serves 3 to 4

- ¼ cup while balsamic vinegar
- 2 tablespoons Dijon mustard
- 1 tablespoon sugar
- ½ teaspoon freshly ground black pepper
- ½ teaspoon garlic salt
- ¼ cup extra-virgin olive oil
- 1½ cups chopped orange, yellow, and red tomatoes
- ½ cucumber, peeled and diced
- 1 small red onion, thinly sliced
- ¼ cup crumbled feta (optional)

1. In a small bowl, whisk the vinegar, mustard, sugar, pepper, and garlic salt. Next, slowly whisk in the olive oil. 2. In a large bowl, add the tomatoes, cucumber, and red onion. Add the dressing. Toss once or twice, and serve with feta crumbles (if using) on top.

Per Serving:
calories: 246 | fat: 18g | protein: 1g | carbs: 19g | fiber: 2g | sodium: 483mg

Roasted Broccoli Panzanella Salad

Prep time: 10 minutes | Cook time: 20 minutes | Serves: 4

- 1 pound (454 g) broccoli (about 3 medium stalks), trimmed, cut into 1-inch florets and ½-inch stem slices
- 3 tablespoons extra-virgin olive oil, divided
- 1 pint cherry or grape tomatoes (about 1½ cups)
- 1½ teaspoons honey, divided
- 3 cups cubed whole-grain crusty bread
- 1 tablespoon balsamic vinegar
- ½ teaspoon freshly ground black pepper
- ¼ teaspoon kosher or sea salt
- Grated Parmesan cheese (or other hard cheese) and chopped fresh oregano leaves, for serving (optional)

1. Place a large, rimmed baking sheet in the oven and preheat to 450°F (235°C) with the pan inside. 2. In a large bowl, toss the broccoli with 1 tablespoon of olive oil until well coated. 3. Carefully remove the hot baking sheet from the oven and spread the broccoli on it. Leave any remaining oil in the bowl. Add the tomatoes to the bowl and toss them in the leftover oil. Drizzle the tomatoes with 1 teaspoon of honey, then transfer them to the baking sheet alongside the broccoli. 4. Roast for 15 minutes, stirring once halfway through. Remove the baking sheet from the oven, add the bread cubes, and return to the oven for an additional 3 minutes. The broccoli should be slightly charred on the edges and fork-tender. 5. Transfer the roasted vegetables and bread to a serving plate or a large, shallow bowl. 6. In a small bowl, whisk together the remaining 2 tablespoons of olive oil, vinegar, the remaining ½ teaspoon of honey, salt, and pepper. Drizzle the dressing over the salad and toss gently to combine. Top with cheese and oregano if desired, then serve immediately.

Per Serving:
calories: 197 | fat: 12g | protein: 7g | carbs: 19g | fiber: 5g | sodium: 296mg

Fresh Caprese Salad with Mozzarella

Prep time: 10 minutes | Cook time: 0 minutes | Serves 6 to 8

For the Pesto:
- 2 cups (packed) fresh basil leaves, plus more for garnish
- ⅓ cup pine nuts
- 3 garlic cloves, minced
- ½ cup (about 2 ounces / 57 g) freshly grated Parmesan cheese
- ½ cup extra-virgin olive oil
- Salt
- Freshly ground black pepper

For the Salad:
- 4 to 6 large, ripe tomatoes, cut into thick slices
- 1 pound (454 g) fresh mozzarella, cut into thick slices
- 3 tablespoons balsamic vinegar
- Salt
- Freshly ground black pepper

1. To make the pesto, in a food processor combine the basil, pine nuts, and garlic and pulse several times to chop. Add the Parmesan cheese and pulse again until well combined. With the food processor running, add the olive oil in a slow, steady stream. Transfer to a small bowl, taste, and add salt and pepper as needed. Slice, quarter, or halve the tomatoes, based on your preferred salad presentation. 2. To make the salad, on a large serving platter arrange the tomato slices and cheese slices, stacking them like fallen dominoes. 3. Dollop the pesto decoratively on top of the tomato and cheese slices. (You will likely have extra pesto. Refrigerate the extra in a tightly sealed container and use within 3 days, or freeze it for up to 3 months.) 4. Drizzle the balsamic vinegar over the top, garnish with basil leaves, sprinkle with salt and pepper to taste, and serve immediately.

Per Serving:
calories: 398 | fat: 32g | protein: 23g | carbs: 8g | fiber: 1g | sodium: 474mg

Arugula and Fennel Salad with Fresh Basil

Prep time: 5 minutes | Cook time: 0 minutes | Serves 4

- 3 tablespoons olive oil
- 3 tablespoons lemon juice
- 1 teaspoon honey
- ½ teaspoon salt
- 1 medium bulb fennel, very thinly sliced
- 1 small cucumber, very thinly sliced
- 2 cups arugula
- ¼ cup toasted pine nuts
- ½ cup crumbled feta cheese
- ¼ cup julienned fresh basil leaves

1. In a medium bowl, whisk the olive oil, lemon juice, honey, and salt until fully combined. Add the fennel and cucumber, toss to coat thoroughly, and let the mixture marinate for about 10 minutes. 2. Place the arugula in a large salad bowl. Add the marinated fennel and cucumber, along with the dressing, and toss everything together until well mixed. Serve immediately, garnished with pine nuts, feta cheese, and fresh basil.

Per Serving:
calories: 237 | fat: 21g | protein: 6g | carbs: 11g | fiber: 3g | sodium: 537mg

Watermelon Burrata Salad

Prep time: 10 minutes | Cook time: 0 minutes | Serves 4

- 2 cups cubes or chunks watermelon
- 1½ cups small burrata cheese balls, cut into medium chunks
- 1 small red onion or 2 shallots, thinly sliced into half-moons
- ¼ cup olive oil
- ¼ cup balsamic vinegar
- 4 fresh basil leaves, sliced chiffonade-style (roll up leaves of basil, and slice into thin strips)
- 1 tablespoon lemon zest
- Salt and freshly ground black pepper, to taste

1. Combine all the ingredients in a large bowl and mix thoroughly. Chill in the refrigerator until cold, then serve.

Per Serving:
1 cup: calories: 224 | fat: 14g | protein: 14g | carbs: 12g | fiber: 1g | sodium: 560mg

Chapter 9 Salads

Zucchini and Creamy Ricotta Salad

Prep time: 5 minutes | Cook time: 2 minutes | Serves 1

- 2 teaspoons raw pine nuts
- 5 ounces (142 g) whole-milk ricotta cheese
- 1 tablespoon chopped fresh mint
- 1 teaspoon chopped fresh basil

For the Dressing:
- 1½ tablespoons extra virgin olive oil
- 1 tablespoon fresh lemon juice
- 1 tablespoon chopped fresh parsley
- Pinch of fine sea salt
- 1 medium zucchini, very thinly sliced horizontally with a mandoline slicer
- Pinch of freshly ground black pepper
- Pinch of fine sea salt
- Pinch of freshly ground black pepper

1. Add the pine nuts to a small pan placed over medium heat. Toast the nuts, turning them frequently, for 2 minutes or until golden. Set aside. 2. In a food processor, combine the ricotta, mint, basil, parsley, and a pinch of sea salt. Process until smooth and then set aside. 3. Make the dressing by combining the olive oil and lemon juice in a small bowl. Use a fork to stir rapidly until the mixture thickens, then add a pinch of sea salt and a pinch of black pepper. Stir again. 4. Place the sliced zucchini in a medium bowl. Add half of the dressing, and toss to coat the zucchini. 5. To serve, place half of the ricotta mixture in the center of a serving plate, then layer the zucchini in a circle, covering the cheese. Add the rest of the cheese in the center and on top of the zucchini, then sprinkle the toasted pine nuts over the top. Drizzle the remaining dressing over the top, and finish with a pinch of black pepper. Store covered in the refrigerator for up to 1 day.

Per Serving:
calories: 504 | fat: 43g | protein: 19g | carbs: 13g | fiber: 3g | sodium: 136mg

Red Pepper, Pomegranate, and Walnut Salad

Prep time: 5 minutes | Cook time: 40 minutes | Serves 4

- 2 red bell peppers, halved and seeded
- 1 teaspoon plus 2 tablespoons olive oil
- 4 teaspoons pomegranate molasses, divided
- 2 teaspoons fresh lemon juice
- ¼ teaspoon kosher salt
- ⅛ teaspoon ground black pepper
- 4 plum tomatoes, halved, seeded, and chopped
- ¼ cup walnut halves, chopped
- ¼ cup chopped fresh flat-leaf parsley

1. Preheat the oven to 450°F (235°C). 2. Brush the bell peppers with 1 teaspoon of olive oil, making sure they are coated evenly. Place them cut-side up on a large rimmed baking sheet. Drizzle 2 teaspoons of pomegranate molasses into the cavities of the peppers. Roast for 30 to 40 minutes, turning once, until the peppers are tender and the skins are charred. Remove from the oven, let them cool to room temperature, then peel off the skins and coarsely chop the peppers. 3. In a large bowl, whisk together the lemon juice, salt, black pepper, the remaining 2 tablespoons of olive oil, and the remaining 2 teaspoons of pomegranate molasses. Add the chopped bell peppers, tomatoes, walnuts, and parsley. Toss everything gently until well combined. Serve at room temperature.

Per Serving:
calories: 166 | fat: 13g | protein: 2g | carbs: 11g | fiber: 3g | sodium: 153mg

Herbed Greek Potato Salad

Prep time: 15 minutes | Cook time: 15 to 18 minutes | Serves 6

- 1½ pounds (680 g) small red or new potatoes
- ½ cup olive oil
- ⅓ cup red wine vinegar
- 1 teaspoon fresh Greek oregano
- 4 ounces (113 g) feta cheese, crumbled, if desired, or 4 ounces (113 g) grated Swiss cheese (for a less salty option)
- 1 green bell pepper, seeded and chopped (1¼ cups)
- 1 small red onion, halved and thinly sliced (generous 1 cup)
- ½ cup Kalamata olives, pitted and halved

1. Put the potatoes in a large saucepan and add water to cover. Bring the water to a boil and cook until tender, 15 to 18 minutes. Drain and set aside until cool enough to handle. 2. Meanwhile, in a large bowl, whisk together the olive oil, vinegar, and oregano. 3. When the potatoes are just cool enough to handle, cut them into 1-inch pieces and add them to the bowl with the dressing. Toss to combine. Add the cheese, bell pepper, onion, and olives and toss gently. Let stand for 30 minutes before serving.

Per Serving:
calories: 315 | fat: 23g | protein: 5g | carbs: 21g | fiber: 3g | sodium: 360mg

No-Mayo Florence Tuna Salad

Prep time: 10 minutes | Cook time: 0 minutes | Serves 4

- 4 cups spring mix greens
- 1 (15-ounce / 425-g) can cannellini beans, drained
- 2 (5-ounce / 142-g) cans water-packed, white albacore tuna, drained (I prefer Wild Planet brand)
- ⅔ cup crumbled feta cheese
- ½ cup thinly sliced sun-dried tomatoes
- ¼ cup sliced pitted kalamata olives
- ¼ cup thinly sliced scallions, both green and white parts
- 3 tablespoons extra-virgin olive oil
- ½ teaspoon dried cilantro
- 2 or 3 leaves thinly chopped fresh sweet basil
- 1 lime, zested and juiced
- Kosher salt
- Freshly ground black pepper

1. In a large bowl, toss together the greens, beans, tuna, feta, tomatoes, olives, scallions, olive oil, cilantro, basil, lime juice, and lime zest. Season with salt and pepper to taste. Mix well to combine all the flavors, and enjoy!

Per Serving:
1 cup: calories: 355 | fat: 19g | protein: 22g | carbs: 25g | fiber: 8g | sodium: 744mg

Turkish Shepherd'S Salad

Prep time: 15 minutes | Cook time: 0 minutes | Serves 6

- ¼ cup extra-virgin olive oil
- 2 tablespoons apple cider vinegar
- 2 tablespoons lemon juice
- ½ teaspoon kosher salt
- ¼ teaspoon ground black pepper
- 3 plum tomatoes, seeded and chopped
- 2 cucumbers, seeded and chopped
- 1 red bell pepper, seeded and chopped
- 1 green bell pepper, seeded and chopped
- 1 small red onion, chopped
- ⅓ cup pitted black olives (such as kalamata), halved
- ½ cup chopped fresh flat-leaf parsley
- ¼ cup chopped fresh mint
- ¼ cup chopped fresh dill
- 6 ounces (170 g) feta cheese, cubed

1. In a small bowl, whisk the oil, vinegar, lemon juice, salt, and black pepper until well blended. 2. In a large serving bowl, combine the tomatoes, cucumber, bell peppers, onion, olives, parsley, mint, and dill. Drizzle the dressing over the vegetables, toss gently to coat, and finish by sprinkling with the cheese.

Per Serving:
calories: 238 | fat: 20g | protein: 6g | carbs: 10g | fiber: 2g | sodium: 806mg

Rustic Tuscan Panzanella

Prep time: 1 hour 5 minutes | Cook time: 0 minutes | Serves 2

- 3 tablespoons white wine vinegar, divided
- 1 small red onion, thinly sliced
- 4 ounces (113 g) stale, dense bread, such as French baguette or Italian (Vienna-style)
- 1 large tomato (any variety), chopped into bite-sized pieces
- 1 large Persian (or mini) cucumber, sliced
- ¼ cup chopped fresh basil
- 2 tablespoons extra virgin olive oil, divided
- Pinch of kosher salt
- ⅛ teaspoon freshly ground black pepper

1. Add 2 tablespoons of the vinegar to a small bowl filled with water. Add the onion and then set aside. 2. In a medium bowl, combine the remaining tablespoon of vinegar and 2 cups of water. Add the bread to the bowl and soak for 2–3 minutes (depending on how hard the bread is) until the bread has softened on the outside but is not falling apart. Place the bread in a colander and gently squeeze out any excess water and then chop into bite-sized pieces. Arrange the bread pieces on a large plate. 3. Drain the onion and add it to plate with the bread. Add the tomato, cucumber, basil, 1 tablespoon of the olive oil, kosher salt, and black pepper. Toss the ingredients carefully, then cover and transfer to the refrigerator to chill for a minimum of 1 hour. 4. When ready to serve, drizzle the remaining 1 tablespoon of olive oil over the top of the salad and serve promptly. This salad can be stored in the refrigerator for up to 5 hours, but should be consumed on the same day it is prepared.

Per Serving:
calories: 325 | fat: 16g | protein: 7g | carbs: 38g | fiber: 4g | sodium: 358mg

Kale Tabbouleh with Lemon and Herbs

Prep time: 15 minutes | Cook time: 0 minutes | Serves 8

- 2 plum tomatoes, seeded and chopped
- ½ cup finely chopped fresh parsley
- 4 scallions (green onions), finely chopped
- 1 head kale, finely chopped (about 2 cups)
- 1 cup finely chopped fresh mint
- 1 small Persian cucumber, peeled, seeded, and diced
- 3 tablespoons extra-virgin olive oil
- 2 tablespoons fresh lemon juice
- Coarsely ground black pepper (optional)

1. Place the tomatoes in a strainer set over a bowl and set aside to drain as much liquid as possible. 2. In a large bowl, stir to combine the parsley, scallions, kale, and mint. 3. Shake any remaining liquid from the tomatoes and add them to the kale mixture. Add the cucumber. 4. Add the olive oil and lemon juice and toss to combine. Season with pepper, if desired.

Per Serving:
1 cup: calories: 65 | fat: 5g | protein: 1g | carbs: 4g | fiber: 1g | sodium: 21mg

Quinoa with Zucchini, Mint, and Pistachios

Prep time: 20 to 30 minutes | Cook time: 20 minutes | Serves 4

For the Quinoa:
- 1½ cups water
- 1 cup quinoa
- ¼ teaspoon kosher salt

For the Salad:
- 2 tablespoons extra-virgin olive oil
- 1 zucchini, thinly sliced into rounds
- 6 small radishes, sliced
- 1 shallot, julienned
- ¾ teaspoon kosher salt
- ¼ teaspoon freshly ground black pepper
- 2 garlic cloves, sliced
- Zest of 1 lemon
- 2 tablespoons lemon juice
- ¼ cup fresh mint, chopped
- ¼ cup fresh basil, chopped
- ¼ cup pistachios, shelled and toasted

1. Make the Quinoa: Bring the water, quinoa, and salt to a boil in a medium saucepan. Reduce to a simmer, cover, and cook for 10 to 12 minutes. Fluff with a fork. Make the Salad: 1. Heat the olive oil in a large skillet or sauté pan over medium-high heat. Add the zucchini, radishes, shallot, salt, and black pepper, and sauté for 7 to 8 minutes. Add the garlic and cook for 30 seconds to 1 minute longer. 2. In a large bowl, mix the lemon zest and lemon juice. Add the quinoa and stir to combine. Add the sautéed zucchini mixture and mix thoroughly. Finally, add the mint, basil, and pistachios, and gently toss everything together.

Per Serving:
calories: 220 | fat: 12g | protein: 6g | carbs: 25g | fiber: 5g | sodium: 295mg

Moroccan Tomato and Roasted Chile Salad

Prep time: 15 minutes | Cook time: 0 minutes | Serves 6

- 2 large green bell peppers
- 1 hot red chili Fresno or jalapeño pepper
- 4 large tomatoes, peeled, seeded, and diced
- 1 large cucumber, peeled and diced
- 1 small bunch flat-leaf parsley, chopped
- 4 tablespoons olive oil
- 1 teaspoon ground cumin
- Juice of 1 lemon
- Sea salt and freshly ground pepper, to taste

1. Set the broiler to high and let it preheat. Broil the peppers and chilies until their skins are charred and blistered. 2. Place the broiled peppers and chilies in a paper bag, seal it tightly, and let them cool. In the meantime, combine the remaining ingredients in a medium bowl and stir until well mixed. 3. After the peppers and chilies have cooled, take them out of the bag. Peel off the blackened skins, remove the seeds, and chop the peppers. Add the chopped peppers to the bowl with the salad mixture. 4. Sprinkle with sea salt and freshly ground black pepper to enhance the flavor. 5. Toss the ingredients thoroughly and let the salad rest for 15–20 minutes to allow the flavors to develop before serving.

Per Serving:
calories: 128 | fat: 10g | protein: 2g | carbs: 10g | fiber: 3g | sodium: 16mg

Flank Steak Spinach Salad

Prep time: 15 minutes | Cook time: 10 minutes | Serves 4

- 1 pound (454 g) flank steak
- 1 teaspoon extra-virgin olive oil
- 1 tablespoon garlic powder
- ½ teaspoon salt
- ½ teaspoon freshly ground black pepper
- 4 cups baby spinach leaves
- 10 cherry tomatoes, halved
- 10 cremini or white mushrooms, sliced
- 1 small red onion, thinly sliced
- ½ red bell pepper, thinly sliced

1. Preheat the broiler and line a baking sheet with aluminum foil. 2. Rub the top of the flank steak with olive oil, garlic powder, salt, and pepper. Let it rest for 10 minutes, then place it under the broiler. Broil for 5 minutes on each side for medium-rare doneness. Once cooked, let the steak rest on a cutting board for 10 minutes. 3. While the steak rests, combine the spinach, tomatoes, mushrooms, onion, and bell pepper in a large bowl, tossing thoroughly. 4. To serve, portion the salad onto 4 dinner plates. Slice the steak diagonally and place 4 to 5 slices over each salad. Serve with your favorite vinaigrette.

Per Serving:
calories: 211 | fat: 7g | protein: 28g | carbs: 9g | fiber: 2g | sodium: 382mg

Parsley Mint Lentil Salad

Prep time: 20 minutes | Cook time: 25 minutes | Serves 6

For the Lentils:
- 1 cup French lentils
- 1 garlic clove, smashed

For the Salad:
- 2 tablespoons extra-virgin olive oil
- 2 tablespoons red wine vinegar
- ½ teaspoon ground cumin
- ½ teaspoon kosher salt
- ¼ teaspoon freshly ground black pepper
- 1 dried bay leaf
- 2 celery stalks, diced small
- 1 bell pepper, diced small
- ½ red onion, diced small
- ¼ cup fresh parsley, chopped
- ¼ cup fresh mint, chopped

Make the Lentils: 1. Put the lentils, garlic, and bay leaf in a large saucepan. Cover with water by about 3 inches and bring to a boil. Reduce the heat, cover, and simmer until tender, 20 to 30 minutes. 2. Drain the lentils to remove any remaining water after cooking. Remove the garlic and bay leaf. Make the Salad: 3. In a large bowl, whisk together the olive oil, vinegar, cumin, salt, and black pepper. Add the celery, bell pepper, onion, parsley, and mint and toss to combine. 4. Add the lentils and mix well.

Per Serving:
calories: 200 | fat: 8g | protein: 10g | carbs: 26g | fiber: 10g | sodium: 165mg

Cauliflower Steak Salad

Prep time: 10 minutes | Cook time: 50 minutes | Serves 4

- 2 tablespoons olive oil, divided
- 2 large heads cauliflower (about 3 pounds / 1.4 kg each), trimmed of outer leaves
- 2 teaspoons za'atar
- 1½ teaspoons kosher salt, divided
- 1¼ teaspoons ground black pepper, divided
- 1 teaspoon ground cumin
- 2 large carrots
- 8 ounces (227 g) dandelion greens, tough stems removed
- ½ cup low-fat plain Greek yogurt
- 2 tablespoons tahini
- 2 tablespoons fresh lemon juice
- 1 tablespoon water
- 1 clove garlic, minced

1. Preheat the oven to 450°F(235°C). Brush a large baking sheet with some of the oil. 2. Place the cauliflower on a cutting board, stem side down. Cut down the middle, through the core and stem, and then cut two 1'-thick "steaks" from the middle. Repeat with the other cauliflower head. Set aside the remaining cauliflower for another use. Brush both sides of the steaks with the remaining oil and set on the baking sheet. 3. Combine the za'atar, 1 teaspoon of the salt, 1 teaspoon of the pepper, and the cumin. Sprinkle on the cauliflower steaks. Bake until the bottom is deeply golden, about 30 minutes. Flip and bake until tender, 10 to 15 minutes. 4. Meanwhile, set the carrots on a cutting board and use a vegetable peeler to peel them into ribbons. Add to a large bowl with the dandelion greens. 5. In a small bowl, combine the yogurt, tahini, lemon juice, water, garlic, the remaining ½ teaspoon salt, and the remaining ¼ teaspoon pepper. 6. Dab 3 tablespoons of the dressing onto the carrot-dandelion mix. With a spoon or your hands, massage the dressing into the mix for 5 minutes. 7. Remove the steaks from the oven and transfer to individual plates. Drizzle each with 2 tablespoons of the dressing and top with 1 cup of the salad.

Per Serving:
calories: 214 | fat: 12g | protein: 9g | carbs: 21g | fiber: 7g | sodium: 849mg

Roasted Golden Beet, Avocado, and Watercress Salad

Prep time: 15 minutes | Cook time: 1 hour | Serves 4

- 1 bunch (about 1½ pounds / 680 g) golden beets
- 1 tablespoon extra-virgin olive oil
- 1 tablespoon white wine vinegar
- ½ teaspoon kosher salt
- ¼ teaspoon freshly ground black pepper
- 1 bunch (about 4 ounces / 113 g) watercress
- 1 avocado, peeled, pitted, and diced
- ¼ cup crumbled feta cheese
- ¼ cup walnuts, toasted
- 1 tablespoon fresh chives, chopped

1. Preheat the oven to 425°F (220°C). Wash and trim the beets, leaving about an inch of the stem intact and the long tail if preferred. Wrap each beet individually in foil. Place the wrapped beets on a baking sheet and roast for 45 to 60 minutes, depending on their size. Check for doneness at 45 minutes by piercing with a fork; if the fork slides in easily, they are ready. 2. Take the beets out of the oven and let them cool. Under cold running water, rub off the skins. Cut the beets into bite-sized cubes or wedges. 3. In a large bowl, whisk together the olive oil, vinegar, salt, and black pepper. Add the watercress and roasted beets, tossing to coat evenly. Gently mix in the avocado, feta, walnuts, and chives. Serve immediately.

Per Serving:
calories: 235 | fat: 16g | protein: 6g | carbs: 21g | fiber: 8g | sodium: 365mg

Chapter 10
Snacks and Appetizers

Chapter 10 Snacks and Appetizers

Delicious Nut and Apple Salad

Prep time: 25 minutes | Cook time: 0 minutes | Serves 4

- 6 firm apples, such as Gala or Golden Delicious, peeled, cored, and sliced
- 1 tablespoon freshly squeezed lemon juice
- 2 kiwis, peeled and diced
- ½ cup sliced strawberries
- ½ cup packaged shredded coleslaw mix, without dressing
- ½ cup walnut halves
- ¼ cup slivered almonds
- ¼ cup balsamic vinegar
- ¼ cup extra-virgin olive oil
- 2 tablespoons sesame seeds, plus more for garnish (optional)
- ¼ teaspoon salt
- ¼ teaspoon freshly ground black pepper

1. In a medium bowl, toss the apple slices with the lemon juice to prevent browning. Add the kiwis, strawberries, coleslaw mix, walnuts, and almonds and toss well to mix. 2. In a small bowl, whisk together the balsamic vinegar, olive oil, and sesame seeds and season with salt and pepper. 3. Pour the dressing over the salad and toss to coat. 4. To serve, spoon into small bowls and top with additional sesame seeds if desired.

Per Serving:
calories: 371 | fat: 21g | protein: 3g | carbs: 49g | fiber: 9g | sodium: 155mg

Black-Eyed Pea "Caviar"

Prep time: 10 minutes | Cook time: 30 minutes | Makes 5 cups

- 1 cup dried black-eyed peas
- 4 cups water
- 1 pound (454 g) cooked corn kernels
- ½ medium red onion, peeled and diced
- ½ medium green bell pepper, seeded and diced
- 2 tablespoons minced pickled jalapeño pepper
- 1 medium tomato, diced
- 2 tablespoons chopped fresh cilantro
- ¼ cup red wine vinegar
- 2 tablespoons extra-virgin olive oil
- 1 teaspoon salt
- ½ teaspoon ground black pepper
- ½ teaspoon ground cumin

1. Add the black-eyed peas and water to the Instant Pot®. Secure the lid, set the steam release to Sealing, press the Manual button, and set the timer for 30 minutes. 2. When the timer goes off, allow the pressure to release naturally for about 25 minutes. Open the lid carefully, drain the peas, and transfer them to a large mixing bowl. Add the remaining ingredients and stir until well combined. Cover the bowl and refrigerate for at least 2 hours before serving.

Per Serving:
½ cup: calories: 28 | fat: 1g | protein: 1g | carbs: 4 | fiber: 1g | sodium: 51mg

Savory Mediterranean Popcorn

Prep time: 5 minutes | Cook time: 2 minutes | Serves 4 to 6

- 3 tablespoons extra-virgin olive oil
- ¼ teaspoon garlic powder
- ¼ teaspoon freshly ground black pepper
- ¼ teaspoon sea salt
- ⅛ teaspoon dried thyme
- ⅛ teaspoon dried oregano
- 12 cups plain popped popcorn

1. In a large sauté pan or skillet, heat the oil over medium heat until it begins to shimmer. Add the garlic powder, pepper, salt, thyme, and oregano, stirring for about 30 seconds until the mixture becomes fragrant. 2. In a large bowl, drizzle the seasoned oil over the popcorn and toss well to evenly coat. Serve immediately.

Per Serving:
calories: 183 | fat: 12g | protein: 3g | carbs: 19g | fiber: 4g | sodium: 146mg

Black Bean Corn Spread

Prep time: 10 minutes | Cook time: 10 minutes | Serves 4

- ½ (15 ounces / 425 g) can black beans, drained and rinsed
- ½ (15 ounces / 425 g) can corn, drained and rinsed
- ¼ cup chunky salsa
- 2 ounces (57 g) reduced-fat cream cheese, softened
- ¼ cup shredded reduced-fat Cheddar cheese
- ½ teaspoon ground cumin
- ½ teaspoon paprika
- Salt and freshly ground black pepper, to taste

1. Preheat the air fryer to 325°F (163°C). 2. In a medium bowl, mix together the black beans, corn, salsa, cream cheese, Cheddar cheese, cumin, and paprika. Season with salt and pepper and stir until well combined. 3. Spoon the mixture into a baking dish. 4. Place baking dish in the air fryer basket and bake until heated through, about 10 minutes. 5. Serve hot.

Per Serving:
calories: 119 | fat: 2g | protein: 8g | carbs: 19g | fiber: 6g | sodium: 469mg

Taste of the Mediterranean Fat Bombs

Prep time: 15 minutes | Cook time: 0 minutes | Makes 6 fat bombs

- 1 cup crumbled goat cheese
- 4 tablespoons jarred pesto
- 12 pitted Kalamata olives, finely chopped
- ½ cup finely chopped walnuts
- 1 tablespoon chopped fresh rosemary

1. In a medium bowl, mix the goat cheese, pesto, and olives thoroughly with a fork. Chill the mixture in the refrigerator for at least 4 hours to allow it to firm up. 2. Once hardened, use your hands to shape the mixture into 6 balls, each about ¾ inch in diameter. The mixture may be sticky, so work quickly. 3. In a small bowl, combine the walnuts and rosemary. Roll each goat cheese ball in the walnut mixture until fully coated. 4. Store the prepared fat bombs in the refrigerator for up to 1 week, or freeze them for up to 1 month.

Per Serving:
1 fat bomb: calories: 235 | fat: 22g | protein: 10g | carbs: 2g | fiber: 1g | sodium: 365mg

Savory Mackerel Goat Cheese Bites

Prep time: 10 minutes | Cook time: 0 minutes | Makes 10 fat bombs

- 2 smoked or cooked mackerel fillets, boneless, skin removed
- 4.4 ounces (125 g) soft goat's cheese
- 1 tablespoon fresh lemon juice
- 1 teaspoon Dijon or yellow mustard
- 1 small red onion, finely diced
- 2 tablespoons chopped fresh chives or herbs of choice
- ¾ cup pecans, crushed
- 10 leaves baby gem lettuce

1. In a food processor, combine the mackerel, goat's cheese, lemon juice, and mustard. Pulse until smooth. Transfer to a bowl, add the onion and herbs, and mix with a spoon. Refrigerate for 20 to 30 minutes, or until set. 2. Using a large spoon or an ice cream scoop, divide the mixture into 10 balls, about 40 g/1.4 ounces each. Roll each ball in the crushed pecans. Place each ball on a small lettuce leaf and serve. Keep the fat bombs refrigerated in a sealed container for up to 5 days.

Per Serving:
1 fat bomb: calories: 165 | fat: 12g | protein: 12g | carbs: 2g | fiber: 1g | sodium: 102mg

Stuffed Cucumber Cups

Prep time: 5 minutes | Cook time: 0 minutes | Serves 2

- 1 medium cucumber (about 8 ounces / 227 g, 8 to 9 inches long)
- ½ cup hummus (any flavor) or white bean dip
- 4 or 5 cherry tomatoes, sliced in half
- 2 tablespoons fresh basil, minced

1. Trim off about ½ inch from each end of the cucumber, then cut the cucumber into 1-inch thick pieces. 2. Using a paring knife or small spoon, carefully scoop out the seeds from the center of each piece to form a hollow cup, making sure not to go all the way through. 3. Fill each cucumber cup with roughly 1 tablespoon of hummus or bean dip. 4. Garnish each cup with a cherry tomato half and a sprinkle of freshly minced basil.

Per Serving:
calories: 135 | fat: 6g | protein: 6g | carbs: 16g | fiber: 5g | sodium: 242mg

Cheese-Stuffed Dates

Prep time: 15 minutes | Cook time: 10 minutes | Serves 12 to 15

- 1 cup pecans, shells removed
- 1 (8-ounce / 227-g)
- container mascarpone cheese
- 20 Medjool dates

1. Preheat the oven to 350°F(180ºC). Put the pecans on a baking sheet and bake for 5 to 6 minutes, until lightly toasted and aromatic. Take the pecans out of the oven and let cool for 5 minutes. 2. Once cooled, put the pecans in a food processor fitted with a chopping blade and chop until they resemble the texture of bulgur wheat or coarse sugar. 3. Reserve ¼ cup of ground pecans in a small bowl. Pour the remaining chopped pecans into a larger bowl and add the mascarpone cheese. 4. Using a spatula, mix the cheese with the pecans until evenly combined. 5. Spoon the cheese mixture into a piping bag. 6. Using a knife, cut one side of the date lengthwise, from the stem to the bottom. Gently open and remove the pit. 7. Using the piping bag, squeeze a generous amount of the cheese mixture into the date where the pit used to be. Close up the date and repeat with the remaining dates. 8. Dip any exposed cheese from the stuffed dates into the reserved chopped pecans to cover it up. 9. Set the dates on a serving plate; serve immediately or chill in the fridge until you are ready to serve.

Per Serving:
calories: 253 | fat: 4g | protein: 2g | carbs: 31g | fiber: 4g | sodium: 7mg

Roasted Chickpeas

Prep time: 5 minutes | Cook time: 15 minutes | Makes about 1 cup

- 1 (15-ounce / 425-g) can chickpeas, drained
- 2 teaspoons curry powder
- ¼ teaspoon salt
- 1 tablespoon olive oil

1. Thoroughly drain the chickpeas and spread them in a single layer on paper towels. Cover with another paper towel and gently press to absorb excess moisture, being careful not to crush them. 2. In a small bowl, combine the curry powder and salt. 3. Transfer the chickpeas to a medium bowl and sprinkle with the seasoning mixture. Stir until the chickpeas are evenly coated. 4. Drizzle with olive oil and mix again to distribute the oil thoroughly. 5. Place the chickpeas in the air fryer basket and cook at 390ºF (199ºC) for 15 minutes, shaking the basket halfway through to ensure even cooking. 6. Allow the chickpeas to cool completely, then store them in an airtight container.

Per Serving:
¼ cup: calories: 181 | fat: 6g | protein: 8g | carbs: 24g | fiber: 7g | sodium: 407mg

Shrimp Pirogues

Prep time: 15 minutes | Cook time: 4 to 5 minutes | Serves 8

- 12 ounces (340 g) small, peeled, and deveined raw shrimp
- 3 ounces (85 g) cream cheese, room temperature
- 2 tablespoons plain yogurt
- 1 teaspoon lemon juice
- 1 teaspoon dried dill weed, crushed
- Salt, to taste
- 4 small hothouse cucumbers, each approximately 6 inches long

1. Pour 4 tablespoons of water into the bottom of the air fryer drawer. 2. Arrange the shrimp in a single layer in the air fryer basket and cook at 390°F (199°C) for 4 to 5 minutes, just until the shrimp are done. Watch carefully to avoid overcooking, as shrimp can become tough quickly. 3. Chop the shrimp into small pieces, no larger than ½ inch, and refrigerate while you prepare the remaining ingredients. 4. In a bowl, use a fork to mash and whip the cream cheese until smooth. 5. Stir in the yogurt and beat until the mixture is creamy. Add the lemon juice, dill weed, and chopped shrimp, stirring until well combined. 6. Taste the mixture and add ¼ to ½ teaspoon of salt if needed. 7. Refrigerate the shrimp mixture until ready to serve. 8. When serving time approaches, wash and dry the cucumbers, then slice them lengthwise. Scoop out the seeds and let them drain upside down on paper towels for 10 minutes. 9. Before filling, pat the cucumber centers dry, then spoon the shrimp mixture into each cucumber half. Cut them crosswise into smaller sections and serve immediately.

Per Serving:
calories: 85 | fat: 4g | protein: 10g | carbs: 2g | fiber: 1g | sodium: 93mg

Manchego Cheese Crackers

Prep time: 15 minutes | Cook time: 15 minutes | Makes 40 crackers

- 4 tablespoons butter, at room temperature
- 1 cup finely shredded Manchego cheese
- 1 cup almond flour
- 1 teaspoon salt, divided
- ¼ teaspoon freshly ground black pepper
- 1 large egg

1. Using an electric mixer, cream together the butter and shredded cheese until well combined and smooth. 2. In a small bowl, combine the almond flour with ½ teaspoon salt and pepper. Slowly add the almond flour mixture to the cheese, mixing constantly until the dough just comes together to form a ball. 3. Transfer to a piece of parchment or plastic wrap and roll into a cylinder log about 1½ inches thick. Wrap tightly and refrigerate for at least 1 hour. 4. Preheat the oven to 350°F(180°C). Line two baking sheets with parchment paper or silicone baking mats. 5. To make the egg wash, in a small bowl, whisk together the egg and remaining ½ teaspoon salt. 6. Slice the refrigerated dough into small rounds, about ¼ inch thick, and place on the lined baking sheets. 7. Brush the tops of the crackers with egg wash and bake until the crackers are golden and crispy, 12 to 15 minutes. Remove from the oven and allow to cool on a wire rack. 8. Serve warm or, once fully cooled, store in an airtight container in the refrigerator for up to 1 week.

Per Serving:
2 crackers: calories: 73 | fat: 7g | protein: 3g | carbs: 1g | fiber: 1g | sodium: 154mg

Classic Hummus with Tahini

Prep time: 5 minutes | Cook time: 0 minutes | Makes about 2 cups

- 2 cups drained canned chickpeas, liquid reserved
- ½ cup tahini
- ¼ cup olive oil, plus more for garnish
- 2 cloves garlic, peeled, or to taste
- Juice of 1 lemon, plus more as needed
- 1 tablespoon ground cumin
- Salt
- Freshly ground black pepper
- 1 teaspoon paprika, for garnish
- 2 tablespoons chopped flat-leaf parsley, for garnish
- 4 whole-wheat pita bread or flatbread rounds, warmed

1. In a food processor, blend together the chickpeas, tahini, oil, garlic, lemon juice, and cumin. Season with salt and pepper, then process until smooth. While the food processor is running, gradually add the reserved chickpea liquid until the hummus reaches your desired consistency. 2. Transfer the hummus to a serving bowl, drizzle with olive oil, and garnish with paprika and chopped parsley. 3. Serve right away with warm pita bread or flatbread, or cover and store in the refrigerator for up to 2 days. Allow to come to room temperature before serving.

Per Serving:
¼ cup: calories: 309 | fat: 16g | protein: 9g | carbs: 36g | fiber: 7g | sodium: 341mg

Steamed Artichokes with Herbs and Olive Oil

Prep time: 10 minutes | Cook time: 10 minutes | Serves 6

- 3 medium artichokes with stems cut off
- 1 medium lemon, halved
- 1 cup water
- ¼ cup lemon juice
- ⅓ cup extra-virgin olive oil
- 1 clove garlic, peeled and minced
- ¼ teaspoon salt
- 1 teaspoon chopped fresh oregano
- 1 teaspoon chopped fresh rosemary
- 1 teaspoon chopped fresh flat-leaf parsley
- 1 teaspoon fresh thyme leaves

1. Rinse the artichokes thoroughly under running water, ensuring water flushes out any debris between the leaves. Cut off the top third of each artichoke and remove any tough outer leaves. Rub all cut surfaces with lemon to prevent browning. 2. Pour water and lemon juice into the Instant Pot® and place the steaming rack inside. Position the artichokes upside down on the rack. Close the lid, set the steam release to Sealing, press the Manual button, and set the timer for 10 minutes. When the timer beeps, allow the pressure to release naturally, which should take about 20 minutes. 3. Press the Cancel button, carefully open the lid, and transfer the artichokes to a cutting board. Slice them in half and arrange the halves on a serving platter. 4. In a small bowl, mix together the olive oil, garlic, salt, oregano, rosemary, parsley, and thyme. Drizzle half of this herb mixture over the artichokes, and serve the remaining mixture in a small bowl for dipping. Serve the artichokes warm.

Per Serving:
calories: 137 | fat: 13g | protein: 2g | carbs: 7g | fiber: 4g | sodium: 158mg

Mexican Potato Skins

Prep time: 10 minutes | Cook time: 55 minutes | Serves 6

- Olive oil
- 6 medium russet potatoes, scrubbed
- Salt and freshly ground black pepper, to taste
- 1 cup fat-free refried black beans
- 1 tablespoon taco seasoning
- ½ cup salsa
- ¾ cup reduced-fat shredded Cheddar cheese

1. Lightly spray the air fryer basket with olive oil. 2. Coat the potatoes with a light spray of oil, season with salt and pepper, and pierce them several times with a fork. 3. Arrange the potatoes in the air fryer basket and air fry at 400ºF (204ºC) for 30 to 40 minutes, or until they are fork-tender. Cooking time may vary based on potato size. While microwaving or baking in a standard oven is an option, the air fryer gives the potatoes a superior crispy skin. 4. As the potatoes cook, mix the beans and taco seasoning in a small bowl and set aside. 5. Once the potatoes are cool enough to handle, slice them in half lengthwise and scoop out most of the flesh, leaving about ¼ inch to maintain the structure of the skins. 6. Season the inside of each skin with salt and pepper, then lightly spray with oil. You may need to work in batches. 7. Place the potato skins, cut-side up, in the air fryer basket and cook until they are golden and crisp, about 8 to 10 minutes. 8. Remove the skins and fill each with ½ tablespoon of the seasoned black beans, followed by 2 teaspoons of salsa and 1 tablespoon of shredded Cheddar cheese. 9. Return the filled skins to the air fryer basket in a single layer and give them a light spray of oil. 10. Air fry for 2 to 3 minutes, or until the cheese melts and becomes bubbly.

Per Serving:
calories: 239 | fat: 2g | protein: 10g | carbs: 46g | fiber: 5g | sodium: 492mg

Baby Artichokes with Lemon-Garlic Aioli

Prep time: 5 minutes | Cook time: 50 minutes | Serves 10

Artichokes:
- 15 baby artichokes
- ½ lemon

Aioli:
- 1 egg
- 2 cloves garlic, chopped
- 1 tablespoon fresh lemon juice
- 3 cups olive oil
- Kosher salt, to taste
- ½ teaspoon Dijon mustard
- ½ cup olive oil
- Kosher salt and ground black pepper, to taste

1. Prepare the Artichokes: Wash and drain the artichokes. Using a paring knife, remove the tough outer leaves around the base and stalk, leaving the tender inner leaves intact. Peel the stalks carefully and trim them to leave about 2 inches below the base. Slice off the top ½ inch of each artichoke. Cut the artichokes in half and rub the cut sides with a lemon half to prevent browning. 2. Fry the Artichokes: In a medium saucepan over medium heat, warm the oil to 280ºF (138ºC) using a deep-fry thermometer. Working in batches, add the artichokes to the hot oil and fry until they become tender, about 15 minutes. Remove with a slotted spoon and drain on a paper towel-lined plate. Repeat until all artichoke halves are fried. 3. Crisp the Artichokes: Increase the oil temperature to 375ºF (190ºC). In batches, fry the pre-cooked artichokes until the edges are browned and crispy, about 1 minute. Transfer them to a paper towel-lined plate and season with salt. Repeat for the remaining artichokes. 4. Prepare the Aioli: In a blender, combine the egg, garlic, lemon juice, and mustard. Pulse until mixed. With the blender running, slowly drizzle in the oil a few drops at a time until the mixture thickens to a mayonnaise-like consistency, about 2 minutes. Transfer the aioli to a bowl and season with salt and pepper to taste. 5. Serve: Plate the warm, crispy artichokes and serve with the aioli on the side for dipping. Enjoy!

Per Serving:
calories: 236 | fat: 17g | protein: 6g | carbs: 21g | fiber: 10g | sodium: 283mg

Spicy White Bean Harissa Dip

Prep time: 10 minutes | Cook time: 1 hour | Makes 1½ cups

- 1 whole head of garlic
- ½ cup olive oil, divided
- 1 (15-ounce / 425-g) can cannellini beans, drained and rinsed
- 1 teaspoon salt
- 1 teaspoon harissa paste (or more to taste)

1. Preheat the oven to 350ºF (180ºC). 2. Cut about ½ inch off the top of a whole head of garlic and lightly wrap it in foil. Drizzle 1 to 2 teaspoons of olive oil over the top of the cut side. Place it in an oven-safe dish and roast it in the oven for about 1 hour or until the cloves are soft and tender. 3. Remove the garlic from the oven and let it cool. The garlic can be roasted up to 2 days ahead of time. 4. Remove the garlic cloves from their skin and place them in the bowl of a food processor along with the beans, salt, and harissa. Purée, drizzling in as much olive oil as needed until the beans are smooth. If the dip seems too stiff, add additional olive oil to loosen the dip. 5. Taste the dip and add additional salt, harissa, or oil as needed. 6. Store in the refrigerator for up to a week. 7. Portion out ¼ cup of dip and serve with a mixture of raw vegetables and mini pita breads.

Per Serving:
¼ cup: calories: 209 | fat: 17g | protein: 4g | carbs: 12g | fiber: 3g | sodium: 389mg

Stuffed Mushrooms

Prep time: 20 minutes | Cook time: 10 to 11 minutes | Serves 10

- ½ cup panko bread crumbs
- ½ teaspoon freshly ground black pepper
- ½ teaspoon onion powder
- ½ teaspoon cayenne pepper
- 1 (8-ounce / 227-g) package cream cheese, at room temperature
- 20 cremini or button mushrooms, stemmed
- 1 to 2 tablespoons oil

1. In a medium bowl, whisk the bread crumbs, black pepper, onion powder, and cayenne until blended. 2. Add the cream cheese and mix until well blended. Fill each mushroom top with 1 teaspoon of the cream cheese mixture 3. Preheat the air fryer to 360ºF (182ºC). Line the air fryer basket with a piece of parchment paper. 4. Place the mushrooms on the parchment and spritz with oil. 5. Cook for 5 minutes. Shake the basket and cook for 5 to 6 minutes more until the filling is firm and the mushrooms are soft.

Per Serving:
calories: 120 | fat: 9g | protein: 3g | carbs: 7g | fiber: 1g | sodium: 125mg

Crispy Kale Chips

Prep time: 5 minutes | Cook time: 30 minutes | Serves 2 to 4

- 2 large bunches kale, ribs removed
- 1 tablespoon extra-virgin olive oil
- 1 teaspoon salt

1. Arrange the oven racks in the upper and middle positions. Preheat the oven to 250°F(120ºC). Line 2 baking sheets with aluminum foil. 2. Rinse the kale and dry very well with a towel or salad spinner. Tear into large pieces. 3. Toss the kale with the olive oil and arrange in a single layer on the baking sheets. Sprinkle with salt. 4. Bake for 20 minutes and then use tongs to gently turn each leaf over. Bake until dry and crisp, another 10 to 15 minutes. Serve warm.

Per Serving:
calories: 141 | fat: 6g | protein: 10g | carbs: 20g | fiber: 8g | sodium: 668mg

Asian Five-Spice Wings

Prep time: 30 minutes | Cook time: 13 to 15 minutes | Serves 4

- 2 pounds (907 g) chicken wings
- ½ cup Asian-style salad dressing
- 2 tablespoons Chinese five-spice powder

1. Trim the wing tips and either discard them or freeze for making stock later. Cut the remaining wing sections in half at the joint. 2. Put the wing pieces into a large resealable plastic bag. Add the Asian dressing, seal the bag, and massage the wings until they are evenly coated with the marinade. Let them marinate in the refrigerator for at least one hour. 3. Take the wings out of the bag and drain any excess marinade. Arrange the wings in a single layer in the air fryer basket. 4. Air fry at 360ºF (182ºC) for 13 to 15 minutes, or until the juices run clear. Shake the basket or stir the wings halfway through cooking to ensure they brown evenly. 5. Once cooked, place the wings on a plate in a single layer. Sprinkle half of the Chinese five-spice powder on one side of the wings, flip them, and sprinkle the rest on the other side. Serve immediately.

Per Serving:
calories: 357 | fat: 12g | protein: 51g | carbs: 9g | fiber: 2g | sodium: 591mg

Smoky Eggplant Dip

Prep time: 10 minutes | Cook time: 1 hour | Makes about 4 cups

- 2 pounds (907 g, about 2 medium to large) eggplant
- 3 tablespoons tahini
- Zest of 1 lemon
- 2 tablespoons lemon juice
- ¾ teaspoon kosher salt
- ½ teaspoon ground sumac, plus more for sprinkling (optional)
- ⅓ cup fresh parsley, chopped
- 1 tablespoon extra-virgin olive oil

1. Preheat the oven to 350ºF (180ºC). Place the eggplants directly on the rack and bake for 60 minutes, or until the skin is wrinkly. 2. In a food processor add the tahini, lemon zest, lemon juice, salt, and sumac. Carefully cut open the baked eggplant and scoop the flesh into the food processor. Process until the ingredients are well blended. 3. Place in a serving dish and mix in the parsley. Drizzle with the olive oil and sprinkle with sumac, if desired.

Per Serving:
calories: 50 | fat: 16g | protein: 4g | carbs: 2g | fiber: 1g | sodium: 110mg

Pea and Arugula Crostini

Prep time: 10 minutes | Cook time: 15 minutes | Serves 6 to 8

- 1½ cups fresh or frozen peas
- 1 loaf crusty whole-wheat bread, cut into thin slices
- 3 tablespoons olive oil, divided
- 1 small garlic clove, finely mined or pressed
- Juice of ½ lemon
- ½ teaspoon salt
- ¼ teaspoon freshly ground black pepper
- 1 cup (packed) baby arugula
- ¼ cup thinly shaved Pecorino Romano

1. Preheat the oven to 350°F(180ºC). 2. Fill a small saucepan with about ½ inch of water. Bring to a boil over medium-high heat. Add the peas and cook for 3 to 5 minutes, until tender. Drain and rinse with cold water. 3. Arrange the bread slices on a large baking sheet and brush the tops with 2 tablespoons olive oil. Bake in the preheated oven for about 8 minutes, until golden brown. 4. Meanwhile, in a medium bowl, mash the peas gently with the back of a fork. They should be smashed but not mashed into a paste. Add the remaining 1 tablespoon olive oil, lemon juice, garlic, salt, and pepper and stir to mix. 5. Spoon the pea mixture onto the toasted bread slices and top with the arugula and cheese. Serve immediately.

Per Serving:
calories: 301 | fat: 13g | protein: 14g | carbs: 32g | fiber: 6g | sodium: 833mg

Pita Pizza with Olives and Feta

Prep time: 15 minutes | Cook time: 10 minutes | Serves 4

- 4 (6-inch) whole-wheat pitas
- 1 tablespoon extra-virgin olive oil
- ½ cup hummus
- ½ bell pepper, julienned
- ½ red onion, julienned
- ¼ cup olives, pitted and chopped
- ¼ cup crumbled feta cheese
- ¼ teaspoon red pepper flakes
- ¼ cup fresh herbs, chopped (mint, parsley, oregano, or a mix)

1. Preheat the broiler to low. Line a baking sheet with parchment paper or foil. 2. Place the pitas on the prepared baking sheet and brush both sides with the olive oil. Broil 1 to 2 minutes per side until starting to turn golden brown. 3. Spread 2 tablespoons hummus on each pita. Top the pitas with bell pepper, onion, olives, feta cheese, and red pepper flakes. Broil again until the cheese softens and starts to get golden brown, 4 to 6 minutes, being careful not to burn the pitas. 4. Remove from broiler and top with the herbs.

Per Serving:
calories: 185 | fat: 11g | protein: 5g | carbs: 17g | fiber: 3g | sodium: 285mg

Chapter 11
Pizzas, Wraps, and Sandwiches

Chapter 11 Pizzas, Wraps, and Sandwiches

Eggplant Parmesan Open Sandwich

Prep time: 10 minutes | Cook time: 10 minutes | Serves 2

- 1 small eggplant, sliced into ¼-inch rounds
- Pinch sea salt
- 2 tablespoons olive oil
- Sea salt and freshly ground pepper, to taste
- 2 slices whole-grain bread, thickly cut and toasted
- 1 cup marinara sauce (no added sugar)
- ¼ cup freshly grated, low-fat Parmesan cheese

1. Preheat broiler to high heat. 2. Salt both sides of the sliced eggplant, and let sit for 20 minutes to draw out the bitter juices. 3. Rinse the eggplant and pat dry with a paper towel. 4. Brush the eggplant with the olive oil, and season with sea salt and freshly ground pepper. 5. Lay the eggplant on a sheet pan, and broil until crisp, about 4 minutes. Flip over and crisp the other side. 6. Lay the toasted bread on a sheet pan. Spoon some marinara sauce on each slice of bread, and layer the eggplant on top. 7. Sprinkle half of the cheese on top of the eggplant and top with more marinara sauce. 8. Sprinkle with remaining cheese. 9. Put the sandwiches under the broiler until the cheese has melted, about 2 minutes. 10. Using a spatula, transfer the sandwiches to plates and serve.

Per Serving:
calories: 355 | fat: 19g | protein: 10g | carbs: 38g | fiber: 13g | sodium: 334mg

Classic Margherita Pizza

Prep time: 10 minutes | Cook time: 10 minutes | Serves 4

- All-purpose flour, for dusting
- 1 pound (454 g) premade pizza dough
- 1 (15-ounce / 425-g) can crushed San Marzano tomatoes, with their juices
- 2 garlic cloves
- 1 teaspoon Italian seasoning
- Pinch sea salt, plus more as needed
- 1½ teaspoons olive oil, for drizzling
- 10 slices mozzarella cheese
- 12 to 15 fresh basil leaves

1. Preheat the oven to 475ºF (245ºC). 2. On a lightly floured surface, roll out the pizza dough to a 12-inch circle and transfer it to a floured pizza pan or baking sheet. 3. In a food processor, blend the tomatoes with their juices, garlic, Italian seasoning, and salt until smooth. Taste and adjust the seasoning if needed. 4. Drizzle the olive oil over the rolled-out dough, then spread the tomato sauce evenly over the dough, leaving a 1-inch border around the edges. Scatter the mozzarella evenly across the sauce. 5. Bake for 8 to 10 minutes, until the crust is golden and fully cooked. Take the pizza out of the oven and let it rest for 1 to 2 minutes. Sprinkle the fresh basil on top just before serving.

Per Serving:
calories: 570 | fat: 21g | protein: 28g | carbs: 66g | fiber: 4g | sodium: 570mg

Mediterranean Eggplant Feta Sandwich

Prep time: 10 minutes | Cook time: 8 minutes | Serves 2

- 1 medium eggplant, sliced into ½-inch-thick slices
- 2 tablespoons olive oil
- Sea salt and freshly ground pepper, to taste
- 5 to 6 tablespoons hummus
- 4 slices whole-wheat bread, toasted
- 1 cup baby spinach leaves
- 2 ounces (57 g) feta cheese, softened

1. Preheat a gas or charcoal grill to medium-high heat. 2. Salt both sides of the sliced eggplant, and let sit for 20 minutes to draw out the bitter juices. 3. Rinse the eggplant and pat dry with a paper towel. 4. Brush the eggplant slices with olive oil and season with sea salt and freshly ground pepper. 5. Grill the eggplant until lightly charred on both sides but still slightly firm in the middle, about 3–4 minutes a side. 6. Spread the hummus on the bread and top with the spinach leaves, feta, and eggplant. Top with the other slice of bread and serve warm.

Per Serving:
calories: 516 | fat: 27g | protein: 14g | carbs: 59g | fiber: 14g | sodium: 597mg

Pesto Chicken Bites Pizza

Prep time: 5 minutes | Cook time: 10 minutes | Serves 4

- 2 cups shredded cooked chicken
- ¾ cup pesto
- 4 English muffins, split
- 2 cups shredded Mozzarella cheese

1. In a medium bowl, toss the chicken with the pesto. Place one-eighth of the chicken on each English muffin half. Top each English muffin with ¼ cup of the Mozzarella cheese. 2. Put four pizzas at a time in the air fryer and air fry at 350ºF (177ºC) for 5 minutes. Repeat this process with the other four pizzas.

Per Serving:
calories: 617 | fat: 36g | protein: 45g | carbs: 29g | fiber: 3g | sodium: 544mg

Turkish Pizza

Prep time: 20 minutes | Cook time: 10 minutes | Serves 4

- 4 ounces (113 g) ground lamb or 85% lean ground beef
- ¼ cup finely chopped green bell pepper
- ¼ cup chopped fresh parsley
- 1 small plum tomato, seeded and finely chopped
- 2 tablespoons finely chopped yellow onion
- 1 garlic clove, minced
- 2 teaspoons tomato paste
- ¼ teaspoon sweet paprika
- ¼ teaspoon ground cumin
- ⅛ to ¼ teaspoon red pepper flakes
- ⅛ teaspoon ground allspice
- ⅛ teaspoon kosher salt
- ⅛ teaspoon black pepper
- 4 (6-inch) flour tortillas

For Serving:
- Chopped fresh mint
- Extra-virgin olive oil
- Lemon wedges

1. In a medium bowl, combine the ground lamb, bell pepper, parsley, chopped tomato, onion, garlic, tomato paste, paprika, cumin, red pepper flakes, allspice, salt, and black pepper, mixing gently until everything is evenly blended. 2. Divide the mixture evenly across the tortillas, spreading it to cover the entire surface of each one. 3. Place one tortilla into the air fryer basket and set the temperature to 400ºF (204ºC). Air fry for 10 minutes, or until the meat is browned and the tortilla edges are crisp and golden. Transfer to a plate and repeat with the remaining tortillas. 4. Serve the lamb pizzas warm, garnished with fresh mint and a drizzle of extra-virgin olive oil, alongside lemon wedges for squeezing.

Per Serving:
calories: 172 | fat: 8g | protein: 8g | carbs: 18g | fiber: 2g | sodium: 318mg

Greek Veggie Wraps

Prep time: 15 minutes | Cook time: 0 minutes | Serves: 4

- 1½ cups seedless cucumber, peeled and chopped (about 1 large cucumber)
- 1 cup chopped tomato (about 1 large tomato)
- ½ cup finely chopped fresh mint
- 1 (2¼ ounces / 64 g) can sliced black olives (about ½ cup), drained
- ¼ cup diced red onion (about ¼ onion)
- 2 tablespoons extra-virgin olive oil
- 1 tablespoon red wine vinegar
- ¼ teaspoon freshly ground black pepper
- ¼ teaspoon kosher or sea salt
- ½ cup crumbled goat cheese (about 2 ounces / 57 g)
- 4 whole-wheat flatbread wraps or soft whole-wheat tortillas

1. In a large bowl, mix together the cucumber, tomato, mint, olives, and onion until well combined. 2. In a small bowl, whisk together the oil, vinegar, pepper, and salt. Drizzle the dressing over the salad, and mix gently. 3. With a knife, spread the goat cheese evenly over the four wraps. Spoon a quarter of the salad filling down the middle of each wrap. 4. Fold up each wrap: Start by folding up the bottom, then fold one side over and fold the other side over the top. Repeat with the remaining wraps and serve.

Per Serving:
calories: 217 | fat: 14g | protein: 7g | carbs: 17g | fiber: 3g | sodium: 329mg

Sautéed Mushroom, Onion, and Pecorino Romano Panini

Prep time: 10 minutes | Cook time: 20 minutes | Serves 4

- 3 tablespoons olive oil, divided
- 1 small onion, diced
- 10 ounces (283 g) button or cremini mushrooms, sliced
- ½ teaspoon salt
- ¼ teaspoon freshly ground black pepper
- 4 crusty Italian sandwich rolls
- 4 ounces (113 g) freshly grated Pecorino Romano

1. Warm 1 tablespoon of olive oil in a skillet over medium-high heat. Add the onion and sauté, stirring frequently, until it starts to soften, about 3 minutes. Stir in the mushrooms, sprinkle with salt and pepper, and continue cooking until the mushrooms are tender and their liquid has evaporated, approximately 7 minutes. 2. To prepare the panini, heat a skillet or grill pan over high heat and brush it with 1 tablespoon of olive oil. Brush the insides of the rolls with the remaining 1 tablespoon of olive oil. Evenly distribute the mushroom mixture across the rolls and top each with ¼ of the grated cheese. 3. Place the sandwiches in the heated pan, and press them down with a heavy pan, like a cast-iron skillet, to flatten. Cook for 3 to 4 minutes until the bottom is crispy and golden. Flip the sandwiches and cook for another 3 to 4 minutes on the other side until golden and crisp. Cut each panini in half and serve immediately while hot.

Per Serving:
calories: 348 | fat: 20g | protein: 14g | carbs: 30g | fiber: 2g | sodium: 506mg

Mediterranean Tuna Salad Sandwiches

Prep time: 10 minutes | Cook time: 5 minutes | Serves 2

- 1 can white tuna, packed in water or olive oil, drained
- 1 roasted red pepper, diced
- ½ small red onion, diced
- 10 low-salt olives, pitted and finely chopped
- ¼ cup plain Greek yogurt
- 1 tablespoon flat-leaf parsley, chopped
- Juice of 1 lemon
- Sea salt and freshly ground pepper, to taste
- 4 whole-grain pieces of bread

1. In a small bowl, thoroughly mix all the ingredients except the bread. 2. Season the mixture with sea salt and freshly ground pepper to your liking. Toast the bread or warm it in a pan until crisp. 3. Assemble the sandwich by spreading the mixture onto the bread and serve right away.

Per Serving:
calories: 307 | fat: 7g | protein: 30g | carbs: 31g | fiber: 5g | sodium: 564mg

Eggplant and Greek Veggie Wraps

Prep time: 10 minutes | Cook time: 20 minutes | Serves 4

- 15 small tomatoes, such as cherry or grape tomatoes, halved
- 10 pitted Kalamata olives, chopped
- 1 medium red onion, halved and thinly sliced
- ¾ cup crumbled feta cheese (about 4 ounces / 113 g)
- 2 tablespoons balsamic vinegar
- 1 tablespoon chopped fresh parsley
- 1 clove garlic, minced
- 2 tablespoons olive oil, plus 2 teaspoons, divided
- ¾ teaspoon salt, divided
- 1 medium cucumber, peeled, halved lengthwise, seeded, and diced
- 1 large eggplant, sliced ½-inch thick
- ½ teaspoon freshly ground black pepper
- 4 whole-wheat sandwich wraps or whole-wheat flour tortillas

1. In a medium bowl, toss together the tomatoes, olives, onion, cheese, vinegar, parsley, garlic, 2 teaspoons olive oil, and ¼ teaspoon of salt. Let sit at room temperature for 20 minutes. Add the cucumber, toss to combine, and let sit another 10 minutes. 2. While the salad is resting, grill the eggplant. Heat a grill or grill pan to high heat. Brush the remaining 2 tablespoons olive oil onto both sides of the eggplant slices. Grill for about 8 to 10 minutes per side, until grill marks appear and the eggplant is tender and cooked through. Transfer to a plate and season with the remaining ½ teaspoon of salt and the pepper. 3. Heat the wraps in a large, dry skillet over medium heat just until warm and soft, about 1 minute on each side. Place 2 or 3 eggplant slices down the center of each wrap. Spoon some of the salad mixture on top of the eggplant, using a slotted spoon so that any excess liquid is drained off. Fold in the sides of the wrap and roll up like a burrito. Serve immediately.

Per Serving:
calories: 233 | fat: 10g | protein: 8g | carbs: 29g | fiber: 7g | sodium: 707mg

Margherita Open-Face Sandwiches

Prep time: 10 minutes | Cook time: 5 minutes | Serves: 4

- 2 (6- to 7-inch) whole-wheat submarine or hoagie rolls, sliced open horizontally
- 1 tablespoon extra-virgin olive oil
- 1 garlic clove, halved
- 1 large ripe tomato, cut into 8 slices
- ¼ teaspoon dried oregano
- 1 cup fresh mozzarella (about 4 ounces / 113 g), patted dry and sliced
- ¼ cup lightly packed fresh basil leaves, torn into small pieces
- ¼ teaspoon freshly ground black pepper

1. Set the broiler to high, positioning the oven rack about 4 inches below the heating element. 2. Arrange the bread slices on a large rimmed baking sheet and broil for about 1 minute until they are lightly toasted. Take the sheet out of the oven. 3. Brush each toasted slice with olive oil and rub with a garlic half to infuse flavor. 4. Return the bread to the baking sheet, top each slice with tomato slices, sprinkle with oregano, and add a layer of cheese. 5. Broil again, setting a timer for 1½ minutes, but check at the 1-minute mark. Remove once the cheese has melted and the edges are just beginning to turn dark brown, which may take 1½ to 2 minutes. 6. Finish each sandwich with fresh basil and a dash of pepper before serving.

Per Serving:
calories: 176 | fat: 9g | protein: 10g | carbs: 14g | fiber: 2g | sodium: 119mg

BBQ Chicken Pita Pizza

Prep time: 5 minutes | Cook time: 5 to 7 minutes per batch | Makes 4 pizzas

- 1 cup barbecue sauce, divided
- 4 pita breads
- 2 cups shredded cooked chicken
- 2 cups shredded Mozzarella cheese
- ½ small red onion, thinly sliced
- 2 tablespoons finely chopped fresh cilantro

1. Measure ½ cup of the barbecue sauce in a small measuring cup. Spread 2 tablespoons of the barbecue sauce on each pita. 2. In a medium bowl, mix together the remaining ½ cup of barbecue sauce and chicken. Place ½ cup of the chicken on each pita. Top each pizza with ½ cup of the Mozzarella cheese. Sprinkle the tops of the pizzas with the red onion. 3. Place one pizza in the air fryer. Air fry at 400°F (204°C) for 5 to 7 minutes. Repeat this process with the remaining pizzas. 4. Top the pizzas with the cilantro.

Per Serving:
calories: 530 | fat: 19g | protein: 40g | carbs: 47g | fiber: 2g | sodium: 672mg

Flatbread Pizza with Roasted Cherry Tomatoes, Artichokes, and Feta

Prep time: 5 minutes | Cook time: 20 minutes | Serves 4

- 1½ pounds (680 g) cherry or grape tomatoes, halved
- 3 tablespoons olive oil, divided
- ½ teaspoon salt
- ½ teaspoon freshly ground black pepper
- 4 Middle Eastern–style flatbread rounds
- 1 can artichoke hearts, rinsed, well drained, and cut into thin wedges
- 8 ounces (227 g) crumbled feta cheese
- ¼ cup chopped fresh Greek oregano

1. Preheat the oven to 500°F (260°C). 2. In a medium bowl, combine the tomatoes with 1 tablespoon of olive oil, salt, and pepper. Spread them on a large baking sheet and roast until the skins blister and crack, about 10 to 12 minutes. Remove the tomatoes from the oven and lower the temperature to 450°F (235°C). 3. Arrange the flatbreads on a baking sheet (use two sheets if needed) and brush the tops with the remaining 2 tablespoons of olive oil. Evenly distribute the roasted tomatoes, artichoke hearts, and cheese over the flatbreads. 4. Bake for 8 to 10 minutes, until the edges are golden brown and the cheese is melted. Finish by sprinkling oregano over the top and serve immediately.

Per Serving:
calories: 436 | fat: 27g | protein: 16g | carbs: 34g | fiber: 6g | sodium: 649mg

Mexican-Style Pizza

Prep time: 10 minutes | Cook time: 7 to 9 minutes | Serves 4

- ¾ cup refried beans (from a 16-ounce / 454-g can)
- ½ cup salsa
- 10 frozen precooked beef meatballs, thawed and sliced
- 1 jalapeño pepper, sliced
- 4 whole-wheat pita breads
- 1 cup shredded pepper Jack cheese
- ½ cup shredded Colby cheese
- ⅓ cup sour cream

1. In a medium bowl, combine the refried beans, salsa, meatballs, and jalapeño pepper. 2. Preheat the air fryer for 3 to 4 minutes or until hot. 3. Top the pitas with the refried bean mixture and sprinkle with the cheeses. 4. Bake at 370°F (188°C) for 7 to 9 minutes or until the pizza is crisp and the cheese is melted and starts to brown. 5. Top each pizza with a dollop of sour cream and serve warm.

Per Serving:
calories: 484 | fat: 30g | protein: 24g | carbs: 32g | fiber: 7g | sodium: 612mg

Mediterranean-Pita Wraps

Prep time: 5 minutes | Cook time: 14 minutes | Serves 4

- 1 pound (454 g) mackerel fish fillets
- 2 tablespoons olive oil
- 1 tablespoon Mediterranean seasoning mix
- ½ teaspoon chili powder
- Sea salt and freshly ground black pepper, to taste
- 2 ounces (57 g) feta cheese, crumbled
- 4 tortillas

1. Coat the fish fillets with olive oil and arrange them in a lightly greased air fryer basket. 2. Air fry at 400°F (204°C) for 14 minutes, flipping the fillets midway through cooking. 3. Fill the pitas with the crispy fish and your preferred toppings, then serve immediately while warm.

Per Serving:
calories: 275 | fat: 13g | protein: 27g | carbs: 13g | fiber: 2g | sodium: 322mg

Chapter 12

Desserts

Chapter 12 Desserts

Toasted Almonds with Honey

Prep time: 15 minutes | Cook time: 5 minutes | Serves 4

- ½ cup raw almonds
- 3 tablespoons good-quality honey, plus more if desired

1. Fill a medium saucepan about three-quarters full with water and bring it to a rolling boil over high heat. Drop in the almonds and boil for 1 minute. Drain them using a fine-mesh sieve and rinse under cold water to stop the cooking process. To remove the skins, rub the almonds inside a clean kitchen towel, then spread them out on a paper towel to dry. 2. Return the saucepan to the stove, add the almonds and honey, and cook over medium heat, stirring frequently, until the almonds turn slightly golden, about 4 to 5 minutes. Take the pan off the heat and let the almonds cool completely for about 15 minutes before serving or storing.

Per Serving:
calories: 151 | fat: 9g | protein: 4g | carbs: 17g | fiber: 2g | sodium: 1mg

Grilled Stone Fruit

Prep time: 15 minutes | Cook time: 6 minutes | Serves 2

- 2 peaches, halved and pitted
- 2 plums, halved and pitted
- 3 apricots, halved and pitted
- ½ cup low-fat ricotta cheese
- 2 tablespoons honey

1. Preheat the grill to medium heat. 2. Lightly oil the grates or spray them with cooking spray. 3. Place the fruit on the grill, cut side down, and cook for 2 to 3 minutes on each side, until the fruit is tender and has light grill marks. 4. Serve the grilled fruit warm, topped with ricotta and a drizzle of honey.

Per Serving:
calories: 263 | fat: 6g | protein: 10g | carbs: 48g | fiber: 4g | sodium: 63mg

Espresso Chocolate Honey Ricotta

Prep time: 5 minutes | Cook time: 0 minutes | Serves 2

- 8 ounces (227 g) ricotta cheese
- 2 tablespoons honey
- 2 tablespoons espresso, chilled or room temperature
- 1 teaspoon dark chocolate chips or chocolate shavings

1. In a medium bowl, whip together the ricotta cheese and honey until light and smooth, 4 to 5 minutes. 2. Spoon the ricotta cheese-honey mixture evenly into 2 dessert bowls. Drizzle 1 tablespoon espresso into each dish and sprinkle with chocolate chips or shavings.

Per Serving:
calories: 235 | fat: 10g | protein: 13g | carbs: 25g | fiber: 0g | sodium: 115mg

Creamy Mascarpone and Fig Toasts

Prep time: 10 minutes | Cook time: 10 minutes | Serves 6 to 8

- 1 long French baguette
- 4 tablespoons (½ stick) salted butter, melted
- 1 (8-ounce / 227-g) tub mascarpone cheese
- 1 (12-ounce / 340-g) jar fig jam

1. Preheat the oven to 350°F(180°C). 2. Slice the bread into ¼-inch-thick slices. 3. Arrange the sliced bread on a baking sheet and brush each slice with the melted butter. 4. Put the baking sheet in the oven and toast the bread for 5 to 7 minutes, just until golden brown. 5. Let the bread cool slightly. Spread about a teaspoon or so of the mascarpone cheese on each piece of bread. 6. Top with a teaspoon or so of the jam. Serve immediately.

Per Serving:
calories: 445 | fat: 24g | protein: 3g | carbs: 48g | fiber: 5g | sodium: 314mg

Dark Chocolate Fruit and Nut Bark

Prep time: 15 minutes | Cook time: 0 minutes | Serves 2

- 2 tablespoons chopped nuts (almonds, pecans, walnuts, hazelnuts, pistachios, or any combination of those)
- 3 ounces (85 g) good-quality dark chocolate chips (about ⅔ cup)
- ¼ cup chopped dried fruit (apricots, blueberries, figs, prunes, or any combination of those)

1. Line a sheet pan with parchment paper. 2. Place the nuts in a skillet over medium-high heat and toast them for 60 seconds, or just until they're fragrant. 3. Place the chocolate in a microwave-safe glass bowl or measuring cup and microwave on high for 1 minute. Stir the chocolate and allow any unmelted chips to warm and melt. If necessary, heat for another 20 to 30 seconds, but keep a close eye on it to make sure it doesn't burn. 4. Pour the chocolate onto the sheet pan. Sprinkle the dried fruit and nuts over the chocolate evenly and gently pat in so they stick. 5. Transfer the sheet pan to the refrigerator for at least 1 hour to let the chocolate harden. 6. When solid, break into pieces. Store any leftover chocolate in the refrigerator or freezer.

Per Serving:
calories: 284 | fat: 16g | protein: 4g | carbs: 39g | fiber: 2g | sodium: 2mg

Crispy Apple Phyllo Tart

Prep time: 15 minutes | Cook time: 30 minutes | Serves 4

- 5 teaspoons extra virgin olive oil
- 2 teaspoons fresh lemon juice
- ¼ teaspoon ground cinnamon
- 1½ teaspoons granulated sugar, divided
- 1 large apple (any variety), peeled and cut into ⅛-inch thick slices
- 5 phyllo sheets, defrosted
- 1 teaspoon all-purpose flour
- 1½ teaspoons apricot jam

1. Preheat the oven to 350°F (180°C). Line a baking sheet with parchment paper, and pour the olive oil into a small dish. Set aside. 2. In a separate small bowl, combine the lemon juice, cinnamon, 1 teaspoon of the sugar, and the apple slices. Mix well to ensure the apple slices are coated in the seasonings. Set aside. 3. On a clean working surface, stack the phyllo sheets one on top of the other. Place a large bowl with an approximate diameter of 15 inches on top of the sheets, then draw a sharp knife around the edge of the bowl to cut out a circle through all 5 sheets. Discard the remaining phyllo. 4. Working quickly, place the first sheet on the lined baking sheet and then brush with the olive oil. Repeat the process by placing a second sheet on top of the first sheet, then brushing the second sheet with olive oil. Repeat until all the phyllo sheets are in a single stack. 5. Sprinkle the flour and remaining sugar over the top of the sheets. Arrange the apples in overlapping circles 4 inches from the edge of the phyllo. 6. Fold the edges of the phyllo in and then twist them all around the apple filling to form a crust edge. Brush the edge with the remaining olive oil. Bake for 30 minutes or until the crust is golden and the apples are browned on the edges. 7. While the tart is baking, heat the apricot jam in a small sauce pan over low heat until it's melted. 8. When the tart is done baking, brush the apples with the jam sauce. Slice the tart into 4 equal servings and serve warm. Store at room temperature, covered in plastic wrap, for up to 2 days.

Per Serving:
calories: 165 | fat: 7g | protein: 2g | carbs: 24g | fiber: 2g | sodium: 116mg

Apricot-Mint Yogurt Parfait

Prep time: 10 minutes | Cook time: 0 minutes | Serves 6

- 4 ounces (113 g) Neufchâtel or other light cream cheese
- 1 (7-ounce / 198-g) container 2% Greek yogurt
- ½ cup plus 2 tablespoons sugar
- 2 teaspoons vanilla extract
- 1 tablespoon fresh lemon juice
- 1 pound (454 g) apricots, rinsed, pitted, and cut into bite-size pieces
- 2 tablespoons finely chopped fresh mint, plus whole leaves for garnish if desired

1. In the bowl of a stand mixer fitted with the paddle attachment, beat the Neufchâtel cheese and yogurt on low speed until well combined, about 2 minutes, scraping down the bowl as needed. Add ½ cup of the sugar, the vanilla, and the lemon juice. Mix until smooth and free of lumps, 2 to 3 minutes; set aside. 2. In a medium bowl, combine the apricots, mint, and remaining 2 tablespoons sugar. Stir occasionally, waiting to serve until after the apricots have released their juices and have softened. 3. Line up six 6-to 8-ounce (170-to 227-g) glasses. Using an ice cream scoop, spoon 3 to 4 tablespoons of the cheesecake mixture evenly into the bottom of each glass. (Alternatively, transfer the cheesecake mixture to a piping bag or a small zip-top bag with one corner snipped and pipe the mixture into the glasses.) Add a layer of the same amount of apricots to each glass. Repeat so you have two layers of cheesecake mixture and two layers of the apricots, ending with the apricots.) Garnish with the mint, if desired, and serve.

Per Serving:
calories: 132 | fat: 2g | protein: 5g | carbs: 23g | fiber: 2g | sodium: 35mg

Blueberry Pomegranate Granita

Prep time: 5 minutes | Cook time: 10 minutes | Serves 2

- 1 cup frozen wild blueberries
- 1 cup pomegranate or pomegranate blueberry juice
- ¼ cup sugar
- ¼ cup water

1. In a saucepan, combine the frozen blueberries and pomegranate juice, then bring the mixture to a boil. Lower the heat and let it simmer for about 5 minutes, until the blueberries begin to soften and burst. 2. While the blueberry mixture simmers, mix the sugar and water in a small, microwave-safe bowl. Microwave for about 1 minute, or until it reaches a vigorous boil. Stir thoroughly until the sugar is fully dissolved, then set the syrup aside to cool slightly. 3. Pour the blueberry mixture and sugar syrup into a blender. Blend on high for about 1 minute, or until the mixture is smooth and the fruit is fully puréed. 4. Transfer the blended mixture to an 8-by-8-inch baking dish or a similarly sized bowl. Ensure the liquid is about ½ inch deep. Allow it to cool for 30 minutes before placing it in the freezer. 5. For the next 2 hours, use a fork to scrape the granita every 30 minutes to prevent it from freezing into a solid block. 6. After 2 hours, the granita is ready to serve. If not serving immediately, store it in a covered container in the freezer for later use.

Per Serving:
calories: 214 | fat: 0g | protein: 1g | carbs: 54g | fiber: 2g | sodium: 15mg

Tangy Strawberry-Pomegranate Sauce

Prep time: 10 minutes | Cook time: 5 minutes | Serves 6

- 3 tablespoons olive oil
- ¼ cup honey
- 2 pints strawberries, hulled and halved
- 1 to 2 tablespoons pomegranate molasses
- 2 tablespoons chopped fresh mint
- Greek yogurt, for serving

1. In a medium saucepan, heat the olive oil over medium heat. Add the strawberries; cook until their juices are released. Stir in the honey and cook for 1 to 2 minutes. Stir in the molasses and mint. Serve warm over Greek yogurt.

Per Serving:
calories: 189 | fat: 7g | protein: 4g | carbs: 24g | fiber: 3g | sodium: 12mg

Refreshing Red Grapefruit Granita

Prep time: 5 minutes | Cook time: 0 minutes | Serves 4 to 6

- 3 cups red grapefruit sections
- 1 cup freshly squeezed red grapefruit juice
- ¼ cup honey
- 1 tablespoon freshly squeezed lime juice
- Fresh basil leaves for garnish

1. Remove as much pith (white part) and membrane as possible from the grapefruit segments. 2. Combine all ingredients except the basil in a blender or food processor and pulse just until smooth. 3. Pour the mixture into a shallow glass baking dish and place in the freezer for 1 hour. Stir with a fork and freeze for another 30 minutes, then repeat. To serve, scoop into small dessert glasses and garnish with fresh basil leaves.

Per Serving:
calories: 94 | fat: 0g | protein: 1g | carbs: 24g | fiber: 1g | sodium: 1mg

Roasted Honey-Cinnamon Apples

Prep time: 15 minutes | Cook time: 20 minutes | Serves 2

- 1 teaspoon extra-virgin olive oil
- 4 firm apples, peeled, cored, and sliced
- ½ teaspoon salt
- 1½ teaspoons ground cinnamon, divided
- 2 tablespoons low-fat milk
- 2 tablespoons honey

1. Preheat the oven to 375°F (190°C) and lightly grease a small casserole dish with olive oil. 2. In a medium bowl, combine the apple slices, salt, and ½ teaspoon of cinnamon, tossing to coat evenly. Arrange the apples in the prepared dish and bake for 20 minutes, until tender. 3. While the apples are baking, warm the milk, honey, and remaining 1 teaspoon of cinnamon in a small saucepan over medium heat, stirring often. Once the mixture simmers, remove it from the heat and cover to keep warm. 4. When ready, divide the baked apple slices between two dessert plates and drizzle the warm sauce over the top. Serve immediately and enjoy.

Per Serving:
calories: 285 | fat: 3g | protein: 2g | carbs: 70g | fiber: 10g | sodium: 593mg

Whipped Greek Yogurt with Chocolate

Prep time: 10 minutes | Cook time: 0 minutes | Serves 4

- 4 cups plain full-fat Greek yogurt
- ½ cup heavy (whipping) cream
- 2 ounces (57 g) dark chocolate (at least 70% cacao), grated, for topping

1. In a stand mixer with the whisk attachment, or using a handheld mixer in a large bowl, beat the yogurt and cream together for approximately 5 minutes, until soft peaks form. 2. Spoon the whipped yogurt mixture evenly into serving bowls and sprinkle with grated chocolate on top. Serve immediately and enjoy!

Per Serving:
calories: 337 | fat: 25g | protein: 10g | carbs: 19g | fiber: 2g | sodium: 127mg

Nut Butter Cup Fat Bomb

Prep time: 5 minutes | Cook time: 0 minutes | Serves 8

- ½ cup crunchy almond butter (no sugar added)
- ½ cup light fruity extra-virgin olive oil
- ¼ cup ground flaxseed
- 2 tablespoons unsweetened cocoa powder
- 1 teaspoon vanilla extract
- 1 teaspoon ground cinnamon (optional)
- 1 to 2 teaspoons sugar-free sweetener of choice (optional)

1. In a mixing bowl, thoroughly blend the almond butter, olive oil, flaxseed, cocoa powder, vanilla extract, cinnamon (if using), and sweetener (if using) with a spatula until you achieve a thick, smooth consistency. 2. Distribute the mixture evenly into 8 mini muffin liners. Place them in the freezer and allow them to set until firm, for at least 12 hours. Keep them stored in the freezer to ensure they hold their shape.

Per Serving:
calories: 239 | fat: 24g | protein: 4g | carbs: 5g | fiber: 3g | sodium: 3mg

Spiced Apple Brown Betty

Prep time: 15 minutes | Cook time: 10 minutes | Serves 8

- 2 cups dried bread crumbs
- ½ cup sugar
- 1 teaspoon ground cinnamon
- 3 tablespoons lemon juice
- 1 tablespoon grated lemon zest
- 1 cup olive oil, divided
- 8 medium apples, peeled, cored, and diced
- 2 cups water

1. Combine crumbs, sugar, cinnamon, lemon juice, lemon zest, and ½ cup oil in a medium mixing bowl. Set aside. 2. In a greased oven-safe dish that will fit in your cooker loosely, add a thin layer of crumbs, then one diced apple. Continue filling the container with alternating layers of crumbs and apples until all ingredients are finished. Pour remaining ½ cup oil on top. 3. Add water to the Instant Pot® and place rack inside. Make a foil sling by folding a long piece of foil in half lengthwise and lower the uncovered container into the pot using the sling. 4. Close lid, set steam release to Sealing, press the Manual button, and set time to 10 minutes. When the timer beeps, let pressure release naturally, about 20 minutes. Press the Cancel button and open lid. 5. Using the sling, remove the baking dish from the pot and let stand for 5 minutes before serving.

Per Serving:
calories: 422 | fat: 27g | protein: 0g | carbs: 40g | fiber: 4g | sodium: 474mg

Ricotta Cheesecake

Prep time: 2 minutes | Cook time: 45 to 50 minutes | Serves 12

- 2 cups skim or fat-free ricotta cheese (one 15-ounce / 425-g container)
- 1¼ cups sugar
- 1 teaspoon vanilla extract
- 6 eggs
- Zest of 1 orange

1. Preheat the oven to 375°F (190°C) and lightly grease an 8-inch square baking pan with butter or nonstick spray. 2. In a medium bowl, mix the ricotta and sugar until combined. Add the eggs one at a time, stirring well after each addition. Mix in the vanilla extract and orange zest until fully incorporated. 3. Pour the ricotta mixture evenly into the greased baking pan. Bake for 45 to 50 minutes, or until the center is set and the edges are lightly golden. 4. Allow the dish to cool in the pan for about 20 minutes before serving. Enjoy warm.

Per Serving:

calories: 160 | fat: 5g | protein: 12g | carbs: 15g | fiber: 0g | sodium: 388mg

Light Baklava Rolls

Prep time: 2 minutes | Cook time: 1 hour 15 minutes | Serves 12

- 4 ounces (113 g) shelled walnuts
- 1¼ teaspoons ground cinnamon
- 1½ teaspoons granulated sugar

Syrup:

- ¼ cup water
- ½ cup granulated sugar
- 5 teaspoons unseasoned breadcrumbs
- 1 teaspoon extra virgin olive oil plus 2 tablespoons for brushing
- 6 phyllo sheets, defrosted
- 1½ tablespoons fresh lemon juice

1. Preheat the oven to 350°F (180°C). 2. Make the syrup by combining the water and sugar in a small pan placed over medium heat. Bring to a boil, cook for 2 minutes, then remove the pan from the heat. Add the lemon juice, and stir. Set aside to cool. 3. In a food processor, combine the walnuts, cinnamon, sugar, breadcrumbs, and 1 teaspoon of the olive oil. Pulse until combined and grainy, but not chunky. 4. Place 1 phyllo sheet on a clean working surface and brush with the olive oil. Place a second sheet on top of the first sheet, brush with olive oil, and repeat the process with a third sheet. Cut the sheets in half crosswise, and then cut each half into 3 pieces crosswise. 5. Scatter 1 tablespoon of the walnut mixture over the phyllo sheet. Start rolling the phyllo and filling into a log shape while simultaneously folding the sides in (like a burrito) until the filling is encased in each piece of dough. The rolls should be about 3½ inches long. Place the rolls one next to the other in a large baking pan, then repeat the process with the remaining 3 phyllo sheets. You should have a total of 12 rolls. 6. Lightly brush the rolls with the remaining olive oil. Place in the oven to bake for 30 minutes or until the rolls turn golden brown, then remove from the oven and promptly drizzle the cold syrup over the top. 7. Let the rolls sit for 20 minutes, then flip them over and let them sit for an additional 20 minutes. Turn them over once more and sprinkle any remining walnut mixture over the rolls before serving. Store uncovered at room temperature for 2 days (to retain crispiness) and then cover with plastic wrap and store at room temperature for up to 10 days.

Per Serving:

calories: 148 | fat: 9g | protein: 2g | carbs: 16g | fiber: 1g | sodium: 53mg

Olive Oil Greek Yogurt Brownies

Prep time: 5 minutes | Cook time: 25 minutes | Serves 9

- ¼ cup extra virgin olive oil
- ¾ cup granulated sugar
- 1 teaspoon pure vanilla extract
- 2 eggs
- ¼ cup 2% Greek yogurt
- ½ cup all-purpose flour
- ⅓ cup unsweetened cocoa powder
- ¼ teaspoon salt
- ¼ teaspoon baking powder
- ⅓ cup chopped walnuts

1. Preheat the oven to 350°F (180°C) and line a 9-inch square baking pan with wax paper. 2. In a small bowl, mix together the olive oil and sugar until fully combined. Stir in the vanilla extract and blend well. 3. In a separate small bowl, beat the eggs, then add them to the olive oil mixture, mixing thoroughly. Add the yogurt and stir until everything is smooth and incorporated. 4. In a medium bowl, whisk together the flour, cocoa powder, salt, and baking powder. Gradually add the olive oil mixture to the dry ingredients, stirring until just combined. Fold in the walnuts and mix until evenly distributed. 5. Pour the brownie batter into the prepared pan, using a spatula to spread it out evenly. Place it in the oven and bake for 25 minutes. 6. Let the brownies cool completely in the pan. Lift them out using the wax paper, remove the paper, and cut into 9 squares. Store the brownies in an airtight container at room temperature for up to 2 days.

Per Serving:

calories: 198 | fat: 10g | protein: 4g | carbs: 25g | fiber: 2g | sodium: 85mg

Dried Fruit Compote

Prep time: 15 minutes | Cook time: 8 minutes | Serves 6

- 8 ounces (227 g) dried apricots, quartered
- 8 ounces (227 g) dried peaches, quartered
- 1 cup golden raisins
- 1½ cups orange juice
- 1 cinnamon stick
- 4 whole cloves

1. Add all the ingredients to the Instant Pot®, stirring well to combine. Secure the lid, set the steam release to Sealing, press the Manual button, and set the timer for 3 minutes. Once the timer goes off, allow the pressure to release naturally for about 20 minutes. Press Cancel and carefully open the lid. 2. Take out and discard the cinnamon stick and cloves. Press the Sauté button and let the mixture simmer for 5–6 minutes. Serve warm, or let it cool before covering and refrigerating for up to a week.

Per Serving:

calories: 258 | fat: 0g | protein: 4g | carbs: 63g | fiber: 5g | sodium: 7mg

Stewed Cinnamon Plums with Greek Yogurt

Prep time: 5 minutes | Cook time: 3 minutes | Serves 6

- 3 cups dried plums
- 2 cups water
- 2 tablespoons sugar
- 2 cinnamon sticks
- 3 cups low-fat plain Greek yogurt

1. Add dried plums, water, sugar, and cinnamon to the Instant Pot®. Close lid, set steam release to Sealing, press the Manual button, and set time to 3 minutes. 2. When the timer beeps, quick-release the pressure until the float valve drops. Press the Cancel button and open lid. Remove and discard cinnamon sticks. Serve warm over Greek yogurt.

Per Serving:
calories: 301 | fat: 2g | protein: 14g | carbs: 61g | fiber: 4g | sodium: 50mg

Pomegranate-Wine Poached Pears

Prep time: 5 minutes | Cook time: 60 minutes | Serves 4

- 4 ripe, firm Bosc pears, peeled, left whole, and stems left intact
- 1½ cups pomegranate juice
- ½ cup pomegranate seeds (seeds from about ½ whole fruit)
- 1 cup sweet, white dessert wine, such as vin santo

1. Slice off a bit of the bottom of each pear to create a flat surface so that the pears can stand upright. If desired, use an apple corer to remove the cores of the fruit, working from the bottom. 2. Lay the pears in a large saucepan on their sides and pour the juice and wine over the top. Set over medium-high heat and bring to a simmer. Cover the pan, reduce the heat, and let the pears simmer, turning twice, for about 40 minutes, until the pears are tender. Transfer the pears to a shallow bowl, leaving the cooking liquid in the saucepan. 3. Turn the heat under the saucepan to high and bring the poaching liquid to a boil. Cook, stirring frequently, for about 15 to 20 minutes, until the liquid becomes thick and syrupy and is reduced to about ½ cup. 4. Spoon a bit of the syrup onto each of 4 serving plates and top each with a pear, sitting it upright. Drizzle a bit more of the sauce over the pears and garnish with the pomegranate seeds. Serve immediately.

Per Serving:
calories: 208 | fat: 0g | protein: 1g | carbs: 46g | fiber: 7g | sodium: 7mg

Chapter 13

Pasta

Chapter 13 Pasta

Spaghetti with Fresh Mint Pesto and Ricotta Salata

Prep time: 5 minutes | Cook time: 15 minutes | Serves 4

- 1 pound (454 g) spaghetti
- ¼ cup slivered almonds
- 2 cups packed fresh mint leaves, plus more for garnish
- 3 medium garlic cloves
- 1 tablespoon lemon juice
- and ½ teaspoon lemon zest from 1 lemon
- ⅓ cup olive oil
- ¼ teaspoon freshly ground black pepper
- ½ cup freshly grated ricotta salata, plus more for garnish

1. Bring a large pot of salted water to a rolling boil over high heat for the pasta. 2. In a food processor, combine the almonds, mint leaves, garlic, lemon juice, lemon zest, olive oil, and pepper. Pulse until a smooth paste forms, then add the cheese and pulse again until fully combined. 3. Once the water is boiling, add the pasta and cook it following the package directions. Drain the pasta well and return it to the pot. Add the pesto and toss until the pasta is evenly coated. Serve hot, garnished with extra mint leaves and cheese, if desired.

Per Serving:
calories: 619 | fat: 31g | protein: 21g | carbs: 70g | fiber: 4g | sodium: 113mg

Couscous with Tomatoes and Olives

Prep time: 5 minutes | Cook time: 3 minutes | Serves 4

- 1 tablespoon tomato paste
- 2 cups vegetable broth
- 1 cup couscous
- 1 cup halved cherry tomatoes
- ½ cup halved mixed olives
- ¼ cup minced fresh flat-leaf parsley
- 2 tablespoons minced fresh oregano
- 2 tablespoons minced fresh chives
- 1 tablespoon extra-virgin olive oil
- 1 tablespoon red wine vinegar
- ½ teaspoon ground black pepper

1. Add the tomato paste and broth to the Instant Pot®, stirring until the paste is fully dissolved. Mix in the couscous. Secure the lid, set the steam release to Sealing, press the Manual button, and set the cooking time to 3 minutes. When the timer finishes, let the pressure release naturally for 10 minutes, then quickly release any remaining pressure and carefully open the lid. 2. Use a fork to fluff the couscous. Add the tomatoes, olives, parsley, oregano, chives, olive oil, vinegar, and pepper, stirring until everything is well combined. Serve warm or let it cool slightly and enjoy at room temperature.

Per Serving:
calories: 232 | fat: 5g | protein: 7g | carbs: 37g | fiber: 2g | sodium: 513mg

Greek Lemon Egg Soup

Prep time: 10 minutes | Cook time: 3 minutes | Serves 6

- 6 cups chicken stock
- ½ cup orzo
- 1 tablespoon olive oil
- 12 ounces (340 g) cooked chicken breast, shredded
- ½ teaspoon salt
- ½ teaspoon ground black pepper
- ¼ cup lemon juice
- 2 large eggs
- 2 tablespoons chopped fresh dill
- 1 tablespoon chopped fresh flat-leaf parsley

1. Add stock, orzo, and olive oil to the Instant Pot®. Close lid, set steam release to Sealing, press the Manual button, and set time to 3 minutes. When the timer beeps, quick-release the pressure until the float valve drops. Open lid and stir in chicken, salt, and pepper. 2. In a medium bowl, combine lemon juice and eggs, then slowly whisk in hot cooking liquid from the pot, ¼ cup at a time, until 1 cup of liquid has been added. Immediately add egg mixture to soup and stir well. Let stand on the Keep Warm setting, stirring occasionally, for 10 minutes. Add dill and parsley. Serve immediately.

Per Serving:
calories: 193 | fat: 5g | protein: 21g | carbs: 15g | fiber: 1g | sodium: 552mg

Pesto Bowtie Pasta Salad

Prep time: 5 minutes | Cook time: 4 minutes | Serves 8

- 1 pound (454 g) whole-wheat bowtie pasta
- 4 cups water
- 1 tablespoon extra-virgin olive oil
- 2 cups halved cherry tomatoes
- 2 cups baby spinach
- ½ cup chopped fresh basil
- ½ cup prepared pesto
- ½ teaspoon ground black pepper
- ½ cup grated Parmesan cheese

1. Add pasta, water, and olive oil to the Instant Pot®. Close lid, set steam release to Sealing, press the Manual button, and set time to 4 minutes. 2. When the timer beeps, quick-release the pressure until the float valve drops and open lid. Drain off any excess liquid. Allow pasta to cool to room temperature, about 30 minutes. Stir in tomatoes, spinach, basil, pesto, pepper, and cheese. Refrigerate for 2 hours. Stir well before serving.

Per Serving:
calories: 360 | fat: 13g | protein: 16g | carbs: 44g | fiber: 7g | sodium: 372mg

Couscous with Pine Nuts, Currants, and Squash

Prep time: 10 minutes | Cook time: 50 minutes | Serves 4

- 3 tablespoons olive oil
- 1 medium onion, chopped
- 3 cloves garlic, minced
- 6 canned plum tomatoes, crushed
- 1 cinnamon stick
- 1 teaspoon ground coriander
- 1 teaspoon ground cumin
- 1 teaspoon salt, divided
- ¼ teaspoon red pepper flakes
- 1½ pounds (680 g) diced butternut squash
- 1 (16-ounce / 454-g) can chickpeas, drained and rinsed
- 4½ cups vegetable broth, divided
- 1-inch strip lemon zest
- ½ cup currants
- 4 cups (about 5 ounces / 142 g) chopped spinach
- Juice of ½ lemon
- ¼ teaspoon pepper
- 1 cup whole-wheat couscous
- ¼ cup toasted pine nuts

1. Heat the olive oil in a medium saucepan set over medium heat. Add the onion and cook, stirring frequently, until softened and lightly browned, about 10 minutes. Stir in the garlic, tomatoes, cinnamon stick, coriander, cumin, ½ teaspoon of the salt, and the red pepper flakes and cook for about 3 minutes more, until the tomatoes begin to break down. Stir in the butternut squash, chickpeas, 3 cups broth, lemon zest, and currants and bring to a simmer. 2. Partially cover the pan and cook for about 25 minutes, until the squash is tender. Add the spinach and cook, stirring, for 2 or 3 more minutes, until the spinach is wilted. Stir in the lemon juice. 3. While the vegetables are cooking, prepare the couscous. Combine the remaining 1½ cups broth, the remaining ½ teaspoon of salt, and the pepper in a small saucepan and bring to a boil. Remove the pan from the heat and stir in the couscous. Cover immediately and let sit for about 5 minutes, until the liquid has been fully absorbed. Fluff with a fork. 4. Spoon the couscous into serving bowls, top with the vegetable and chickpea mixture, and sprinkle some of the pine nuts over the top of each bowl. Serve immediately.

Per Serving:
calories: 549 | fat: 19g | protein: 16g | carbs: 84g | fiber: 14g | sodium: 774mg

Simple Pesto Pasta

Prep time: 10 minutes | Cook time: 10 minutes | Serves 4 to 6

- 1 pound (454 g) spaghetti
- 4 cups fresh basil leaves, stems removed
- 3 cloves garlic
- 1 teaspoon salt
- ½ teaspoon freshly ground black pepper
- ¼ cup lemon juice
- ½ cup pine nuts, toasted
- ½ cup grated Parmesan cheese
- 1 cup extra-virgin olive oil

1. Boil a large pot of salted water. Add the spaghetti and cook for 8 minutes until tender. 2. In a food processor with a chopping blade, combine the basil, garlic, salt, pepper, lemon juice, pine nuts, and Parmesan cheese, and purée until smooth. 3. With the processor running, slowly pour the olive oil through the top opening, processing until all the oil is fully incorporated. 4. Save ½ cup of pasta water before draining. Transfer the drained spaghetti to a bowl, add the pesto and reserved pasta water, and toss well to coat. Serve warm.

Per Serving:
calories: 1067 | fat: 72g | protein: 23g | carbs: 91g | fiber: 6g | sodium: 817mg

Fast Shrimp Fettuccine

Prep time: 10 minutes | Cook time: 10 minutes | Serves 4 to 6

- 8 ounces (227 g) fettuccine pasta
- ¼ cup extra-virgin olive oil
- 3 tablespoons garlic, minced
- 1 pound (454 g) large shrimp (21-25), peeled and deveined
- ⅓ cup lemon juice
- 1 tablespoon lemon zest
- ½ teaspoon salt
- ½ teaspoon freshly ground black pepper

1. Bring a large pot of salted water to a boil. Add the fettuccine and cook for 8 minutes. 2. In a large saucepan over medium heat, cook the olive oil and garlic for 1 minute. 3. Add the shrimp to the saucepan and cook for 3 minutes on each side. Remove the shrimp from the pan and set aside. 4. Add the lemon juice and lemon zest to the saucepan, along with the salt and pepper. 5. Reserve ½ cup of the pasta water and drain the pasta. 6. Add the pasta water to the saucepan with the lemon juice and zest and stir everything together. Add the pasta and toss together to evenly coat the pasta. Transfer the pasta to a serving dish and top with the cooked shrimp. Serve warm.

Per Serving:
calories: 615 | fat: 17g | protein: 33g | carbs: 89g | fiber: 4g | sodium: 407mg

Spicy Broccoli Pasta Salad

Prep time: 10 minutes | Cook time: 10 minutes | Serves 2

- 8 ounces (227 g) whole-wheat pasta
- 2 cups broccoli florets
- 1 cup carrots, peeled and shredded
- ¼ cup plain Greek yogurt
- Juice of 1 lemon
- 1 teaspoon red pepper flakes
- Sea salt and freshly ground pepper, to taste

1. Cook the pasta until al dente, following the package instructions, then drain it well. 2. Once the pasta has cooled, place it in a large bowl and add the veggies, yogurt, lemon juice, and red pepper flakes. Stir everything together until fully combined. 3. Taste the mixture and season with sea salt and freshly ground pepper to your preference. 4. Serve the dish either at room temperature or chilled, depending on your preference.

Per Serving:
calories: 473 | fat: 2g | protein: 22g | carbs: 101g | fiber: 13g | sodium: 101mg

Lamb Meatball Rigatoni

Prep time: 15 minutes | Cook time: 3 to 5 hours | Serves 4

- 8 ounces (227 g) dried rigatoni pasta
- 2 (28-ounce / 794-g) cans no-salt-added crushed tomatoes or no-salt-added diced tomatoes
- 1 small onion, diced
- 1 bell pepper, any color, seeded and diced
- 3 garlic cloves, minced, divided
- 1 pound (454 g) raw ground lamb
- 1 large egg
- 2 tablespoons bread crumbs
- 1 tablespoon dried parsley
- 1 teaspoon dried oregano
- 1 teaspoon sea salt
- ½ teaspoon freshly ground black pepper

1. In a slow cooker, combine the pasta, tomatoes, onion, bell pepper, and 1 clove of garlic. Stir to mix well. 2. In a large bowl, mix together the ground lamb, egg, bread crumbs, the remaining 2 garlic cloves, parsley, oregano, salt, and black pepper until all of the ingredients are evenly blended. Shape the meat mixture into 6 to 9 large meatballs. Nestle the meatballs into the pasta and tomato sauce. 3. Cover the cooker and cook for 3 to 5 hours on Low heat, or until the pasta is tender.

Per Serving:
calories: 653 | fat: 29g | protein: 32g | carbs: 69g | fiber: 10g | sodium: 847mg

Rotini with Red Wine Marinara

Prep time: 10 minutes | Cook time: 25 minutes | Serves 6

- 1 pound (454 g) rotini
- 4 cups water
- 1 tablespoon olive oil
- ½ medium yellow onion, peeled and diced
- 3 cloves garlic, peeled and minced
- 1 (15-ounce / 425-g) can crushed tomatoes
- ½ cup red wine
- 1 teaspoon sugar
- 2 tablespoons chopped fresh basil
- ½ teaspoon salt
- ¼ teaspoon ground black pepper

1. Pour the pasta and water into the Instant Pot®. Secure the lid, turn the steam release to Sealing, select the Manual function, and adjust the timer to 4 minutes. Once the timer finishes, quickly release the pressure by turning the steam release until the float valve drops. Open the lid, press Cancel, drain the pasta thoroughly, and set it aside. 2. Rinse out the pot, then place it back in the unit. Select the Sauté function and add the oil to heat. Stir in the onion and sauté for approximately 10 minutes until it starts to caramelize. Add the garlic and stir for 30 seconds. Mix in the tomatoes, red wine, and sugar, allowing it to simmer for 10 minutes. Finally, add the basil, salt, pepper, and the cooked pasta. Serve hot.

Per Serving:
calories: 320 | fat: 4g | protein: 10g | carbs: 59g | fiber: 4g | sodium: 215mg

Chapter 14
Staples, Sauces, Dips, and Dressings

Chapter 14 Staples, Sauces, Dips, and Dressings

Bagna Cauda

Prep time: 5 minutes | Cook time: 20 minutes | Serves 8 to 10

- ½ cup extra-virgin olive oil
- 4 tablespoons (½ stick) butter
- 8 anchovy fillets, very finely chopped
- 4 large garlic cloves, finely minced
- ½ teaspoon salt
- ½ teaspoon freshly ground black pepper

1. In a small saucepan, warm the olive oil and butter over medium-low heat until the butter has completely melted. 2. Add the anchovies and garlic, stirring until well combined. Season with salt and pepper, then lower the heat to a gentle simmer. Let the mixture cook for around 20 minutes, stirring occasionally, until the anchovies have broken down and the sauce is aromatic. 3. Serve warm as a drizzle over steamed vegetables, a dip for raw veggies or cooked artichokes, or as a salad dressing. Store any leftovers in an airtight container in the refrigerator for up to 2 weeks.

Per Serving:
calories: 145 | fat: 16g | protein: 1g | carbs: 0g | fiber: 0g | sodium: 235mg

Basic Brown-Onion Masala

Prep time: 20 minutes | Cook time: 6½ hours | Makes 4 cups

- 2 tablespoons rapeseed oil
- 6 onions, finely diced
- 8 garlic cloves, finely chopped
- 1¾ pounds (794 g) canned plum tomatoes
- 3-inch piece fresh ginger, grated
- 1 teaspoon salt
- 1½ teaspoons turmeric
- Handful fresh coriander stalks, finely chopped
- 3 fresh green chiles, finely chopped
- 1 teaspoon chili powder
- 1 teaspoon ground cumin seeds
- 1 cup hot water
- 2 teaspoons garam masala

1. Preheat the slow cooker to high (or use the sauté function if available). Pour in the oil and allow it to heat up. Add the onions and cook for a few minutes until they develop a rich brown color, which will create a deeply flavorful base. 2. Stir in the garlic and continue cooking on high for another 10 minutes. 3. Add the tomatoes, ginger, salt, turmeric, coriander stalks, chopped chiles, chili powder, cumin seeds, and water. 4. Cover the slow cooker and let it cook on low for 6 hours. 5. Remove the lid and give everything a good stir. Allow the masala to cook uncovered for an additional 30 minutes to thicken and reduce. 6. Once finished cooking, mix in the garam masala. 7. Use immediately, or portion it into small containers or freezer bags for storage. Defrost as needed.

Per Serving:
calories: 286 | fat: 8g | protein: 7g | carbs: 52g | fiber: 8g | sodium: 656mg

Refreshing Cucumber Yogurt Dip

Prep time: 5 minutes | Cook time: 0 minutes | Serves 2 to 3

- 1 cup plain, unsweetened, full-fat Greek yogurt
- ½ cup cucumber, peeled, seeded, and diced
- 1 tablespoon freshly squeezed lemon juice
- 1 tablespoon chopped fresh mint
- 1 small garlic clove, minced
- Salt and freshly ground black pepper, to taste

1. In a food processor, combine the yogurt, cucumber, lemon juice, mint, and garlic. Pulse several times to combine, leaving noticeable cucumber chunks. 2. Taste and season with salt and pepper.

Per Serving:
calories: 55 | fat: 3g | protein: 3g | carbs: 5g | fiber: 0g | sodium: 38mg

Tomatillo Salsa

Prep time: 5 minutes | Cook time: 15 minutes | Serves 4

- 12 tomatillos
- 2 fresh serrano chiles
- 1 tablespoon minced garlic
- 1 cup chopped fresh cilantro leaves
- 1 tablespoon vegetable oil
- 1 teaspoon kosher salt

1. Peel off and discard the papery husks from the tomatillos, then rinse them under warm running water to wash away the sticky residue. 2. Arrange the tomatillos and peppers in a baking pan and place it in the air fryer drawer. Set the air fryer to 350°F (177°C) and cook for 15 minutes. 3. Move the roasted tomatillos and peppers to a blender. Add the garlic, cilantro, vegetable oil, and salt, blending until the mixture is nearly smooth. (If you're not serving it right away, skip the salt and add it just before serving.) 4. Serve immediately or transfer to an airtight container and refrigerate for up to 10 days.

Per Serving:
calories: 68 | fat: 4g | protein: 1g | carbs: 7g | fiber: 2g | sodium: 585mg

Zesty Orange Mustard Dressing

Prep time: 5 minutes | Cook time: 0 minutes | Serves 2

- ¼ cup extra-virgin olive oil
- 2 tablespoons freshly squeezed orange juice
- 1 orange, zested
- 1 teaspoon garlic powder
- ¾ teaspoon za'atar seasoning
- ½ teaspoon salt
- ¼ teaspoon Dijon mustard
- Freshly ground black pepper, to taste

1. In a jar, combine the olive oil, orange juice and zest, garlic powder, za'atar, salt, and mustard. Season with pepper and shake vigorously until completely mixed.

Per Serving:
calories: 284 | fat: 27g | protein: 1g | carbs: 11g | fiber: 2g | sodium: 590mg

Herbed Italian Salad Dressing

Prep time: 5 minutes | Cook time: 0 minutes | Serves 12

- ¼ cup red wine vinegar
- ½ cup extra-virgin olive oil
- ¼ teaspoon salt
- ¼ teaspoon freshly ground black pepper
- 1 teaspoon dried Italian seasoning
- 1 teaspoon Dijon mustard
- 1 garlic clove, minced

1. In a small jar, combine the vinegar, olive oil, salt, pepper, Italian seasoning, mustard, and garlic. Close with a tight-fitting lid and shake vigorously for 1 minute. 2. Refrigerate for up to 1 week.

Per Serving:
calories: 82 | fat: 9g | protein: 0g | carbs: 0g | fiber: 0g | sodium: 71mg

Whole-Wheat Pizza Dough

Prep time: 10 minutes | Cook time: 10 to 12 minutes | Makes 1 pound (454 g)

- ¾ cup hot tap water
- ½ teaspoon honey
- 1 envelope quick-rising yeast, (2¼ teaspoons)
- 1 tablespoon olive oil, plus more for oiling the bowl
- 1 cup whole-wheat flour
- 1 cup all-purpose flour
- 1 teaspoon salt

1. Set the oven to preheat at 500°F (260°C). 2. In a non-reactive bowl, combine hot water and honey, stirring until mixed. Sprinkle the yeast over the top, stir gently, and let it sit for about 10 minutes until it becomes foamy. Add 1 tablespoon of olive oil and stir to incorporate. 3. In a food processor or stand mixer fitted with a dough hook, mix the whole-wheat flour, all-purpose flour, and salt. While the machine is running, slowly pour in the yeast-water mixture until the dough forms a soft, tacky ball. If the dough is too dry, add warm water 1 tablespoon at a time, mixing in between, until the consistency is right. If the dough is too wet, add all-purpose flour 1 tablespoon at a time until it feels correct. Knead by processing for an additional minute. 4. Lightly oil a large bowl with olive oil, place the dough inside, and turn it to coat with oil. Cover the bowl with a clean dish towel and let it rise in a warm spot for 1 hour, or until it has doubled in size. 5. Shape the dough into your desired form using your hands or a rolling pin. Add toppings of your choice, then bake in the preheated oven for 10 to 12 minutes until the crust is crisp and lightly browned.

Per Serving:
2 ounces / 57 g: calories: 135 | fat: 2g | protein: 5g | carbs: 24g | fiber: 3g | sodium: 294mg

Arugula and Walnut Pesto

Prep time: 5 minutes | Cook time: 0 minutes | Serves 8 to 10

- 6 cups packed arugula
- 1 cup chopped walnuts
- ½ cup shredded Parmesan cheese
- 2 garlic cloves, peeled
- ½ teaspoon salt
- 1 cup extra-virgin olive oil

1. In a food processor, combine the arugula, walnuts, cheese, and garlic and process until very finely chopped. Add the salt. With the processor running, stream in the olive oil until well blended. 2. If the mixture seems too thick, add warm water, 1 tablespoon at a time, until smooth and creamy. Store in a sealed container in the refrigerator.

Per Serving:
calories: 292 | fat: 31g | protein: 4g | carbs: 3g | fiber: 1g | sodium: 210mg

Aromatic Herbed Oil

Prep time: 5 minutes | Cook time: 0 minutes | Serves 2

- ½ cup extra-virgin olive oil
- 1 teaspoon dried basil
- 1 teaspoon dried parsley
- 1 teaspoon fresh rosemary leaves
- 2 teaspoons dried oregano
- ⅛ teaspoon salt

1. Pour the oil into a small bowl and stir in the basil, parsley, rosemary, oregano, and salt while whisking the oil with a fork.

Per Serving:
calories: 486 | fat: 54g | protein: 1g | carbs: 2g | fiber: 1g | sodium: 78mg

Textured Yogurt Crunch Dip

Prep time: 5 minutes | Cook time: 0 minutes | Serves 2 to 3

- 1 cup plain, unsweetened, full-fat Greek yogurt
- ½ cup cucumber, peeled, seeded, and diced
- 1 tablespoon freshly squeezed lemon juice
- 1 tablespoon chopped fresh mint
- 1 small garlic clove, minced
- Salt
- Freshly ground black pepper

1. In a food processor, combine the yogurt, cucumber, lemon juice, mint, and garlic. Pulse several times to combine, leaving noticeable cucumber chunks. 2. Taste and season with salt and pepper.

Per Serving:
calories: 128 | fat: 6g | protein: 11g | carbs: 7g | fiber: 0g | sodium: 47mg

Zesty Lemon Dill Dressing

Prep time: 2 minutes | Cook time: 0 minutes | Serves 6 to 8

- 4 large cloves of garlic
- ½ cup fresh dill
- ½ cup parsley
- 1 tablespoon sherry vinegar or red wine vinegar
- 1 tablespoon lemon juice
- ½ teaspoon salt
- ½ cup extra-virgin olive oil

1. Put the garlic, dill, parsley, lemon juice, vinegar, and salt into a blender. Add olive oil and process until smooth. Refrigerate covered up to a day. (I put it into a Ball jar with a tight-fitting top so I can shake it to use later but it stays emulsified.)

Per Serving:
calories: 165 | fat: 18g | protein: 0g | carbs: 1g | fiber: 0g | sodium: 198mg

Melitzanosalata (Greek Eggplant Dip)

Prep time: 10 minutes | Cook time: 3 minutes | Serves 8

- 1 cup water
- 1 large eggplant, peeled and chopped
- 1 clove garlic, peeled
- ½ teaspoon salt
- 1 tablespoon red wine vinegar
- ½ cup extra-virgin olive oil
- 2 tablespoons minced fresh parsley

1. Pour water into the Instant Pot®, place the rack inside, and set the steamer basket on top of the rack. 2. Add the eggplant to the steamer basket, secure the lid, and turn the steam release to Sealing. Press the Manual button and set the timer for 3 minutes. Once the timer beeps, quick-release the pressure by turning the steam release until the float valve drops. Press Cancel and open the lid. 3. Move the steamed eggplant to a food processor, then add garlic, salt, and vinegar. Pulse about 20 times until the mixture becomes smooth. 4. With the food processor running, slowly drizzle in the oil until fully blended. Mix in the parsley and serve at room temperature.

Per Serving:
calories: 134 | fat: 14g | protein: 1g | carbs: 3g | fiber: 2g | sodium: 149mg

Green Olive Tapenade with Harissa

Prep time: 5 minutes | Cook time: 0 minutes | Makes about 1½ cups

- 1 cup pitted, cured green olives
- 1 clove garlic, minced
- 1 tablespoon harissa
- 1 tablespoon lemon juice
- 1 tablespoon chopped fresh parsley
- ¼ cup olive oil, or more to taste

1. Finely chop the olives by hand or pulse them in a food processor until they form a coarse paste. 2. Mix in the garlic, harissa, lemon juice, parsley, and olive oil, stirring or pulsing until everything is thoroughly blended.

Per Serving:
¼ cup: calories: 215 | fat: 23g | protein: 1g | carbs: 5g | fiber: 2g | sodium: 453mg

Sherry Vinaigrette

Prep time: 5 minutes | Cook time: 0 minutes | Makes about ¾ cup

- ⅓ cup sherry vinegar
- 1 clove garlic
- 2 teaspoons dried oregano
- 1 teaspoon salt
- ½ teaspoon freshly ground black pepper
- ½ cup olive oil

1. In a food processor or blender, add the vinegar, garlic, oregano, salt, and pepper. Blend until the garlic is finely minced and everything is fully combined. While the machine is running, slowly drizzle in the olive oil in a steady stream until the mixture emulsifies. Use right away or cover and refrigerate for up to one week.

Per Serving:
calories: 74 | fat: 8g | protein: 0g | carbs: 0g | fiber: 0g | sodium: 194mg

Appendix 1: Measurement Conversion Chart

VOLUME EQUIVALENTS (DRY)

US STANDARD	METRIC (APPROXIMATE)
1/8 teaspoon	0.5 mL
1/4 teaspoon	1 mL
1/2 teaspoon	2 mL
3/4 teaspoon	4 mL
1 teaspoon	5 mL
1 tablespoon	15 mL
1/4 cup	59 mL
1/2 cup	118 mL
3/4 cup	177 mL
1 cup	235 mL
2 cups	475 mL
3 cups	700 mL
4 cups	1 L

WEIGHT EQUIVALENTS

US STANDARD	METRIC (APPROXIMATE)
1 ounce	28 g
2 ounces	57 g
5 ounces	142 g
10 ounces	284 g
15 ounces	425 g
16 ounces (1 pound)	455 g
1.5 pounds	680 g
2 pounds	907 g

VOLUME EQUIVALENTS (LIQUID)

US STANDARD	US STANDARD (OUNCES)	METRIC (APPROXIMATE)
2 tablespoons	1 fl.oz.	30 mL
1/4 cup	2 fl.oz.	60 mL
1/2 cup	4 fl.oz.	120 mL
1 cup	8 fl.oz.	240 mL
1 1/2 cup	12 fl.oz.	355 mL
2 cups or 1 pint	16 fl.oz.	475 mL
4 cups or 1 quart	32 fl.oz.	1 L
1 gallon	128 fl.oz.	4 L

TEMPERATURES EQUIVALENTS

FAHRENHEIT (F)	CELSIUS (C) (APPROXIMATE)
225 °F	107 °C
250 °F	120 °C
275 °F	135 °C
300 °F	150 °C
325 °F	160 °C
350 °F	180 °C
375 °F	190 °C
400 °F	205 °C
425 °F	220 °C
450 °F	235 °C
475 °F	245 °C
500 °F	260 °C

Appendix 2: The Dirty Dozen and Clean Fifteen

The Environmental Working Group (EWG) is a nonprofit, nonpartisan organization dedicated to protecting human health and the environment Its mission is to empower people to live healthier lives in a healthier environment. This organization publishes an annual list of the twelve kinds of produce, in sequence, that have the highest amount of pesticide residue-the Dirty Dozen-as well as a list of the fifteen kinds ofproduce that have the least amount of pesticide residue-the Clean Fifteen.

THE DIRTY DOZEN

- The 2016 Dirty Dozen includes the following produce. These are considered among the year's most important produce to buy organic:

Strawberries	Spinach
Apples	Tomatoes
Nectarines	Bell peppers
Peaches	Cherry tomatoes
Celery	Cucumbers
Grapes	Kale/collard greens
Cherries	Hot peppers

- The Dirty Dozen list contains two additional itemskale/collard greens and hot peppers-because they tend to contain trace levels of highly hazardous pesticides.

THE CLEAN FIFTEEN

- The least critical to buy organically are the Clean Fifteen list. The following are on the 2016 list:

Avocados	Papayas
Corn	Kiwi
Pineapples	Eggplant
Cabbage	Honeydew
Sweet peas	Grapefruit
Onions	Cantaloupe
Asparagus	Cauliflower
Mangos	

- Some of the sweet corn sold in the United States are made from genetically engineered (GE) seedstock. Buy organic varieties of these crops to avoid GE produce.

Appendix 3: Recipes Index

A

Amaranth Salad	20
Apple-Spiced Oatmeal	15
Apricot-Mint Yogurt Parfait	85
Aromatic Herbed Oil	95
Artichoke Quinoa Delight	22
Arugula and Fennel Salad with Fresh Basil	67
Arugula and Walnut Pesto	95
Asian Five-Spice Wings	77
Asian Glazed Meatballs	37

B

Baby Artichokes with Lemon-Garlic Aioli	76
Bagna Cauda	94
Baked Ricotta with Pears	17
Baked Tofu with Sun-Dried Tomatoes and Artichokes	59
Basic Brown-Onion Masala	94
BBQ Chicken Pita Pizza	81
Beef Brisket with Onions	39
Beet and Watercress Salad with Orange Zest	54
Black Bean Corn Spread	73
Black Chickpea Snack	25
Blackened Zucchini with Kimchi-Herb Sauce	50
Black-Eyed Pea "Caviar"	73
Blueberry Pomegranate Granita	85
Braised Fennel	52
Braised Greens with Olives and Walnuts	55
Braised Short Ribs with Fennel and Pickled Grapes	38
Braised Whole Cauliflower with North African Spices	51
Brown Rice Salad with Zucchini and Tomatoes	25

C

Caesar Whole Cauliflower	53
Caprese Eggplant Stacks	59
Cauliflower Steak Salad	71
Cauliflower with Lemon Tahini Sauce	50
Cheese-Stuffed Dates	74
Chili Tilapia	47
Chili-Spiced Trout with Sautéed Salad	45
Citrusy Spinach Salad	66
Classic Hummus with Tahini	75
Classic Margherita Pizza	79
Coconut Chicken Bites	27
Couscous with Pine Nuts, Currants, and Squash	91
Couscous with Tomatoes and Olives	90
Creamy Farrotto with Asparagus and Mushrooms	60
Creamy Lima Bean Soup	24
Creamy Mascarpone and Fig Toasts	84
Crispy Apple Phyllo Tart	85
Crispy Eggplant Rounds	60
Crispy Flounder Fillets	41
Crispy Kale Chips	77
Crispy Mediterranean Pan-Style Pizza	61
Crunchy Almond-Coated Salmon	47
Crunchy Pita and Veggie Salad	66
Crunchy Stone Age Loaf	57

D

Dakos (Cretan Salad)	65
Dark Chocolate Fruit and Nut Bark	84
Date and Pistachio Rice Pilaf	24
Delicious Nut and Apple Salad	73
Delicious Polenta with Chard and Eggs	14
Dried Fruit Compote	87
Duck with Fennel Root	27

E

Egg and Pepper Pita	13
Egg Baked in Avocado	11
Eggplant and Greek Veggie Wraps	81
Eggplant Caponata	54
Eggplant Parmesan Open Sandwich	79
Eggplants Stuffed with Walnuts and Feta	61
Endive Boats with Quinoa Salad	22
Espresso Chocolate Honey Ricotta	84

F

Fast Shrimp Fettuccine	91
Fava Beans with Ground Meat	20

Feta and Spinach Stuffed Chicken Breasts	29
Filipino Crispy Pork Belly	37
Flank Steak and Blue Cheese Wraps	35
Flank Steak Spinach Salad	70
Flatbread Pizza with Roasted Cherry Tomatoes, Artichokes, and Feta	81
Flavorful Herb-Marinated Chicken	30
Flavorful Scallops with Dandelion Greens	43
Flavorful Venetian Pasta with Beans	21
Fragrant Rice Pilaf with Dill	52
Fresh Caprese Salad with Mozzarella	67

G

Garbanzo and Pita No-Bake Casserole	23
Garlic Basil Prawns with Tomatoes	41
Garlicky Broiled Sardines	46
Garlicky Swiss Chard and White Bean Medley	53
Garlic-Lemon Chicken and Potatoes	27
Garlic-Mint Zucchini Bites	50
Giant Beans with Tomato and Parsley	24
Glazed Carrots	54
Gluten-Free Granola Cereal	12
Golden Apple Tahini Toast	15
Gorgonzola Sweet Potato Burgers	53
Grape Chicken Panzanella	32
Greek Breakfast Power Bowl	12
Greek Lemon Egg Soup	90
Greek Meatball Soup	36
Greek Stuffed Tenderloin	34
Greek Veggie Wraps	80
Greek Yogurt Parfait	11
Greek-Style Roast Turkey Breast	29
Green Olive Tapenade with Harissa	96
Grilled Stone Fruit	84

H

Hearty Almond Date Oatmeal	14
Hearty Beef, Mushroom, and Green Bean Broth	37
Hearty Mediterranean Farro Bowl	62
Herb and Cheese Filled Portobellos	60
Herb and Cheese Fritters	13
Herb Halibut in Parchment	45
Herb-Crusted River Trout	42
Herb-Crusted Tilapia Fingers	47
Herbed Greek Potato Salad	68
Herbed Italian Salad Dressing	95
Herbed Polenta	23

Herb-Infused Fasolakia	55
Herb-Infused Trout with Parsley	46

I

Indian Eggplant Bharta	50
Italian Fish	42
Italian Tuna Roast	44

K

Kagianas	16
Kale and Chickpea Delight	19
Kale Tabbouleh with Lemon and Herbs	69
Kale with Lemon-Tahini Dressing	54

L

Lamb Chops with Fresh Zucchini Slaw	35
Lamb Meatball Rigatoni	92
Lemon Chicken	27
Lemon Mahi-Mahi	45
Lemon Mushroom Chicken Piccata	32
Lemon-Infused Chicken with Asparagus	31
Lentil and Rice Pilaf	19
Lentil and Spinach Medley	22
Light Baklava Rolls	87
Lightened-Up Eggplant Parmigiana	55
Linguine with Roasted Brussels Sprouts	60

M

Manchego Cheese Crackers	75
Margherita Open-Face Sandwiches	81
Mediterranean Breakfast Pita Sandwiches	12
Mediterranean Bulgur Mix	23
Mediterranean Eggplant Feta Sandwich	79
Mediterranean Lamb Burger with Feta	38
Mediterranean Omelet	14
Mediterranean Tuna Salad Sandwiches	80
Mediterranean-Pita Wraps	82
Melitzanosalata (Greek Eggplant Dip)	96
Mexican Potato Skins	76
Mexican-Style Pizza	82
Mini Shrimp Frittata Bites	11
Mini Spinach Mushroom Quiche Cups	15
Moist Greek Yogurt Corn Bread	19
Moroccan Tomato and Roasted Chile Salad	70

Moroccan-Style Couscous	52

N

No-Mayo Florence Tuna Salad	68
Nut Butter Cup Fat Bomb	86
Nutty Brown Rice with Cherries and Apricots	20
Nutty Freekeh Pilaf with Walnuts	51
Nutty Fruit Oatmeal	12

O

Olive Oil Breakfast Cakes with Berry Syrup and Lemon	15
Olive Oil Greek Yogurt Brownies	87
One-Pan Parsley Chicken and Potatoes	30
One-Pot Shrimp Fried Rice	46
Ouzo Mussels	47

P

Pan-fried Fresh Sardines	41
Pan-Fried Spicy Mussels with Tomato and Basil	48
Paprika-Spiced Fish	42
Parmesan Garlic Cauliflower	51
Parmesan-Crusted Filet Mignon	39
Parsley Mint Lentil Salad	70
Pea and Arugula Crostini	77
Pepper Steak	36
Pesto Bowtie Pasta Salad	90
Pesto Chicken Bites Pizza	79
Pine Nut and Currant Cabbage Rolls	52
Pistachio Mint Pesto Pasta	62
Pita Pizza with Olives and Feta	77
Pomegranate-Wine Poached Pears	88
Pork Milanese	38
Pork Rind Fried Chicken	28
Potato Vegetable Hash	56

Q

Quinoa Lentil Balls with Tomato Sauce	62
Quinoa Salad with Chicken, Chickpeas, and Spinach	22
Quinoa with Almonds and Cranberries	61
Quinoa with Zucchini, Mint, and Pistachios	69

R

Red Pepper, Pomegranate, and Walnut Salad	68
Red Pepper, Spinach, and Feta Muffins	16
Refreshing Cucumber Yogurt Dip	94
Refreshing Red Grapefruit Granita	86
Rice Pilaf	25
Ricotta and Fruit Bruschetta	17
Ricotta Cheesecake	87
Roasted Broccoli Panzanella Salad	67
Roasted Chickpeas	74
Roasted Golden Beet, Avocado, and Watercress Salad	71
Roasted Honey-Cinnamon Apples	86
Rotini with Red Wine Marinara	92
Rustic Tuscan Panzanella	69
Rustic Vegetable and Brown Rice Bowl	63

S

Salmon Cakes with Bell Pepper and Lemon Yogurt	41
Salmon with Tarragon-Dijon Sauce	44
Sautéed Lentil Spinach Curry	19
Sautéed Mushroom, Onion, and Pecorino Romano Panini	80
Sautéed Tomato Rice	20
Savory Broccoli Crust Pizza	59
Savory Chicken and Mushroom Medley	30
Savory Farro with Nuts and Dried Fruit	17
Savory Herb Lamb Loin Chops	35
Savory Herbed Lima Beans	23
Savory Mackerel Goat Cheese Bites	74
Savory Mediterranean Popcorn	73
Savory Pork Chops with Peppers and Onions	34
Sheet Pan Roasted Chickpeas and Vegetables with Harissa Yogurt	63
Sherry Vinaigrette	96
Shrimp and Asparagus Risotto	43
Shrimp Pirogues	75
Shrimp Saganaki with Feta	42
Shrimp with Arugula Pesto and Zucchini Noodles	45
Sicilian Baked Cod with Herbed Breadcrumbs	47
Simple Pesto Pasta	91
Skillet Greek Turkey and Rice	29
Smoky Eggplant Dip	77
Spaghetti with Fresh Mint Pesto and Ricotta Salata	90
Spiced Apple Brown Betty	86
Spiced Crispy Mediterranean Chickpeas	63
Spiced Eggplant with Harissa Yogurt	53
Spiced Flank Steak with Harissa Couscous	37
Spiced Moroccan Tuna Steaks	44
Spiced Potatoes with Chickpeas	13
Spiced Squash with Halloumi	57
Spiced Yogurt Beets with Hazelnuts	56

Spicy Black Beans with Root Veggies	25
Spicy Broccoli Pasta Salad	91
Spicy Creole Crayfish	46
Spicy White Bean Harissa Dip	76
Spinach and Feta Breakfast Bake	14
Spinach and Feta Stuffed Chicken Breasts	28
Spinach and Paneer Cheese	56
Spinach Arugula Nectarine Salad	65
Steamed Artichokes with Herbs and Olive Oil	75
Steel-Cut Oats with Flax, Dates, and Walnuts	17
Stewed Cinnamon Plums with Greek Yogurt	88
Stuffed Cube Steak Rolls	35
Stuffed Cucumber Cups	74
Stuffed Flank Steak	34
Stuffed Mushrooms	76
Stuffed Pepper Stew	62
Stuffed Shrimp	44
Sumac Chicken with Cauliflower and Carrots	30
Sun-Dried Tomato and Spinach Egg Wrap	13
Sunshine Overnight Oats	15
Sweet and Tangy Mango Chutney Chicken	28

T

Tangy Asparagus and Broccoli	59
Tangy Chicken Jalfrezi	31
Tangy Four-Bean Salad	66
Tangy Italian Cabbage Slaw	65
Tangy Strawberry-Pomegranate Sauce	85
Taste of the Mediterranean Fat Bombs	74
Tex-Mex Chicken Roll-Ups	28
Textured Yogurt Crunch Dip	96
Toasted Almonds with Honey	84
Tomatillo Salsa	94
Tortellini with Roasted Red Pepper Sauce	61
Tricolor Tomato Salad	66
Tuna Steaks with Olive Tapenade	48
Tuna Tortilla with Roasted Peppers	17
Turkish Egg Bowl	16
Turkish Pizza	80
Turkish Shepherd'S Salad	69
Tuscan Bread and Tomato Salad	65

V

Vegetable Burgers	63
Veggie Breakfast Hash with Eggs	11
Velvety Thyme-Infused Polenta	25

W

Warm Fava Bean Dip with Pita Wedges	16
Watermelon Burrata Salad	67
Wedding Soup	36
Whipped Greek Yogurt with Chocolate	86
White Beans with Kale	23
White Beans with Rosemary, Sage, and Garlic	51
Whole Roasted Garlic	55
Whole-Wheat Pizza Dough	95
Wild Mushroom Farrotto	21
Wild Rice and Mushroom Soup	24
Wild Rice and Orange Salmon Bowl	43

Y

Yellow and White Hearts of Palm Salad	66

Z

Zesty Farro Bowl with Avocado	21
Zesty Lemon Dill Dressing	96
Zesty Mustard-Glazed Lamb Chops	36
Zesty Orange Mustard Dressing	95
Zesty Spanish Lemon and Garlic Chicken	29
Zesty Spanish Rice Bowl	20
Zucchini and Creamy Ricotta Salad	68
Zucchini Fritters	56

Made in United States
Troutdale, OR
03/13/2025